Words of praise for
NAPOLEON ON PROJECT MANAGEMENT
by Jerry Manas

"As a U.S. Marine Corps officer for 30 years, I always looked on military operations as projects—albeit of a more dangerous and uncertain variety. This book, which I found to be engaging and never dull, draws powerful, practical relationships between Napoleon's war planning, execution, control and leadership, and modern project management principles. It is a bright light on the project management landscape!"

—BILL BAHNMAIER, Col, USMC (Ret), and retired Professor of Defense Acquisition Management, Defense Acquisition University

"An insightful, well-done and much-too-rare examination of the value of revisiting the lessons of history. While others chase the 'newest, latest, greatest,' Jerry Manas reminds us that we may be overlooking invaluable thought leadership that preceded us. He inevitably challenges us to apply these ageless lessons not only at work, but at home, in our community, in worship and in athletics as well."

—JEROME JEWELL, Productivity Improvement Consultant

"Don't overlook this book! Comparing Napoleon and project management may be unique; but isn't that what we're looking for—new and fresh insights? This book has relevant content to all of us in the industry. Read it and see how helpful this text can be to your career in project management. You'll learn a lot."

—JOAN KNUTSON, Author, lecturer, and consultant, PM Guru Unlimited
Author of *Succeeding in Project-Driven Organizations* (John Wiley and Sons)

"Who can resist a book that highlights Mr. Manas's clever integration of the awe-inspiring figure of Napoleon to the most important concepts that are the foundation of the science of project management? If you are looking for a deep yet easy read that brings alive the timeless events of 19ᵗʰ century Europe to splash color on a potentially dry subject like project management, this book is a *must read.* Managing a project is in many ways akin to fighting a war, and indeed sometimes seems more like the conquest of Europe or even Waterloo than it does like just another business initiative."

—GUS CICALA, CEO, Project Assistants, Inc.

"This book takes us on an inspirational tour of Napoleon's life and works, bringing us insightful and valuable project management lessons. Jerry Manas's academic and well-read understanding of both history and project management has provided us an excellent tool for learning. I urge all those interested in improving their ability to perform projects successfully to read and reread this remarkable study."

—TOM VANDERHEIDEN, Chairman, PMI Aerospace & Defense SIG,
Consultant to the Aerospace and Defense industry

"An intriguing perspective from which to view the concepts of project management. These concepts are as valid today as they were 200 years ago."

—PETER PACITTI, Assistant Vice President/Project Manager, PNC Bank

"Jerry's method of associating real-life historical events to modern-day project management methods is brilliant. This is a must read for anyone in the field of project management who has grown weary of the repetitive nature of currently published material. I was engaged and simultaneously entertained. As a past president of a very large component of the Project Management Institute, I have read many articles and books in this field. No author has taken the fresh approach that Jerry has in correlating real project management examples to a previously unconsidered and unrelated field, military tactics. It should also be noted that Jerry's material has been researched extensively and depicts a very accurate account of the actual events. It's great to see someone doing something different that presents project management in the perspective and relative importance that it deserves."

—PHILLIP LONG, Chief Solutions Architect, LogicaCMG

NAPOLEON
ON
PROJECT
MANAGEMENT

Timeless Lessons
in Planning, Execution,
and Leadership

by Jerry Manas

NELSON BUSINESS
A Division of Thomas Nelson Publishers
Since 1798
www.thomasnelson.com

To Sharon and Elizabeth—
For making me realize what counts in life.

Published in Nashville, Tennessee, by Thomas Nelson, Inc.

Nelson Books titles may be purchased in bulk for educational, business, fund-raising, or sales promotional use. For information, please e-mail SpecialMarkets@ThomasNelson.com.

Library of Congress Cataloging-in-Publication Data

Manas, Jerry.
   Napoleon on project management : timeless lessons in planning, execution, and leadership / by Jerry Manas.
      p. cm.
   Includes bibliographical references.
   ISBN 0-7852-1285-X (hardcover)
   1. Project management. 2. Napoleon I, Emperor of the French, 1769-1821. 3. Executive ability. 4. Leadership. 5. Business planning. I. Title.
   HD69.P75M3645 2006
   658.4'04--dc22

                              2005035694

      ISBN: 0-7852-1285-X

Printed in the United States of America
06 07 08 09 QW 6 5 4 3 2

CONTENTS

FOREWORD

Those who have studied Napoleon's career are usually left in awe of the sheer brilliance, work ethic, and tenacity of the man. No doubt there are many lessons to be learned. But how do we apply them to modern-day project management? Jerry Manas has made a careful study of Napoleon's career, learned those lessons, and, in engaging style, combines history and business in this unique work.

When Napoleon took over as first consul, France was in a dreadful state. Over a million people had died during the French Revolution. France was beleaguered, surrounded by enemies, not least of whom were the expatriates who had lost power and clamored for a restoration of the old monarchy. The recently formed government was in a state of collapse, the economy of France was in a shambles, and another revolution was breaking out.

Napoleon had undoubtedly been a brilliant young general, but what did he know about politics and diplomacy, much less governing and business? As it shortly turned out, everything.

The master of organization determined to turn chaos into order. One can measure his success by the fact that by the time he was elected emperor, he was wildly popular among civilians as well as the army.

Jerry Manas has approached *Napoleon on Project Management* as would Napoleon—clearly, methodically, relentlessly, and accurately. Mr. Manas makes the case that Napoleon's diplomatic skills were first rate, an unappreciated talent. He uses, among other examples, the Egyptian campaign, where Napoleon's innate curiosity and analysis of multiple constituencies (his army and the Egyptians) resulted in tactics to address key issues of concern to each. That sounds a lot like a top marketer with outstanding PR skills.

When it came to warfare, Napoleon claimed that he "listened to no one," but we know that to be an exaggeration. What he meant was *he made his own decisions*; no management by committee for him! However, Napoleon was constantly in communication with his commanders, adjusting his battle plan according to events, which accounts in large measure for his phenomenal success. The author identifies what traits he used, why, and with what results. It's more than instructive; it's an education.

And results, after all, are what Napoleon was all about. Between his assumption of power and the end of the disastrous Russian campaign, Napoleon restored France to solvency, and then to great wealth. As Manas points out, he met with shopkeepers, mayors, industrialists, and troopers, always listening; and he achieved miracles in jump-starting a formerly moribund economy—not to mention a starving, shoeless army.

Napoleon's mastery of prioritization was perfected in warfare, but employed in business and politics as well. Manas uses as one example the army created for the invasion of England. Austria decided to take advantage of Napoleon by attacking him on the eastern front while he was tied up with England. Napoleon responded by changing his strategy to conform to breaking events, and marched his army across Europe to meet the enemy on his own ground. The author points out the research, flexibility, decentralized command (but centralized planning), and economy of force that achieved such breathtaking results. Mr. Manas explains how the reader can apply the same methods when managing projects in a competitive market.

As you read *Napoleon on Project Management*, keep in mind that he was fighting (and beating) coalitions of the greatest military powers on earth. It took them nearly twenty years and a disaster of cataclysmic proportions in Russia to defeat him.

In addition to words and examples from Napoleon himself, Mr. Manas uses many examples from business experts to explain and supplement the lessons of the master. He then pulls the lessons together into a statement of the *Six Winning Principles* that Napoleon followed—and which any astute manager can learn by reading this book.

As I started the draft, I thought that, although the premise was sound, such a book would be difficult and very likely boring. I can give no greater accolade to Jerry Manas's achievement than to simply say that he has succeeded in his goal, and boring it's not. The Emperor would approve.

But enough of this . . . On to Napoleon's unrivaled career and the many lessons to be learned from—as Will Durant observed—perhaps the greatest practical mind the world has ever known.

Advance!

DOUGLAS JAMES ALLAN
President
The Napoleonic Society of America

INTRODUCTION

What is it about Napoleon Bonaparte that has led recognized leaders to study his principles and countless books on management and leadership to quote his maxims? How did such a renowned military genius, who rose from obscurity to rule all of Western Europe, fall so quickly and suffer such defeat? Most importantly, what lessons can today's leaders and project managers learn from Napoleon's successes and failures?

According to Stephen Covey, author of *The Seven Habits of Highly Effective People*, "Project Management continues to be a critical function in organizations. Almost any new product, service, system, or technology must be introduced and implemented through a formal project management process."[1] All the leading business and information technology research groups, such as the Gartner Group, Forrester Research, Cutter Consortium, and Meta Group, have targeted formal project management as a key factor behind organizational success.

Napoleon knew all about formal project management techniques. He not only successfully led more than fifty military campaigns, but he also led hundreds of development and rebuilding efforts throughout Europe, including financial reforms, construction of roads, infrastructure setup, bridges, marinas, museums, and more—all during a period of constant warfare. And he succeeded by using sound principles and techniques that are as applicable today as they were then. Napoleon used advanced project portfolio-management practices before the term "portfolio management" even existed, except he used the practices to manage an entire empire. Furthermore, he did all this without e-mail, telephones, or computers. Surely, Napoleon's vast accomplishments must contain a wealth of lessons. And indeed they do.

There are lessons in the way Napoleon conducted extensive research before each campaign and in the way he organized his army for maximum effectiveness. There are lessons in the way he turned chaos into order and in the way he communicated to his troops, allies, and the general public. There are lessons in the way he motivated his soldiers, building fierce loyalty amid challenging times. And there are lessons in the way he kept track of all the activities in his vast empire, using simple and effective means. Perhaps most importantly, there are lessons in the way he began his fall at the very height of his power.

These lessons not only address issues that many project managers struggle with, such as adequate planning and leadership skills, but also address needs that a general leader faces regarding the achievement of objectives through sound project management principles. In other words, these lessons can help us achieve better leadership through stronger project management, and better project management through stronger leadership. Throughout this book, we'll explore the principles that led to Napoleon's rise and the weaknesses that led to his fall. We'll learn techniques that every project manager or leader can use to assure a successful completion of his or her project—be it a software project, a military battle, a sports event, a film project, or the creation of a new product.

Of course, like Napoleon, we each want to achieve lasting success and leave our mark on the world. As leaders, we have a unique opportunity to make a difference with every endeavor we attempt. And as project managers, we have an opportunity to proudly leave our signatures on each of our undertakings.

An excellent way to turn these opportunities into achievements is to study the events that led to Napoleon's rise, the key principles that enabled his repeated success, and the ill-fated actions that caused his downfall. We can augment this study by learning modern techniques for improving upon Napoleon's methods. Our goal is not merely to imitate Napoleon; it is to be better than Napoleon.

PART I

The Rise to Power

CHAPTER I

The Skills to Succeed

My business is to succeed, and I'm good at it. I create my
Iliad by my actions, create it day by day. —Napoleon

Napoleon Bonaparte perhaps achieved more objectives with amazing success than anyone else in history. He undertook an effort to bring order to France in a time of postrevolutionary chaos. He led numerous battles and continuously emerged victorious, often against larger armies. He rose from relative obscurity to become the ruler of all Western Europe in but a few years, using an army that had never before achieved such greatness. He implemented efforts to build alliances, eventually increasing his army to an unprecedented six hundred thousand strong. He created a civil code that is still in use and provided the inspiration for many civil codes worldwide.

It is through countless documents and memoirs, written by Napoleon and many others, that we get a sense of what made Napoleon so successful. As a result, we can gain a good understanding of the methods that brought him such success and the skills that made him rise above the pack. And it is these same skills that will make us successful in our organizations today. Let's begin by examining the skills Napoleon viewed as essential for any leader—particularly as they apply to project management.

NAPOLEON'S TIMELESS TOOLS
FOR PROJECT MANAGEMENT

The formal title of "project manager" is not required to benefit from project management lessons. On the contrary, anyone who must lead an endeavor—whether as a CEO, a sports coach, a film director, or any other type of leader—can benefit from these universal lessons. So, when we refer to project managers, we are referring to all leaders who choose to manage their efforts as "projects." And, according to today's experts, ranging from Tom Peters to the Gartner Group, management-by-projects is the surest path to achieving organizational (and yes, even personal) goals. The lessons from Napoleon's rise and fall can show us how to be successful with this approach both in our organizations and in our personal lives.

As our journey progresses, we will explore how Napoleon rose to power, how he grew his empire as much through shrewd diplomacy as through victories in battle, and how he lost it all with several costly mistakes—mistakes that many of us make in our daily working lives. We will examine the Six Winning Principles that guided Napoleon to repeated success, and look at case studies detailing where he went wrong. But first, we will begin with the basics, as Napoleon walks us through his philosophies on leadership. In this way, we will build a solid foundation before embarking on our journey. Following are excerpts from Napoleon's memoirs, written as he contemplated the abilities and values that he felt made him successful: developing solid skills, such as a good memory and knowledge of mathematics; upholding key values, such as calmness and predictability; being visible to those you lead; and understanding the nature of politics.

A GOOD MEMORY

A singular thing about me is my memory. As a boy, I knew the logarithms of thirty or forty numbers; in France, I not only knew the names of the officers of all the regiments, but also where the corps had been recruited, had distinguished themselves; I even knew their spirit.

Napoleon knew, as do most modern salespeople, that a good memory is critical in building relationships. The best salespeople not only know their customers' names, but know their customers' family members' names, their likes, dislikes, hobbies, and any other bits of information that help build a relationship. Using the same approach, a project manager can develop better relationships with stakeholders, project team members, peers, and management.

A good memory is also valuable for team selection—for example, remembering certain nuances about individuals that would make them more or less valuable at one task or another. Remembering people's past successes in general is important. All too often, managers judge people by only their most recent activity, ignoring all of their past accomplishments and capabilities. It is also critical to remember the factors that motivate each individual, as each person's needs may be different.

Remembering things about people is only one benefit of having a good memory. Another is the ability to remember the small details that can make or break a project—for example, some obscure fact that may come back to cause havoc later. The saying "The devil is in the details" holds true when talking about project management. Napoleon perused relevant data and detailed reports from the field daily (and often throughout the night). It is to his credit that he was able to recall these small details on a moment's notice, often giving the impression of spontaneous ingenuity.

An area that most project managers ignore is the art of making presentations. Building memory skills can go a long way toward avoiding the overused crutch of PowerPoint. There is nothing worse than making a presentation with your back to the audience and reading bullets from a slide projection—other than perhaps having to sit through such a presentation. A good presentation should appear natural and energetic, with tools like PowerPoint slides used as props to illustrate key points through meaningful graphics, rather than the presenter merely narrating bullets the audience can read for themselves—although handouts should always be provided. A presentation should be built on a good memory and should avoid the overuse of notes and bulleted slides.

Perhaps Peter Norvig's humorous parody of Abraham Lincoln giving the Gettysburg Address as a PowerPoint presentation illustrates this point best (http://www.norvig.com/Gettysburg/). Norvig is the Director of Search Quality at Google, Inc., and a fellow and councilor of the American Association for Artificial Intelligence. His parody is included as part of Edward Tufte's course on information presentation.

So, how can you improve upon your memory and utilize it as efficiently as possible throughout all these activities? Today, people try all kinds of things to improve their memories, from herbal remedies to mental exercises. Probably the best way to remember things is to use the association method, since we all tend to remember things by associating them with something—usually a word or a visual cue. In effect, by doing this, we are subconsciously building bridges in our minds between the cues and the memory associations.

Another method that helps solidify things in our minds is repetition—which is the reason actors and singers learn their lines by endless practice, and the reason advertisements use jingles and catchphrases. Through association and repetition, we can remember key facts that would otherwise be lost to oblivion.

Even with the above methods, there is no reason to leave things to chance when you can simply write something down, even if it's a small "trigger" key word, assuming you remember to look at what you've written. Today, we have all sorts of tools for keeping track of things, from appointment books to Personal Digital Assistants

(PDAs). In addition to calendars and to-do lists, all PDAs come with a memo section that is invaluable for capturing notes about people, projects, ideas, or anything else you may need to recall at a moment's notice. Of course, when you are giving a presentation, it is ideal not to rely on the use of notes, but index cards with brief trigger words are quite acceptable. It is hard to dispute that a good memory can do well to serve any leader, whether in business or otherwise, and fortunately there are many tools and techniques that can help.

THE POWER OF MATHEMATICS

To be a good general, a man must know mathematics; it is of daily help in straightening one's ideas. Perhaps I owe my success to my mathematical conceptions; a general must never imagine things; that is the most fatal of all. My great talent, the thing that marks me most, is that I see things clearly; it is the same with my eloquence, for I can distinguish what is essential in a question from every angle.

Mathematics probably isn't high on most project managers' and leaders' lists of important skills to build. Yet, almost all phases of a project—project selection, task estimates, risk analysis, decision making during project execution, and so forth—require some sort of mathematical skills.

For project selection, knowledge of return on investment (ROI), the internal rate of return (IRR), and other selection techniques is essential. For cost estimates, it is important to calculate costs accurately, including variations based on risk factors. For quality analysis, it is critical to understand statistical sampling and control charts. For proper decision making, it is important to understand risk probability and have the ability to perform decision-tree analysis. Planning should not be based on hunches, but, as much as possible, on calculations and actual facts.

During project execution, you should be able to calculate where you should be versus where you are in terms of budget and schedule. A tool such as Earned Value Management can help you determine this as early as 15 percent into the project. A good book on this is *Earned Value Project Management*, by Quentin W. Fleming and Joel M. Koppelman.[1]

For all of these needs—since many of us are not armchair mathematicians—it's useful to keep a list of handy calculations and algorithms, most of which are included in any Project Management Professional (PMP) exam study guide. A couple of good ones that include all the calculations a project manager would need, among other tools and techniques vital to any project manager, are: *PMP Exam Prep* (4th edition), by Rita Mulcahy; and *Preparing for the Project Management Professional (PMP) Certification Exam* (2nd edition), by Michael W. Newell. Type the most useful calculations into your PDA or notebook, and you will be well equipped for success.

As Napoleon so astutely pointed out, a great leader cannot underestimate the value of building the mathematical skills necessary to make proper decisions, whether selecting, planning, or executing a project. Facts and calculated estimates are always better than guesses and hunches.

STAYING COOL AND COLLECTED

The first qualification in a general-in-chief is a cool head—that is, a head which receives just impressions, and estimates things and objects at their real value. He must not allow himself to be elated by good news, or depressed by bad. The impressions he receives . . . should be so classified as to take up only the exact place in his mind that they deserve to occupy; since it is upon a just comparison and consideration of the weight due to different impressions that the power of reasoning and of right judgment depends . . .

*I could listen to intelligence of the death of my wife, of my son, or all
of my family, without a change of feature. Not the slightest sign of emotion, or alteration of countenance, would be visible. Everything would
appear indifferent and calm. But when alone in my room, then I suffer.
Then the feelings of the man burst forth.*

Napoleon was often surprisingly candid in his memoirs, such as in
this case, revealing how he suffered internally while appearing cool
and collected to others. He often spoke of this as a necessary trait
for a great leader. This is an extreme example and probably a great
exaggeration, but the point is that a leader cannot appear vulnerable
to subordinates—or worse yet, unpredictable. People do not trust a
leader who is inconsistent, irrational, or weak.

It is important for the leader to show strength and confidence if
problems arise, either with the project or with some external factor
that could impact the team or the leader. Nothing can unravel a
team more quickly than a leader who overreacts or becomes disillusioned. That is not to say the leader
should display false bravado or in-
appropriate cheerfulness, but merely
a solid, even temperament.

> Nothing can unravel a
> team more quickly
> than a leader who
> overreacts or becomes
> disillusioned.

In addition, Napoleon pointed out
the importance of categorizing and
weighing news, not only according to
its rightful value, but also after considering potentially varying impres-
sions of the same news. There may be unseen benefits in what
appears to be bad news, and there may be dangers lurking behind
seemingly good news. Overreacting to good news or bad news can
take away from the true picture and can have an unpredictable
impact on the morale of a team.

For example, a leader may want to rejoice when a major milestone is achieved, and certainly there is some benefit to celebrating small victories, but the project is not over until all the loose ends are resolved and the expected results have been delivered. The team must still maintain focus.

A leader may go on a tirade or appear convinced that a project cannot succeed upon hearing that a team member forgot to do something or that a stakeholder issued a complaint, but the fact is that these are merely triggers to see if a process needs correction or if communication needs to be improved. A negative or cynical attitude tends to spread throughout a team like a disease and becomes a self-fulfilling prophecy. Cooler heads must prevail.

So, the next time you find yourself getting all worked up or disillusioned, take time to examine the facts from all angles. Keep things in proper perspective. Consider the impact of your reaction on your team's morale and the potential effect on their behavior. If you find yourself becoming elated by good news before the project is finished, just be cautious that the team doesn't misinterpret your elation as an opportunity to relax and lose focus. Most importantly, don't let your emotions—good or bad—get in the way of sound judgment.

"Go Amongst the Soldiers"

Nature formed all men equal. It was always my custom to go amongst the soldiers and the rabble, to converse with them, hear their little histories, and speak kindly to them. This I found to be the greatest benefit to me.

One of the things that made Napoleon so popular with his troops was that he was always visible. He'd frequently go to the front lines and mingle with the troops, first to inspire them, but second to get a sense of how they were feeling and what was on their minds. This relates to building relationships by finding out the details of your team members' lives. Many companies in today's business atmosphere have a "be visible" policy for their managers. Some companies call it "management by wandering around" or MBWA—a term used at Hewlett-Packard and popularized in the landmark book *In Search of Excellence* by Tom Peters and Robert Waterman.[2] As the correlation with Napoleon's theories can testify, this is certainly a good approach to adopt.

One thing to be cautious of when wandering around, though, is not to micromanage. There is a tremendous difference between being visible and micromanaging. It is one thing to mingle, to ask how things are going or if there is anything you can do to help. In this way, you are in a position to remove any barriers your team is facing. It is another to hover over people's backs and nitpick about what they are doing wrong. Better to ask if help is needed.

If a correction in course is needed, clarify the objective privately or generically to the team—if you feel the team could benefit from the clarification. Training could also be suggested as needed. Another way to get a point across is to schedule a joint working session where you can work with the team member (or team) to accomplish something; meanwhile, they're learning from you during the session in a noncombative way.

There are three primary purposes for mingling with your team: (1) to build relationships with them, which in turn builds trust; (2) to see if there are any barriers that you can remove for the team; and (3) to get a sense of the team's morale. It is important not to let micromanagement undermine these goals.

THE FUTILITY OF TYRANNY

Rule cannot be despotic because there is neither a feudal system, a mediatory body, nor a precedent on which it can act. As soon as a government becomes tyrannical, it must suffer in public opinion and will never regain confidence. Therefore, a Council is necessary for unforeseen cases, and the Senate is most suitable for this purpose. In my opinion, there is no such thing as despotism pure and simple. Ideas are relative. If a sultan has heads cut off at his pleasure, his own head is in most danger of all, for that very reason, of suffering the same fate.

Napoleon was perceived by many to be tyrannical in his own right (he was strict, but always observed caution regarding treatment of his soldiers and staff). But even he knew that in truth, power is given and not taken. A project manager or leader cannot let the position go to his or her head. Power must be earned by building trust and respect. Trust and respect must be earned through actions and fair treatment of others. That is true power.

Although a sense of purpose is good, one can become overly ambitious, tossing all good judgment aside to achieve that purpose. Even Napoleon realized the dangers of absolute power and suggested some sort of council for keeping things in check—in his case, the Senate. In business, of course, we have executive boards and various leadership councils for this purpose.

Following this principle, a project manager would be wise to appoint a core team, especially for large projects, to ensure that all things are considered and to balance ideas. It is quite easy to come up with an idea and be certain it is correct until someone points out the dangers or some new perspective.

There can be only one leader; it is ineffective to lead by committee. Full consensus usually cannot be achieved, and operations can become stagnant. The leader must consider the opinions and perspectives of the core team, yet must be able to make the final decision if needed. That is not to say the team should not work together first to solve a problem, nor is it to say the leader should totally disregard the wishes of the team. As Napoleon pointed out, any leader who uses a position of power to act against public opinion is in danger of losing that power.

The issue of a leader having the ultimate authority is a tricky one, and some may point to modern democratic governments where a senate and/or some other ruling body has the power to veto or even remove a president or prime minister. For example, let's examine the United States government's system of checks and balances. The president can veto bills approved by Congress; the Supreme Court can declare a law passed by Congress or an action by the president unconstitutional; and Congress can impeach the president or federal court justices and judges.

> As Napoleon pointed out, any leader who uses a position of power to act against public opinion is in danger of losing that power.

This is indeed a valid precaution against any one individual or group running away with power, although it's not foolproof. But with the exception of a public company with an executive board and shareholders, there is nothing close to it in the corporate world, and there probably never will be. The best we can do is get as close as we can to a situation where everybody must answer to somebody.

In the leader's case, as Napoleon pointed out, becoming tyrannical serves no one and will usually lead to failure, through recognition of such by superiors or peers or through lack of support by subordinates. The most enlightened leaders will implement a 360-degree feedback system, in which the leader gathers feedback from peers, subordinates, and his or her manager, and then compares it with his or her own self-evaluation and makes adjustments accordingly. There are countless software products available on the Internet exclusively for this purpose, as will be evident if you do a search on "360 feedback." A simple Zoomerang survey would work quite adequately. Zoomerang is a valuable, inexpensive tool that allows you to tailor and send surveys via the Internet. It collects and categorizes the results for you, and you can download them as needed. Zoomerang is available at www.zoomerang.com.

Even with all the best intentions and listening to the feedback of others, sometimes a leader faces a dilemma when the apparent right decision is an unpopular one. A tricky subject we will explore next is how far to go in pleasing the majority versus making the right decision.

POPULARITY

What is popularity? What is gentleness? . . . One must serve a nation worthily, but not take pains to flatter the people. To win them, you must do them good. For nothing is more dangerous than to echo people's opinions and say just what they want to hear. When afterwards, they do not get all they want, they get restless and believe you have broken your word. And if you oppose them, they hate you in proportion as they think themselves deceived.

The first duty of a prince is doubtless to do what the people wish, but the common people scarcely ever want what they say they do. Their will and needs should less be expressed by them than felt by the ruler . . .

My policy consists in ruling according to the will of the great majority. In this way, I believe one recognizes the sovereignty of the people. In order to end the war in La Vendee, I made myself a Catholic, as a Mussulman I managed to establish myself in Egypt, and as an Ultramontanist I won all hearts in Italy. If I were ruling a Jewish people, I would restore the Temple of Solomon.

At first glance, Napoleon's ideas appear to conflict with one another: be aware of public opinion, but don't merely echo it in your decisions; perceive what is best for the people, rather than listen to what they are saying. Napoleon was admitting that it is vital to be aware of public opinion, yet he was cautioning not to blindly follow it. Just because the great majority feels a certain way does not mean they are correct. Yet, Napoleon said that his policy was to rule according to the great majority.

Is this an inconsistency, or was Napoleon merely throwing the public a bone, echoing the Roman sentiment for keeping the masses happy with bread and circuses? Upon deeper examination, it appears instead that Napoleon was saying yes, it is vital to be aware of public opinion; it is even valuable to cater to public opinion wherever possible; yet it is equally important not to blindly follow public opinion, as the public is not always aware of all circumstances, nor are they always correct.

Does this mean that a leader should follow his or her instinct, even if it seems as if the world is opposed? Again the answer is no, as Napoleon has already warned us of the dangers of going against public opinion. It is the rare case indeed that a leader has been successful going against public opinion in the interest of doing what is right. Former United States President Franklin Delano Roosevelt's decision to temporarily close banks during the Great Depression to allow time to regroup would seem to be an example of this.

When the right decision appears to be over the heads of your audience—a project manager's audience may be peers, subordinates, or customers—the answer, and certainly the safest solution, would seem to be to first verify that you are indeed right and they are wrong. And then, assuming that to be the case, you need to convince them. To verify that you are right, it is important to hear the viewpoints of others. This is where the core team approach comes in handy. It is also important to consider the long-term consequences and potentially damaged relationships that could occur; success in business, as in life, is all about relationships.

If you still believe your decision is correct after reviewing the dangers, the next step is to convince people that they are wrong and you are right. This is the equivalent of convincing a conservative market that they need a new, disruptive technology—one that forces them to do things differently and enter a new paradigm of behavior. Not doing this, but attempting to force the decision, is a risky endeavor.

Fortunately, there are several valuable tools available for creating a compelling case for an unpopular decision:

- *High-tech marketing guru Geoffrey Moore's Crossing the Chasm model.* This model is used for marketing disruptive technologies. Moore suggests fully walking through a hypothetical scenario to test the idea's value and effectiveness, finding a champion to back and test the idea, and marketing to increasingly broader audiences using past successes and peer-group pressure to convince them. The "chasm" represents the gap between the early adopters and the early majority.[3]

- *Information design guru Edward Tufte's approach to presenting data and information.* Tufte provides details in several books. In his book *Visual Explanations: Images and Quantities, Evidence and Narrative*, he illustrates how scientists could have convinced NASA not to make the ill-fated decision to launch the space shuttle *Challenger* by clearly showing causality in a simple, graphic manner.[4]

- *Change-management gurus Dean Anderson and Linda Ackerman-Anderson's Transformational Change model.* This model is detailed in their books *Beyond Change Management* and *The Change Leader's Roadmap*, which stress the need to address the people issues and consider stakeholder perspectives when introducing a paradigm-shifting change.[5]

These tools are not mutually exclusive, as each illustrates a unique point when trying to turn an unpopular decision into a popular one.

Moore's Crossing the Chasm model addresses the marketing perspective, Tufte's model addresses the presentation perspective, and the Andersons' Transformational Change model addresses the people issues involved. Any leader or project manager would be wise to study all three approaches.

At this point, some project managers may be asking how this applies to them. After all, they are merely implementing a project. The problem comes when the project is introducing a product or a result that is unpopular. Unhappy or unconvinced people, whether they are customers, peers, or team members, can be one of the most disruptive barriers to the successful completion of a project. It is the project manager's responsibility to remove barriers to success, and therefore the project manager must address these issues in whatever way possible. These tools can help, and they will be covered in more detail later in this book.

Another thing that can help ensure stakeholder buy-in is to create a compelling vision of the project's desired product or result. Although circumstances were certainly with him, Napoleon did this effectively when he created the vision of an organized and free society instead of the postrevolutionary chaos that existed. In the next chapter, we will explore this in more detail.

Meanwhile, to answer the question posed by Napoleon: What is popularity and what is gentleness when one is faced with leadership decisions? It is listening to public opinion; keeping the great majority happy; maintaining good relations with customers, peers, and subordinates; and at the same time,

- recognizing when a change is needed, even when the majority may not see it;
- doing sanity checks to assure that your thinking is sound; and
- convincing the stakeholders that change is needed.

Doing this effectively is the mark of a true leader, and one that will have a lasting impact on his or her organization.

EXECUTIVE SUMMARY

The lessons to be learned from Napoleon's career are timeless—just as applicable to a modern-day project manager or business leader as to a military general in the nineteenth century. Napoleon's advice is as relevant today as it was two hundred years ago—the value of a good memory and mathematical skills, the importance of being calm and visible, and the virtues of making difficult but informed decisions and selling them accordingly. With this solid foundation laid, we can begin the next leg of our journey and discover how Napoleon used these skills and philosophies to become the ruler of all Western Europe—and how we can use the same skills to assure success for our projects.

MARCHING ORDERS

DEVELOP A GOOD MEMORY

Increase your memory through association, repetition, and use of a PDA or memo system. It will help you to:

- build relationships by remembering people's names and interests.
- select the right people for your team by remembering their backgrounds, work habits, strengths, and weaknesses.
- motivate your team by remembering people's individual needs.
- recall small details that might come back to haunt you later.
- make better presentations by avoiding the overuse of PowerPoint as a crutch.

HARNESS THE POWER OF MATHEMATICS

Calculate—do not guess. Increase your mathematical skills by taking statistics classes and learning useful algorithms. This can help you:

- select the right projects, based on calculated costs and benefits.
- produce accurate estimates that consider risk and probability.
- judge quality using statistical controls and measures.
- determine the impact of adding resources, by calculating the additional communication channels required.
- plan for potential problems using risk-probability analysis.
- make better decisions using risk and decision-tree analysis.
- predict cost and schedule overruns as early as 15 percent into the project using earned value analysis.

STAY COOL AND COLLECTED

Remain cool and collected at all times. This can help you:

- promote a positive atmosphere.
- avoid unnecessary panic by your team.
- inspire others to act the same way.

GO AMONG THE SOLDIERS

Be visible to your team. Use the MBWA (management by wandering around) approach. This can help you:

- inspire your team.
- build trust by getting to know your team personally.
- be available to address questions.
- get a sense of how your team is feeling—their concerns and needs.
- remove barriers that may be impeding your team's success.

UNDERSTAND THE FUTILITY OF TYRANNY

Don't let a position of power trick you into thinking you can go it alone. Appointing a core team can help you:

- balance out ideas and gain various perspectives.
- build trust and respect by demonstrating participative leadership.
- become more efficient by sharing the leadership workload with others.
- implement a 360-degree feedback process. This allows you to
  —see how you are perceived by others.
  —make needed adjustments to your style.
  —grow as a leader and manager.

CATER TO POPULARITY—WITHIN REASON

Listen to public opinion, but recognize when a change is needed.

- Do sanity checks to ensure that your thinking is sound.

If your project's proposed product is unpopular, confirm the idea is a good one, then implement tools to sell it to the public. Consider the marketing, presentation, and people angles. This can help you:

- be certain that you are implementing the most effective solution.
- decrease resistance to your initiative.
- maintain relationships that are crucial for ongoing success.

CHAPTER 2

A Compelling Vision

Sprung from the lower ranks of society
I became an emperor, because circumstances,
opinion, were with me. —Napoleon

Napoleon had it easy. He had an ambitious vision of a free and united Europe unconstrained by monarchy—and that vision jelled perfectly with the desires of the French people. In the chaos following the French Revolution, with rebels and royalists still battling, the people were more than ready to accept someone who could give them a sense of order and hope and yet still meet their needs for equality. And this was precisely what Napoleon offered. After all, it was Napoleon who said, "A leader is a dealer in hope."

To fully appreciate this phrase, it is important to understand that the word *hope* does not signify unsupported optimism or dreaming of the impossible. *Hope* implies a sense of expectation. And to give people a sense of expectation, you must give them a clear vision of what will come—a picture they can grasp.

A vision without a purpose—a need to fill—is not compelling to anyone except its creator. Any vision of a desired end state therefore must have a purpose—a problem or need that it is meant to address. In Napoleon's case, the need was clear and shared by all. As project managers, we are not always so fortunate and must work harder to define and communicate the problem and to craft a clear picture of the future.

But even with a problem to solve and a clear vision of what the end state should look like, we still need a strategy—a way to get from the problem to the desired result. There is a saying: "A vision without a strategy is a hallucination." We need to develop a solution to the problem—ideally several alternate solutions, from which the best can be chosen.

We have defined three elements of a compelling vision:

1. A problem to solve—a need to fill, giving rise to a purpose
2. A strategy to solve the problem
3. A vision of the future—a clear picture of the end state of the solution

These three stages also need a basis for reliable and consistent direction. If this problem-strategy/solution-vision combination serves as the ship's compass, then guiding values are needed to serve as the rudder. Ken Blanchard and Jesse Stoner recognized this in their book *Full Steam Ahead!* in which they tout the importance of having "a significant purpose, clear values, and a picture of the future" as the key ingredients of any compelling vision.[1] In Napoleon's case, the values of liberty, equality, and fraternity—the battle cry of the French Revolution—served as the rudder that would guide his actions, at least for a while.

For the time being, Napoleon had all the necessary elements for success: he had a problem to solve, a strategy to address it, a vision of the future, and guiding values to live by. We can learn much by examining each of these in more detail. We will start where we should always begin when establishing a vision—with a problem to be solved.

THE PROBLEM TO SOLVE:
POSTREVOLUTIONARY CHAOS

Napoleon said in his memoirs: "My throne was raised by the unanimous wishes of the French people." Indeed it was. In order to understand the problem that so rapidly needed to be solved, it is important to understand the environment at the time. In the late eighteenth century, the French people were tired of injustice and inequality after years of being ruled by a royal and privileged class, so they rebelled. This led to the overthrow of the Bourbon dynasty, in particular, Louis XVI. You probably know this as the French Revolution.

The storming of the Bastille prison by the revolutionaries on July 14, 1789, marked a symbolic victory against tyranny, but chaos persisted for several more years. Although the revolutionaries formed a new government, royalists posed a serious threat—backed by the kings and queens of other countries, who were not about to see an antimonarchy precedent set in France. More threats came from revolutionaries who favored total anarchy and from those who grew impatient with the slowness of change.

By 1793, a new government was formed in France, led by a ruthless left-wing extremist, Robespierre. Not only did he have anyone suspected of being a royalist beheaded, but he also began murdering even the moderate left. All over France, people rebelled against the new government, bringing France into further turmoil. Eventually, Robespierre's own people sent him to the guillotine, and the Terror—as this era was called—was over.

THE ARRIVAL OF NAPOLEON

In 1795, a new constitution was created and a new government, called the Directory, was formed. The government leaders were faced with two difficult tasks. First, they needed to protect France's new-found freedom by heading off the persistent royalist plots, many aided by England. Second, they needed to bring a sense of order to this chaotic environment—an environment torn apart by civil war between royalists and revolutionaries. And the people *wanted* order. They *needed* order. After years of suffering the whims of a privileged monarchy, and later the ruthlessness of an unbalanced extremist, consistent rules would have been a blessing. Unfortunately, this weak and unpopular government was not up to the task. Enter Napoleon Bonaparte.

Napoleon earned a good reputation in the French army, deftly defeating France's adversaries one by one, beginning with dislodg-ing the English from Toulon, an important Mediterranean port. Napoleon also won respect in that battle. When his superior officer wanted to postpone an attack because of bad weather, the French government offered Napoleon the chance to assume command and issue an immediate attack. He declined, saying that he had full con-fidence in his senior officer and instead would convince him of the need to go forward. Napoleon did exactly as he promised, and the battle was won. The senior officer sang Napoleon's praises, writing to the Ministry of War of Napoleon's intelligence, bravery, and character. Napoleon eventually worked his way up the military and political ladders through a combination of rousing victories, word of mouth, and clever propaganda.

In 1799, a few members of the government secretly identified Napoleon as the only man capable of saving France. The sole way to do this, they said, was through a coup. Napoleon agreed to their plan, after assuring that the most influential military figures approved. The coup was successful, and a new government was formed. This government would be a consulate of three members, with Napoleon as First Consul. A few years later, the 3.5 million people of France who voted would unanimously elect him to this position for life.

His mission? To bring order to France; to protect the values of the French Revolution—liberty, equality, and fraternity; and to craft a new and brighter future for France, where privilege by heredity would have no rank. This was the problem to solve—Napoleon's reason for being. France was in desperate need of change, and Napoleon was the one to help bring it about.

IDENTIFYING THE PROBLEM:
TOOLS FOR SUCCESS

This has been an interesting story, and it clearly illustrates the pressing need at the time. But what of us, as project managers? How can we learn from this? First, Napoleon rose to power by addressing a problem—in his case, the postrevolutionary chaos of France. It is the same in business. A project, whether undertaken to provide a product, service, or result, exists to solve a problem— be it a gap in the market, a needed improvement, or a risk or a fear that needs to be addressed.

The challenge for the project manager is to determine the specifics of the problem to be solved, with the ultimate goal of communicating the need the project is meant to address. This is often done as part of the business case for the project, and in theory is done before the project manager is even assigned. In reality, however, the business case is often weak, if one exists at all, and it is critical for the project manager to assist the customer with completing the business case. Not only does this help assure that the project is aligned with a true need, but it helps motivate the team and get stakeholders on board as well.

For Napoleon, the problem was clear. But because we are not always so fortunate, we need a few tools to help us get to the bottom of the real problem. One tool for extrapolating the real problem is the application of the Five Why's, popularized by Peter

Senge, author of *The Fifth Discipline*. This involves asking, "Why?" five times until you get to the root of the problem.[2]

Another tool is the business case, often part of a request/governance system or portfolio management system. Ideally, the need should be tied to some fundamental business driver. This is where it helps to have some business acumen. A small but powerful book, *What the CEO Wants You to Know*, by Ram Charan, is an excellent tool for building business acumen. Charan's book explains business in its most fundamental terms, using a fruit vendor as an example, and should be mandatory reading for anyone in business, including project managers.[3] A mission statement is another tool that is good to have, once the problem is identified and the need documented. A mission statement is not meant to be an inspiring paragraph of fluffy words that everybody ignores—as spoofed in numerous Dilbert cartoons—but rather a statement of purpose. An effective mission statement should address the question: Why do we exist?—at least from the perspective of the project. This differs from a vision statement, which depicts what the end state is supposed to look like and addresses the question: Where are we going? The vision statement should be developed after the mission statement, since it is hard to know where you are going until you know why you are going there.

There was no doubt about the problem facing Napoleon and his staff. As project managers, we need to get to that same point. Once we've identified and communicated the problem, the next step is to develop a solution. In Napoleon's case, this meant getting organized. This next step will often be the same for us as well.

DEVELOPING A STRATEGY: GETTING ORGANIZED

Before a vision can be crafted, there must be a problem to address, ultimately elaborated into specific requirements. In addition, there must be a solution to the problem—and this becomes the foundation of any vision. Napoleon's solution was to first organize with his core team—the consulate—which, in addition to Napoleon, included Emmanuel Sieyès and Roger Ducos. They knew that quick and frequent communication was critical, and they addressed the people of France with this simple initial statement, which also served to communicate the guiding principles of their regime:

> *People of France: Swear with us to be true to the Republic one and indivisible, founded on equality, liberty, and the representative system.*

Note that the consulate specifically mentions "the representative system." The original battle cry of the French Revolution was "Liberty, Equality, Fraternity!" This is a key point in that without a strong representative system, a constitution giving rights of equality and liberty would forever be in jeopardy.

The problem was clearly identified and the guiding principles were communicated. The next order of business was to create a capable organization. The consulate assigned a Ministry of Finance, a Ministry of War, a Ministry of the Interior, and a Senate and legislative body.

Momentum was key, and a financial system was the first order of business. Napoleon declared, "Every day must be marked by one step forward in the creation of a general system of finance." For motivation, Napoleon ordered that a plan be devised to place all captured enemy flags under the dome of the Invalides (now Napoleon's resting place) and that the chronology of each victory be engraved on marble tablets. He also had the Ministry of War draw up a plan of operations for the new army. Things were quickly getting in order.

In the coming months, Napoleon's administration would create the Bank of France and a new constitution. They introduced the constitution with a brief but powerful statement. It managed to address the people's fears, emphasize strong guiding principles, paint a picture of stability, and declare an important symbolic milestone—the end of the French Revolution and the beginning of the new future—all in six short sentences:

> *To the people of France: A constitution is submitted to you. It will bring to an end the uncertainties that attended the provisional government in all its dealings, exterior, military, and interior. The Constitution is based on the true principles of representative government, on the sacred rights of property, of equality, of liberty.*
>
> *The powers it provides for are strong and stable, as they should be to guarantee the rights of citizens and the interests of the State.*
>
> *Citizens, the Revolution is now anchored to the principles which gave it birth. The Revolution is finished.*

Napoleon and his consulate continued to implement further improvements, including the creation of the Legion of Honor and the establishment of educational reforms, such as uniforms for teachers and students, and classes in the letters, arts, and sciences. In 1804, the Code Napoleon was established, which introduced a civil code that is still in use today in France and provided the inspiration for many civil codes worldwide. This code introduced principles such as separation of church and state, freedom of religion, no recognition of privileges of birth, rules of inheritance, divorce laws, and, most important, equality of all in the eyes of the law. In essence, Napoleon *organized* things.

CHOOSE A CORE TEAM
AND COMMUNICATE EARLY

Project managers can learn many lessons from Napoleon's steps for getting organized. First, Napoleon wasn't alone. He had a core team to work with—the consulate. As the First Consul and leader, however, he set the pace and was able to make final decisions. It is wise for project managers to assemble a small core team, especially for large projects, as we discussed in Chapter 1.

Next, Napoleon met with his core team to draft a quick communication. At this point, the ultimate vision didn't need to be part of the communication, merely a brief statement of purpose—a call to action. Early and frequent communication is critical when managing projects. In fact, according to the Project Management Institute, 90 percent of a project manager's job is communication, and rightfully so.[4] As Napoleon knew, people need to feel a sense of order, and this need is met by frequent communication.

ESTABLISH AN ORGANIZATION

Once the core team is assembled and stakeholders have been addressed, the next step is to establish an organization capable of not only carrying out the work, but often contributing to defining the work as well. Napoleon needed an organization appropriate for managing a country. In our cases, the organization may need to be tailored for each instance, because the need will differ by project. For example, a project for developing a software product might require an architectural lead, a testing lead, a quality/configuration lead, a security lead, and leaders for other major areas. A project for designing a new building might consist of a planning lead, an engineering lead, a construction lead, an administrative lead, and so forth. Often, these leads are added to the core team.

DEVELOP SOLUTIONS

The next step is to begin developing solutions with the assistance of the core team. We can assume that Napoleon and his staff spent hours going over the current situation and various plans and alternatives before deciding on the appropriate course of action. Their solutions initially were to develop the constitution and a system of finance, and then to rebuild their military. Later, other needs were addressed. It is at this point that we, too, work with constituents to review alternatives and propose one or more solutions. The ultimate vision hasn't necessarily been established yet, but this process should get the team going in that direction.

This brings us to another issue to consider at this stage: momentum. Remember, Napoleon stated that each day had to be marked by one step forward in the development of a financial system. He knew people sometimes tend to get lax just as things are getting organized. The project manager must be the catalyst for keeping things moving. This is also a time to use any sources of motivation, just as Napoleon had requested captured flags to be hung in the Invalides and victories to be engraved on marble tablets. This early in the game it is not always practical or feasible, but it is something to think about.

This is also a good time to develop any administrative tools necessary for carrying out the project, just as Napoleon asked the Ministry of War to develop a plan of operations and asked other leaders to develop appropriate plans, forms, and operating procedures. With the need defined, the team assembled, a solution chosen, and tools and procedures in place, the foundation is set. It is now time to begin crafting and communicating a clear vision of the end state.

A VISION OF THE FUTURE:
NAPOLEON'S VISION

We began this chapter talking about Napoleon's vision of a free and united Europe. But this vision didn't come out of nowhere. It evolved. An overall vision of a better and glorious France certainly would have been tempting, but much too broad to start with. Napoleon needed to focus on only a few important things, beginning with improving France's economy. Thus, he began to build his vision for a more prosperous France. He concentrated on the thirty-six thousand communes of France, with each commune representing one thousand people. This gave him thirty-six thousand points of measurement.

Napoleon called for his Ministry of the Interior to draft a spreadsheet showing the status of these communes, listing them under the following categories: those with assets, those whose accounts merely balanced, and those in debt. He also asked that the spreadsheet include the situation within each commune, depicting the number of incidents and gravity for each major issue—what we refer to today in risk management as "probability and impact." This would allow him to focus on only the critical issues and establish a good set of requirements.

Napoleon called for the removal of mayors who were not in line with the reforms, knowing that alignment of all management was critical to success. He established an annual system of rewards for those who reached midterm milestones. He then was able to declare his short- and long-term visions. The short-term vision was to have all communes out of debt within five years. The long-term vision was to make all communes prosperous within ten years, bringing those communes whose accounts merely balanced to the category of "communes with assets." Here was the vision—clear, measurable, and realistic.

The economy began to improve, and with systems in place to sustain those improvements, Napoleon began to focus on a broader vision. Specifically, he wanted to create a federation of nations and put an end to monarchy once and for all. He recalled that vision, which could, for all intents and purposes, be called a "United States of Europe":

One of my favorite ideas was the fusion, the federation of the nations, which had been separated by revolution and politics. There are in Europe more than 30 million French, 15 million Spaniards, as many Italians, and 30 million Germans. I wanted to unite them all into one strong, national body. The accomplisher of this work would be awarded by Posterity with its most beautiful wreath, and I felt myself strong enough and called on to undertake this work. When this was done, people could devote themselves to the realization of the ideal, at present only a dream, of a higher civilization. Then there would be no more vicissitudes to fear, for there would be only one set of laws, one kind of opinion, one view, one interest, the interest of mankind. Then perhaps one could realize for Europe the thought of an amphictyony, a North American Congress.

Unfortunately, somewhere along the way, through a combination of circumstances, deals gone wrong, and the lure of power, Napoleon lost his way. But the point is: he had a vision, and so must we.

Our vision needs to begin realistically. We don't want to create a pie-in-the-sky illusion. Remember, Napoleon built his vision over time. He started with specific goals and objectives, detailing not only how to get the communes out of debt, but what the whole situation should look like in five years. He then went on to establish his ten-year vision—having all communes profitable. As things began to fall into place, only then could he focus on the broader vision of a united Europe, and even that was only after fate, circumstance, or whatever it was, led to the assimilation of other countries into Napoleon's empire.

To create a vision of our own that can evolve and flourish over time, we should account for and consider some other factors. First, as project managers, we must understand our roles and limitations with regard to the vision, and, at the very least, we must communicate the vision and ensure that it is realistic and measurable. Next, we need to assure that every team member and participant is truly working cohesively and in support of the vision. And to facilitate that, we must understand how to inspire team members with our own passion for the project. We must keep our eyes on the strategic goals, and not just focus on short-term needs, to help sustain the longevity of the vision and thus the results of the project. Finally, we must establish a routine for monitoring the overall status of the project against the vision and for being sure the vision still makes sense. Let's explore each of these areas in more detail.

The Nature of Project Management and Vision

How can we as project managers—and our leadership teams, if applicable—create a compelling vision if the projects are usually assigned by way of a charter?

The answer is that we won't always have the opportunity to *create* the vision, but we can—and must—*understand* and *articulate* it. If we don't understand the problem that is being addressed, the rationale for doing the project, and what the end result is supposed to look like—by way of customer-driven requirements—then we won't be able to relay it to our team. And we will be fighting an uphill battle to get our team and our stakeholders on board.

How can we get this data? There are several ways. Much of it should be found in the business case that was used to accept the project. If there isn't one, it may be a good time to institute a formal request and approval process that requires the requester to state the problem the project is meant to address, any tangible or intangible benefits, and any known risks. This is also useful in determining which projects to undertake. Many organizations have a formal portfolio management and governance process to address this. The problem can also be confirmed via surveys of the user community, management, and the project's sponsor, or via a series of meetings. Make certain the project's sponsor agrees as to the people who should be consulted. This will ensure that the project is meeting the needs of all stakeholders.

In some fields, design samples or mock-ups are used to toss around for comment and feedback. This is ideal, in that the vision can be fine-tuned based on people's feedback. To avoid a runaway project, what we call "scope creep," an agreement must be made in advance as to how many times it will go back and forth before agreeing on the scope of the vision.

Finally, to guarantee that the parameters of a vision—the supporting goals and objectives—are optimized for success, they should abide by certain basic rules. Remember Napoleon's goal of improving France's economy? Notice that this goal was qualitative and not quantitative. Goals state what we want to accomplish in general terms. Objectives, which support the goals, are more detailed. Napoleon's key objectives—getting the communes out of debt within five years and making them all prosperous within ten years—observed the modern-day rules that we refer to as SMART. That is, they were Specific, Measurable, Aligned (with the goals and overall vision), Realistic, and Time-bound. Just like Napoleon's, our objectives, and our overall vision, should follow these basic guidelines.

TEAM COHESION AND VISION

Napoleon knew the importance of ensuring that the management team was on board with his vision. He offered incentives for those who embraced the vision and dismissal for those who didn't. As project managers, we don't often have that amount of latitude, nor is it the best method we have today, but it is critical to have your leadership team buy into the vision, and Napoleon knew that.

It would be incorrect to assume that Napoleon made all of his decisions in isolation just because he expected his managers to support his vision. Quite the contrary. In his memoir, *Napoleon: How He Did It*, Baron Fain, Napoleon's secretary, said: "After his rise to commander-in-chief, he feared nothing so much as revealing the opinions of his bygone youth, and his policy in this respect went so far as to cultivate and even to seek out men of opposing opinion."[5] In other words, he made sure he had buy-in from others, before expecting his managers to follow his lead—at least until his later years, when the trappings of power took hold.

One way we can assure buy-in is to make certain that our vision is inclusive to begin with—that it considers the needs of all stakeholders. Books such as Dean Anderson and Linda Ackerman-Anderson's *Beyond Change Management* and Peter Senge's *The Fifth Discipline* suggest using a Whole System Model that considers the vision from the perspectives of all stakeholders, with the ideal situation being a cocreated or shared vision.[6] Kaplan and Norton echo this in their landmark book, *The Balanced Scorecard*, which suggests tying vision and strategy to four perspectives: Learning and Growth, the Business Process, the Customer, and the Financial Perspective.[7] These books should be the foundation for anyone seeking to craft a truly inclusive vision. Napoleon could have benefited from them, especially later in his career.

Fundamentally, Napoleon excelled at awareness, so no doubt he would have admired these studies—especially since they provide an organized, systematic way of keeping others' perspectives in mind. The key point is that just as it is important to be aware of changing circumstances and external events, it is critical to be aware of how a project impacts people, systems, and the future. There are a million ways that an otherwise well-run project could meet resistance and be seen as a failure, even if it ends up on time and on budget. Project management is about much more than just managing the triple constraint of time, cost, and scope. Ultimately, it is about people.

Passion and Vision

Speaking of people, there is nothing that makes a vision more compelling and a team more cohesive than passion. If a vision is based on some passionate need or drive, or is meant to ease a deep-seated fear, it is automatically compelling. Napoleon knew all too well what the French people were feeling after the Revolution. He had been there in Corsica, so he was able to play to the people's feelings.

> *I was born when my country was dying. Thirty thousand Frenchmen disgorged upon our shores, and drowning the throne of Liberty in a sea of blood—such was the hateful spectacle that offended my infant eyes. My cradle was surrounded, from the very day of my birth, by the cries of the dying, the groans of oppression, and the tears of despair.*[8]

At age twenty, Napoleon wrote the above letter to General Paoli, a former family friend and freedom fighter on Corsica, Napoleon's birthplace. At the time of the letter, Napoleon was a young soldier just returning from holiday, and Paoli was in exile. The letter continued:

> *Our compatriots, weighed down by the triple chain of soldier, lawyer, and tax collector, live despised—despised by those who wield the power of government.*[9]

Napoleon wrote the letter seeking feedback about a campaign of protest he intended to begin. It is no surprise that Napoleon, who practically grew up fighting oppression, was passionate about the mission of fighting monarchy, or that he was able to inspire others to this mission. We can apply this to business. When undertaking a project, is there some passionate need or fear that the project addresses? Can one be identified—and not fabricated? If so, it can be a powerful tool for making a vision compelling. If you can show people an example that clearly illustrates the need, all the better. As John P. Kotter and Dan S. Cohen said in the book *The Heart of Change: Real Life Stories of How People Change Their Organizations*, "People change less because they are given analysis and facts about why change is needed and more because we show them a truth that influences their feelings."[10]

What they are saying is that emotions motivate people more than statistics. One way to help trigger emotions is through stories. People tend to remember stories. They are *moved* by stories, which is why Jesus spoke in parables. Consider also what Harry Beckwith has to say in his book *What Clients Love*:

> Stories . . . reach places that no description can: people's hearts. Consider, for example, the many attempts to define "love." One author devised one popular definition, calling love "unconditional positive regard."[11]

What kind of stories can we tell? Perhaps stories of past events or other companies or projects, either those we should emulate or those we should avoid. The bottom line is: if we can find a story or an example that clearly shows the need for our project and inspires some sort of emotion, we'll be well on our way to getting people on board—with dedication and passion.

COST REDUCTION AND VISION

When Napoleon became the First Consul, it was a time of economic uncertainty in France, much like most of our world today. Knowing this, he created a vision that at the end of five years, all communes would either have their accounts in balance or have assets. Napoleon had a spreadsheet devised to analyze the situation and used it to craft a plan to get things in order. He even had a ten-year goal of all communes becoming profitable, ultimately leading to a prosperous and economically independent France.

Certainly these improvements would involve cost reductions. But they were tied to a need and sold as such, and were in harmony with other, more uplifting goals, rewards, and milestones. These uplifting goals included the civil codes and reforms that supported Napoleon's guiding principles of equality, liberty, and the representative system. Napoleon never lost sight of France's future. Today's companies would be wise to follow the same path.

In our own times of economic uncertainty, it is not surprising that cost cutting has become epidemic across the globe. Unfortunately, this is making its way into vision statements everywhere. A target cost reduction could indeed be part of a vision statement, but unless framed correctly, it's not very motivating. It is a challenge to project managers to make a vision that is centered on cost reduction sound compelling, just as it is a challenge for organizations to consider long-term strategies during economic uncertainty. Consider the following excerpt from an article by Jonathan Tate of PricewaterhouseCoopers, titled "Strange Days: Are Businesses Equipped to Catch Opportunity in an Unpredictable World?":

> Most cost cutting appears to be driven by the need to placate share-holders and analysts rather than by a real need to contain costs. Companies are failing to differentiate between good costs and bad costs, and shareholder appeasement is winning out over long-term strategic management. Managers worldwide are resorting to "slash and burn cost-cutting" instead of approaching cost control strategically and for the long term . . . Very few of these reductions are actu-

ally helping because many of the actions taken are done so without a clear vision or understanding of what adds value to the business and what does not . . . "This ambiguity and lack of direction has a severely negative impact on staff loyalty and the best people will often be tempted away to more forward-thinking competitors," according to Kevin Delaney, a PwC Partner in Human Resources Consulting.[12]

The solution would seem to be to consider target cost reductions only as needed, and in the context of the long-term vision, much as Napoleon did. It is better to focus on improvement initiatives or a strategic need, with cost reduction as a by-product. The trick is to frame it appropriately. For example, Napoleon's true goal was not to cut costs; it was to get France out of debt and for France to become ultimately prosperous. Cutting costs was merely a stepping-stone toward a more positive and uplifting goal—and one geared toward the future. Since many of today's organizations tend to focus only on the short-term needs, it becomes even more critical for the project manager to identify and articulate whatever vision there is, and to frame it in the context of a brighter future.

CHECKING YOUR VISION

Napoleon's vision evolved over time. As circumstances changed, old visions were no longer appropriate and new ones began to take hold. Once the communes were out of debt and the empire grew, he was able to focus on loftier visions that would have been unthinkable earlier.

The same holds true in project management. Ensuring that the vision is SMART (Specific, Measurable, Aligned, Realistic, and Time-bound) can help to avoid miscues. But even then, circumstances can change, and what seemed reasonable at one time may no longer be valid. Of course, to know this, we must keep tabs on how things are going. We can assume, based on Napoleon's documented passion for staying on top of changing events and altering plans accordingly, that he regularly checked that his vision and all related plans were still sound. In some cases, he had key performance indicators that let him know if things were on target. For example, since he was striving to improve France's economy, he used the price of wheat across the country as an economic indicator. Every two weeks he would check for trends and comparisons, along with the average price for all of France and the two counties representing the highest and lowest prices. In this way, he could see if his debt-reduction plans were working, and if his five-year vision was still appropriate.

For today's project managers, a simple and effective way to monitor our high-level vision is to have a periodic vision check, perhaps at certain milestones throughout the project. During such a checkpoint, which is ideally done with the project team and/or key stakeholders, it is good to ask questions such as: Are we on track? Is the vision still appropriate? Is there a more realistic or better vision that can be defined? If changes are needed and the vision itself is not under the control of the project manager, as is often the case, then perhaps it is a good time to suggest scope changes to the project sponsors. Of course, at the more detailed project plan level, we have specific performance indicators we can use to monitor how we are doing against schedule and budget (using the Earned Value method), but from a macro level we are just concerned about making sure the overall vision remains sound.

To ensure that a vision remains realistic throughout the length of a project, spot checks are often needed to assure that it still makes sense. Often, circumstances change or new information is obtained that will lead to a better, more appropriate vision.

EXECUTIVE SUMMARY

We have explored the need to define the problem, devise a strategy, and craft a clear and inclusive vision that considers long-term objectives. We have also benefited from seeing Napoleon and his consulate do likewise, following the postrevolutionary chaos in France. The next step would be a heavy and ongoing campaign of communication. Napoleon knew that the consulate needed to address their stakeholders—including their people, their allies, and, most of all, their enemies.

This combination of organization, planning, and communication paid off in dividends. By 1810, the French Empire had almost complete domination over the European continent. Only England and the Spanish guerrillas resisted. Next, we'll explore how careful and exhaustive diplomacy and networking led to such unprecedented success, and how we as project managers can do the same.

MARCHING ORDERS

DEFINE THE PROBLEM

Always start by defining the problem or need being addressed.

- Use the Five Why's: ask "Why?" five times until you get to the root of the problem.
- Consider a formal business case as part of a request/ governance process. This helps confirm the problem's criticality and validity.
- Write a mission statement that declares the problem being addressed—the project's reason for being.

DEVELOP A STRATEGY

Organize for success.

- Build a core team and subteam leads as needed.

- Address stakeholders early and often.
- Define and communicate guiding principles.
- Establish processes, systems, and tools.
- Maintain momentum; look for sources of motivation.

Strategize on a solution.
- Determine the requirements.
- Analyze the situation, focusing on the critical issues. This may require a preliminary risk analysis.
- Define alternate strategies and select the best one.

CREATE A VISION

Craft a clear and inclusive vision.
- If you are not in a position to create the vision, be sure that you understand and can articulate the vision.
- Remember SMART—Specific, Measurable, Aligned, Realistic, Time-bound.
- Build a shared or cocreated vision if possible. At the very least, consider the perspectives of all stakeholders.
- Find the passionate need or fear that the project addresses. Sell the vision with examples and stories that clearly show the need.
- If cost reduction must be part of the vision, be sure it is framed in context with a long-term strategy and combined with positive rewards and other uplifting goals and milestones.

Check your vision with periodic vision checks.
- Ask if the vision is on track and still appropriate.
- Adjust the vision as needed.
- If you are not in control of the vision, consider submitting a scope change request as needed.

CHAPTER 3

―――⟨◈⟩―――

Diplomacy and Networking

In military operations I consult nobody; in diplomatic operations I consult everybody.—NAPOLEON

When people hear the name Napoleon, diplomacy is usually the last thing that comes to mind. Yet it is diplomacy and networking, even more so than expertise on the battlefield, that enabled Napoleon to rise to the position of First Consul for Life and eventually to the position of emperor.

Once he became First Consul, Napoleon's focus was on peace. This was evident in his meetings with his Council of State, his endless letters of diplomacy, and the ultimate treaties with the Church and even his archrival, England. And peace he did achieve for a time, no small feat considering that his empire changed the way of life for virtually all of Europe.

As project managers and leaders, we also can benefit from networking and building relationships. Projects can run more smoothly—from the project selection and approval process to implementation and ultimately postproject evaluations—if stakeholders are on our side. And "stakeholders" means customers, functional managers, team members, senior managers, technicians, vendors, contractors, end users—anyone who can impact the success or perceived success of our project. How can we best do this? We have much to learn from Napoleon's methods of diplomacy, so let's see how he went about winning friends and influencing enemies.

First, we'll examine Napoleon's early days as a general, when he built crucial diplomatic skills during the Italian and Egyptian campaigns. Then we'll return to Napoleon as First Consul, where we'll explore how he turned enemies, particularly the Roman Catholic Church and his archrival England, into allies. Finally, we'll take an up-close look at how Napoleon conducted his Council of State meetings, which will give us valuable lessons in exercising diplomacy when running meetings with our project teams and stakeholders.

PREPARING FOR DIPLOMATIC SUCCESS

By the time Napoleon was First Consul, he was no stranger to diplomacy. He had built these skills over time as he elevated through the ranks—partly through his well-known successes on the battlefield, but greatly because of knowing the right people at the right time and making politically astute choices. Let's examine this more closely by looking back at Napoleon's days as a general. First we'll examine the Italian campaign, which resulted in a treaty with Austria and the establishment of two sister republics in Italy. Then we'll take a look at the Egyptian campaign, which doubled as a scientific expedition. Each brings us valuable lessons.

THE ITALIAN CAMPAIGN

Toward the end of the French Revolution, Napoleon had sensed the government's new constitution gaining momentum. He embraced the movement and had an opportunity to contribute his considerable artillery skills, thus gaining recognition by the new leadership—not to mention the reputation he had built from his bravery and integrity in battles such as Toulon. Meanwhile, France's enemies, Austria and Piedmont, who were committed to restoring the royalist regime, were just north of Italy preparing to invade France.

Opportunity knocks. Sensing a golden opportunity, Napoleon asked his leadership for permission to command the army against Austria and Piedmont in northern Italy. At this time he reported to Paul Barras, who was happy with the job Napoleon was doing commanding the Army of the Interior and was reluctant to part with Napoleon. Barras also knew, however, that Napoleon was planning to propose marriage to Josephine, a mutual friend and Barras's former mistress. Barras suspected he had much to gain from such a wedding, not only in removing his own entanglements with Josephine, but from the fact that he would have another ally in the noble class—Josephine was of noble birth, as was Barras. Napoleon, being in the right place at the right time and knowing the right people, was given command of the French army in Italy as a wedding present. Thus began the Italian campaign, and the first real test of Napoleon's diplomatic skills.

Building a reputation. Napoleon won the battles (turning an army of misfits into a motivated fighting force), but the real lessons here concern Napoleon's diplomatic negotiations. First, despite the fact that some unscrupulous government leaders wanted Napoleon to secure all sorts of monetary gains in a treaty with Piedmont, Napoleon negotiated a moderate treaty. Napoleon kept his integrity and principles intact and followed up with this statement to the Piedmontese:

> *People of Italy! The French army has come to break your chains . . . We shall respect your property, your religion, and your customs. We wage war with generous hearts, and turn ourselves only against the tyrants who seek to enslave us.*

Next, under orders to oust the pope once the papal states were under control, Napoleon instead decided to secure the pope's friendship and offered another moderate treaty. Even the Bourbon spies were surprised by his moderation.

Napoleon wasn't trying to destroy or conquer a peaceful country. He was trying to protect France and its new philosophies from a very real and impending threat and liberate the Italian people in the process. Keeping this goal in mind, he knew that he could catch more flies with honey. Napoleon was in essence turning enemies into allies. Many others have tried such a thing before and since and have failed.

What made the difference was that Napoleon followed up by keeping his promises. Once he defeated the Austrians, he completely rebuilt Italy, lobbying for funding, planting trees, abolishing feudal dues, establishing freedom of the press, working with the people to adopt a new flag—inspired by the French Tricolor and still the flag of Italy today—cutting down on crime, and declaring two Italian republics representing the north and the south. Staying true to his principles, he also abolished any persecution of people based on their class, whether it was the despised noble class or people of certain cultures, such as Jews, who before that had to wear the Star of David and remain in a locked ghetto at night; or Muslims, who were treated as second-class citizens. These reforms proved so successful that other regions of Italy petitioned to join the republics. It is through such diplomacy that Napoleon turned enemies into friends.

Managing up. Napoleon's diplomacy also extended to his superiors, as he knew he needed to "manage up" as well as "manage down." Several times during the Italian campaign, he had to make a strong case to his directors. At one point, they wanted to split the war effort, giving command of the battles in the north to another general while Napoleon led the campaigns in the south. Napoleon, having been burned before, lobbied to keep sole command. He remembered an incident during his first major battle, in which the mission was foiled because a senior officer he shared command with refused to provide cover in bad weather. He had learned then that unity of command was critical, and this time he was able to make his case, astutely stating, "One bad general is better than two good ones."

After the battles were won, Napoleon lobbied again, this time to get funds and support to help win the peace and rebuild Italy. He had seen too many failures in that area in Corsica, his homeland, and knew that civil war could ensue otherwise. Fortunately, he was given what he wanted, but only after a government spy reported that Napoleon was indeed not politically tied to any party nor his own ambitions, other than retaining the reputation he had won. The spy said in his report, "He has only one guide—the Constitution."

On October 17, 1797, Napoleon signed the Treaty of Campo Formio with Austria, resulting in Austria's recognition of the two Italian republics. Napoleon returned to France to critical acclaim unprecedented for a general and made this statement to his directors:

Religion, the feudal system, and monarchy have in turn governed Europe for twenty centuries, but from the peace you have just concluded dates the era of representative governments.

Napoleon was by then not only a general—he was a diplomat.

LESSONS FROM THE ITALIAN CAMPAIGN

There are several valuable lessons to be gleaned from the Italian campaign. First, let's remember how Napoleon came to lead this campaign. He began by embracing the movement for the new constitution. He gained visibility by being competent in the battlefield and demonstrated that he was to be counted on when it came to the new philosophy of France. We, too, can increase visibility for ourselves and for our teams by embracing change and ensuring our projects are aligned with an important strategic goal. This takes awareness of key movements in our organizations.

Also, Napoleon sought the opportunity to lead the Italian campaign and was given approval based only on his directors' perceived gains from Napoleon's relationship with Josephine. We, too, should seek visible opportunities and not be afraid to take on something that stretches our abilities. After all, we'll have the support of stakeholders and subject-matter experts. And while we can't always marry somebody to gain favor at work, we can increase our influence by networking as much as possible, either informally or through various organizational groups.

Napoleon's actions during and after the campaign also bring some good lessons. Napoleon made a strong case for retaining sole command. As Napoleon knew, unity of command is critical in joint operations. Many diplomatic issues can be avoided by first determining who has ultimate authority over multiple related initiatives. In the project management field, this can be translated to mean there ultimately can be only one project manager for each project, and where there are several related projects, the overall command is best grouped as part of one program—a group of related projects with a central administration point.

> A good rule of thumb is to try to focus on the positive, speak from experience, and always come prepared with a solution. Napoleon did all three.

Furthermore, Napoleon was able to gain credibility, not only with his superiors, but also with the local country's leadership and population, by sticking with good principles and not being afraid to speak up when he felt the wrong decisions were being made. We, too, need to speak up when necessary and make a case based on logic and not emotions. The confidence this can inspire and the integrity it shows can pay off in dividends. Be cautious, however, that you have the complete picture. Often, an inexperienced project manager will make a strong case to senior management, not knowing or considering all perspectives, only to find that there were other circumstances governing management's decisions. A good rule of thumb is to try to focus on the positive, speak from experience, and always come prepared with a solution. Napoleon did all three.

THE EGYPTIAN ADVENTURE

Following the Italian campaign and upon his return to France, Napoleon was put in charge of commanding the army against England, the only country still at war with France. After surveying the situation and seeing the futility of trying to invade England, which had total command of the seas, Napoleon proposed striking at England another way. He proposed invading and occupying Egypt. This served several purposes: it would put France within striking distance of the English in India; it would free Egypt from the control of the foreign elite class, the Mamelukes, who favored England; and, finally, it would enable France to learn about Egyptian history and in return teach the Egyptians modern medicine and technology.

As an added benefit, since the Mamelukes weren't exactly popular in Egypt, this was diplomatically a low risk, as long as relations could be maintained with nearby Turkey. Unfortunately, Napoleon's treacherous foreign minister, Tallyrand, never fulfilled his assigned diplomatic duties in Turkey, which caused some problems. But that's another story.

Although there were some military setbacks—Napoleon's fleet was destroyed by England, leaving his troops and him stranded in

Egypt fighting the invading Turks—diplomatically this was Napoleon's finest hour.

On the long journey to Egypt, Napoleon studied whatever he could about the people, the terrain, and past battles. Most notably, he studied the Koran. Once the Egyptians realized that Napoleon had taken the time to learn their customs and their ways, and as they saw the improvements he was able to bring, they accepted him as one of their own. Napoleon also made sure his troops followed sound principles. Upon arriving in Egypt, he made the following speech:

> *The people among whom we are going are Mahometans; the chief article of their creed is: God is God, and Mahomet is his prophet. Do not contradict them; deal with them as we have dealt with the Jews, with the Italians; show respect for their muftis and their imams, as you have for rabbis and bishops. The legions of Rome protected all religions. You will meet with customs different from those of Europe; you must learn to accept them.*

More than a conquest, the Egyptian campaign was an educational expedition, both for the French and the Egyptians. Napoleon's team of researchers, which included the greatest minds in France, discovered the Rosetta stone, which had text in three different scripts— hieroglyphs, demotic (modern Egyptian), and Greek. This enabled the first interpretation of hieroglyphics, which until then had never been solved. An entire universe of Egyptian history was opened. Modern Egypt evolved from this discovery and from other medical and scientific advancements Napoleon's team brought.

LESSONS FROM THE EGYPTIAN CAMPAIGN

We, as project managers and leaders, can also benefit from this expedition. First, remember that Napoleon studied the people and culture of Egypt, even studying the entire Koran. Just as in military battles, where he studied the topography intently before an invasion, here he studied the "topography" of the people and their culture. When he went to Egypt, he became an Egyptian, at one point even wearing the local attire. We, too, can do this—on many levels—whether learning the language of business, the culture of various organizations or functional groups, the perspectives and interests of senior management, personal details about our team members or customers, or the language or culture of our global stakeholders.

For example, someone in the marketing department may prefer to see only a high-level summary of issues, while an engineer may want to see the fine details. Senior management is typically interested in things that affect the bottom line. People from certain Latin American countries may have loose rules regarding time. These are all things that can be learned from books on business acumen, global cultures, or other topics related to understanding a specific group. The more we can learn about the perspectives of the people we deal with, the more successful we will be in any diplomatic endeavor. The key is to do the necessary homework.

Let's also remember that Napoleon had several reasons for targeting Egypt: to strike a blow to England, to liberate Egypt from a strict foreign ruling class, and to exchange scientific advancements for an understanding of Egyptian history and knowledge. Our projects, too, often have more advantages than are readily apparent. In the search to bring projects in on time and on budget and to meet financial objectives, let's not forget the intangible benefits that our projects often provide, whether it is customer loyalty, customer satisfaction, employee satisfaction, or another benefit that is hard to measure but can pay back in multiple ways. Where possible, it is a good idea to try to quantify these intangible benefits by giving them some estimated value—perhaps identifying the cost of not doing the project, or measuring the cost of errors, lost time, or the number of employee or customer defections, just to list a few examples.

There is no doubt that the Italian and Egyptian campaigns shaped Napoleon's diplomatic career. It is also plain to see that his diplomatic skills were just as important on his road to success as his renowned military prowess. And now that we've seen these formative events, let's revisit Napoleon's subsequent rise to First Consul. Then we'll see how he used these newfound skills to address some other brewing situations.

CREATING ALLIES

Near the end of 1799, Napoleon's time in Egypt was cut short when he received news that his government had made a mess of France through their mismanagement and improprieties. France was on the brink of a civil war, and now England had taken advantage of the situation, amassing additional allies, including Russia, Turkey, Naples, and Austria.

Adding fuel to the fire, the French government had broken relations with the Church, disillusioned after years of oppression and corruption by the clergy. As a result, most churches were closed, and people began to rebel. This was the situation Napoleon faced when he was asked to become First Consul after his return from Egypt. He had a real mess on his hands with threats from afar and unrest in France.

From the time Napoleon was named First Consul, he had been working to rebuild France by addressing financial issues, establishing a Senate and a new constitution, creating the Bank of France, establishing educational reforms, and creating a civil code with the help of his Council of State. Surely these things helped to get France under control. Now he had a few more issues to address.

PEACE WITH THE CHURCH AND ENGLAND

First, Napoleon knew he needed to resolve France's internal religious wars, which were still going on despite the valiant rebuilding efforts. He began studying reports and conducting surveys to see what the people really wanted. It was evident that the people wanted their churches back and that the government had misread what the people wanted, especially those in the south.

Napoleon negotiated a treaty with the pope, declaring Catholicism the majority religion in France as endorsed by the consulate—carefully worded to protect freedom of religion—and reopening the Roman Catholic churches. In exchange, the pope would recognize Napoleon's authority to appoint new bishops, who would be chosen on merit and worthiness, thus ending the supposed corruption issue. This treaty was called the Concordat.

After the Concordat, Napoleon had to deal with another problem. England was still determined to restore a Bourbon king to power in France. Wanting to secure peace once and for all, Napoleon decided to send a Christmas message to England's King George III:

Is the war that for eight years past has devastated the four quarters of the world to be eternal? Is there no possibility of coming to an agreement? How can the two most enlightened nations of Europe, both more powerful than is needed to secure their safety and independence, sacrifice their trade, their prosperity, and their domestic happiness to some vague notion of superiority? How can they fail to see that peace is the first necessity and the greatest of glories? Your Majesty must see in this overture nothing but my sincere desire by prompt action to effectively contribute . . . to a general conciliation.

King George III and his First Minister, William Pitt, were not impressed. Bitter over their defeat in the American Revolution and concerned about Napoleon's gains, including sister republics in Italy, Holland, and Switzerland, they were not about to appear soft and negotiate with this upstart from France. They also had allegiance to certain French nobles in exile. Most importantly, if Napoleon were to establish peace in Europe and spread his revolutionary principles, where would that leave England?

They responded to Napoleon with a demand to restore the Bourbon monarchy and to return to the borders of 1789. Having received England's response, Napoleon began writing diplomatic letters to other countries throughout Europe, confirming existing friendships and securing new ones. The people of England began to pressure their government for peace. It wasn't until Pitt resigned that his replacement, Addington, finally gave them what they wanted.

In March 1802, England signed the Treaty of Amiens with Napoleon, agreeing to a mutual return of gained territory by both sides to their rightful owners. Triumphantly announcing both the Concordat with the Church and the Treaty of Amiens with England, Napoleon was more popular than ever in France. The assemblies proposed that Napoleon be named "Consul for Life" (in essence, dictator), and the French people overwhelmingly voted in favor of this, by a margin of 3.5 million to eight thousand. Napoleon was on top of the world, and all of Europe was at peace. It would remain so for more than a year.

In his days as First Consul, Napoleon consulted all levels of stakeholders—the people, his government, his allies, his staff, and his enemies. He always sought popular opinion. He communicated frequently, through letters and face-to-face meetings. He established relationships on all levels, and perhaps of most importance, with his soldiers. When issues surfaced, he addressed them head-on, trying to avoid potential conflicts by inviting the other party to dinner to discuss the issue at hand, and at times even calling in a mediator—as we'll see in the next chapter. Napoleon had to wear many hats, including soldier, leader, planner, and administrator, but none were as critical to his success as that of diplomat and communicator.

LESSONS FROM NAPOLEON'S PEACE EFFORTS

We've covered quite a bit here, from Napoleon's efforts to make peace with the Church and England to his rise to Consul for Life. Clearly, we can see that without considerable diplomatic accomplishments, Napoleon would not have arrived at this place. There are some specific lessons worth pointing out from these endeavors that can help us make our projects more successful.

FIND OUT WHAT YOUR CUSTOMERS WANT

Let's note Napoleon's initial step when trying to resolve issues with the Church—he found out what the people wanted. As project managers, we often have a charter that says what the project is supposed to deliver, and we jump right into developing a solution. All too often, we don't take the time to find out what is really wanted or needed. Moreover, sometimes customers come with a desired solution, and even they don't quite know what they need or if it is the best solution to their problem. We must dig deeper to determine what they really lack or what is causing them difficulty. In this case, Napoleon sensed that the people needed their religion back, and he confirmed this with a survey.

It takes effort to find out what customers want and even more effort to balance that with the needs of other stakeholders, assuming we even remember to poll the stakeholders for their needs. We've already examined the requirement for a needs-based vision, but without involving stakeholders up front in determining the needs, a project is sunk from the start. Before we can develop technical specifications, which elaborate on how to do something; or even functional specifications, which detail what must be done, we must first get feedback on what the people want—and that means all stakeholders. A written process for identifying stakeholders and their goals, including checklists of standard questions to ask, can be of help in accomplishing that.

Prioritize Customers and Their Needs

Another thing to consider is that not everyone's voice should necessarily be equal. Some people have more at stake or have more influence. Some in the organization tend to speak louder than others—or at least are heard louder than others. It is a good idea to have some sort of system for ranking stakeholders based on influence and need, and prioritizing stakeholder wishes accordingly. Likewise, these prioritized needs can be used to identify and prioritize the design elements that must go into your project.

A tool called "House of Quality," part of the Quality Function Deployment tool used in Six Sigma, can help facilitate all of this. Six Sigma is a quality methodology created by Motorola and popularized by GE under CEO Jack Welch. The House of Quality tool involves listing the customers' requirements by priority and identifying which design essentials can best meet those needs. It is a way to ensure that "the people's voices" are heard and are incorporated into the product, and is especially valuable when developing a complex product that needs to meet the demands of a varied audience.

Let's use coffee as an example. If your customers have stated the requirements for their coffee in order of desirability—hot, strong, flavorful, and so forth—the next step would be to weigh this against the importance of various customers. For instance, customers who rarely drink coffee may not weigh as heavily in the decision. Once you have a good, prioritized set of requirements, with the customers' importance levels factored in, the next step would be to identify design elements to meet those requirements. For instance, if strong coffee is a high-priority requirement, you would want to be sure that you use fine grounds.

BUILD SUPPORT FROM THE GROUND UP

Let's also remember that when Napoleon tried to make peace with England, the English government initially replied quite negatively. Knowing that further pursuit would be fruitless, Napoleon began to ensure peace with other regions of Europe. It wasn't until Addington replaced Pitt in England, and with pressure from other parts of Europe and the people of England themselves, that England finally agreed to a deal. There is a crucial lesson here.

Despite our best intentions, there are going to be some people or groups that will resist our ideas or efforts, often for reasons beyond our knowledge. The best thing to do, after it becomes apparent that diplomatic efforts will not succeed, is to invest those diplomatic efforts elsewhere. Several things can result from this.

First, you can build enough of a critical mass that either you'll gain sufficient influence yourself, or there will be pressure from the masses for your "opponent" to be more amenable to your pursuits. Second, your opponent could end up being replaced by the time that happens or at least may lose influence, putting things more in your favor. Even marketing people recognize the value in this approach. Geoffrey Moore, in *Crossing the Chasm*, points out the futility of trying to sell to "laggards" or skeptics. Instead, he suggests going after the true fans, then the champions who may have something to gain from your idea, then those who are willing to buy in if they see others on board, and so forth.[1] Before long, you have critical mass and the skeptics become irrelevant.

COMMUNICATE FREQUENTLY
AND EFFECTIVELY

Napoleon spent countless hours communicating to all levels of stakeholders, addressing conflicts head-on when they arose and consulting his constituents when faced with major decisions that could have diplomatic impact. Communication is key in any project, no matter how small. A project that meets all other criteria for success could be viewed as a dismal failure if communication is inadequate. Think of the adage "If a tree falls in the forest and nobody's there to hear it, did it make a sound?" The same is true when managing projects, which is why the Project Management Institute rightfully considers communication to be 90 percent of a project manager's job. Perception is everything.

Even with the best communication, occasionally conflicts occur. When they do arise, address them immediately and face-to-face, as Napoleon did, not via e-mail or written communication. Use the proven conflict management skills of raising your concern, letting the other person state his or her position, offering your position, and working together to solve the problem. Many conflicts can be resolved by focusing on true, collaborative problem solving—as opposed to compromising, withdrawing, or forcing—and by avoiding "you" messages in favor of "I" messages. Conflicts are acceptable and sometimes are needed in order to get broad viewpoints. Unresolved conflicts are not.

As for consulting constituents, as Napoleon did time and time again, we, too, must consult others when making key decisions that could have political impact. Just as we included stakeholders up front in determining project goals, we need to include them in other key decisions that could impact them. If we make them part of the solution and/or decision, they'll be less likely to criticize it later.

And now that we've discussed the need to involve stakeholders early and often, let's explore another element of dealing with stake-holders, one that we face routinely in our work lives—running effective meetings. Fortunately, Napoleon's Council of State meetings offer us many lessons for this routine yet frequently mismanaged affair.

RUNNING EFFECTIVE MEETINGS

During Napoleon's time as First Consul, a good part of his day was spent dictating and answering letters, issuing orders, checking ministers' reports, reviewing budgets, and performing various other administrative duties. Another major task Napoleon performed— initially daily and later several times a week—was to conduct his Council of State meetings, with the purpose of reviewing and drafting laws and decrees, starting with what would become a new civil code. Council members were civilians chosen by Napoleon from all over France and from various ranks, each chosen for an area of specialty. In this way, the right people would be gathered to make effective decisions. Napoleon's government was truly inclusive and thus represented the will of the people.

One can imagine that there were varying opinions when it came to creating a civil code. During the meetings, Napoleon would let others talk freely about an issue, and then would offer his thoughts. Although he always read in advance on the topics at hand, he wasn't afraid to admit he knew nothing about a certain subject and would often ask the experts to explain the basic concepts. He would continue to ask questions until he understood enough to offer intelligent input. He also encouraged finding the most efficient way to do something and was not interested in reinventing the wheel.

The council voted on decisions, with Napoleon usually abiding by the majority vote and occasionally spending time to make his case if he disagreed. Meetings were long, but this was by necessity, as there was much to do.

INCLUDE THE RIGHT PEOPLE

Napoleon's Council of State meetings carry some valuable lessons for us as project managers. First, when conducting meetings or even when assembling a team, it is important that we, too, include the right people—and this may mean including people from various departments or different ranks. This inclusiveness will not only ensure that key areas will be adequately addressed, but it also will serve to get the proper buy-in early in the project.

We need to consider who actually needs to be at any given meeting, as there may be more efficient ways of communicating with certain audiences. There are some proven project management tools today that help facilitate this. A communication plan can help identify what types of communication are needed and the most receptive audience for each, the communication method (e-mail, face-to-face, etc.), and the appropriate frequency of the communication (weekly, monthly, as needed, etc.).

Another good tool is a RACI (pronounced "racie") chart, which identifies roles and responsibilities. For each major deliverable, a RACI chart outlines who is responsible (the doers), who is accountable (there can be only one owner), who needs to be consulted, and who needs to be informed. Combined, these documents can help manage all stakeholder communications, including who needs to attend which meetings.

PREPARE . . . PREPARE . . . PREPARE

In preparing for meetings, we should learn as much as possible about the topics at hand, create a formal agenda, and distribute it to all invitees. Napoleon immersed himself in a topic before conducting meetings and still learned more from the subject-matter experts at the meeting.

ASK QUESTIONS AND STATE YOUR CASE

At the meeting, after presenting the topic(s) to be discussed, it is a good rule to let the experts discuss the issues at hand and then weigh in once the various sides have been heard. Also, like Napoleon, don't be afraid to ask questions or request an explanation of anything you don't understand. There is nothing wrong with asking what may seem to be a basic question. Often others in the room are wondering the same thing. That's not to say you shouldn't read up on the topic in advance of the meeting to become as literate as possible on the subject. It is often the less-experienced project managers, lacking confidence, who tend not to ask questions, then leave the meeting not having offered anything and not fully understanding what was discussed.

There is a difference between asking questions and entering a debate on a topic that you know little about. Consider this fatherly advice Napoleon once bestowed upon a young prince:

> *Speak as little as possible; you have not sufficient knowledge, and your education has been too much neglected for you to plunge into impromptu debate. Learn how to listen, and remember that silence often produces as much effect as knowledge. Don't blush to ask questions, however. Though a viceroy, you are but twenty-three years old, and whatever flattery may tell you, people are perfectly aware of just how much you know, and think better of you for what you may become than for what they know you to be.*

At first, this may seem like conflicting advice, but what Napoleon was saying is that the less experience you have in an area, the better it is to listen and avoid debate—but do not hesitate to ask plenty of questions. This is sound advice for any of us.

If the majority of people at a meeting, however, reach a decision that you do not agree with and you feel you understand the issues reasonably well, it can't hurt to try to make your case. Either you will raise issues that nobody thought about, or they will convince you that their decision is the correct one. It is generally a good idea, if at all possible, to concede to the majority after presenting your case. It is the manager's right and responsibility to make the ultimate decision, but keep in mind that going against the majority is not without diplomatic risk. These are all guidelines that Napoleon tried to follow during his Council of State meetings and his communications with people in general. They certainly are applicable to us today.

EXECUTIVE SUMMARY

Napoleon rose to the position of First Consul for Life as much from his diplomatic skills as his successes on the battlefield. Although we may not become First Consuls for Life, we can achieve great success in the project management field using these valuable lessons in diplomacy, such as the importance of networking, learning the language of our stakeholders, and understanding the people aspect of our projects. We can also build more credibility by running effective meetings, which requires that we engage the right people at the right time, listen to all parties before judging, and ask plenty of questions.

So far, we've seen how Napoleon's efforts allowed him to subdue a revolution, change the face of Europe, and end up with a peaceful continent—a peace that would last for more than a year. We've also seen how Napoleon's campaigns to this point were defensive in nature, just as he professed in his memoirs. We will next explore the period known as the Napoleonic Wars, a series of campaigns that resulted, against all odds, in Napoleon's territory growing to unprecedented proportions. We will see how Napoleon became emperor, how coalition after coalition formed against him, and how he consistently came out on top.

These great campaigns, widely known as the greatest achievements of Napoleon's military career, offer us many lessons as applicable to today's business world as they have been to military leaders for years. We'll discover how Napoleon structured his *Grande Armée* for speed and flexibility, and how they were able to conquer armies much greater in number. We'll see firsthand the importance of acting quickly, providing focus, and enabling decentralized command and control. Most of all, we'll learn how we can use these principles and techniques to bring success to our projects.

MARCHING ORDERS

PREPARE FOR DIPLOMATIC SUCCESS
Embrace change.
- If your organization is moving in a certain direction, assuming it's of sound principles, embrace it. Immerse yourself in it.
- Don't be afraid to take on a major initiative that may seem over your head. Make good use of subject-matter experts.

Get to know people at all levels.
- Many jobs are won or lost based on relationships with peers, subordinates, and management.
- Try networking with various groups within and outside your organization. These can be formal groups or informal social gatherings.
- Many positive relationships are built during classes.

Speak up.
- Don't be afraid to make a case for something you believe will make or break the success of your project, especially when it adheres to good principles. But first, hear the other side to assure you have the complete picture.
- Focus on the positive, speak from experience, and always come prepared with a solution.

Aim for unity of command to avoid unnecessary disputes.
- Determine who has overall command when there are multiple operations that are dependent upon one another. Ideally, there should ultimately be only one project manager.
- Consider grouping related projects under one program, where each project can have its own project manager, but program level oversight consolidates redundant efforts and ensures alignment.

Learn the language of your stakeholders, including:
- business acumen—or the acumen of whatever field you're in.
- organizational, functional, or department-specific cultures.
- foreign cultures and languages.
- personal details about team members and customers.

Consider intangible "people" benefits your project will deliver.
- Find the intangible benefits that can impact all levels of stakeholders.
- Try to quantify the benefits by giving them an estimated value, or perhaps use the cost of not doing the project.

CREATE ALLIES

Find out what is important to people.
- Bring stakeholders in early to get a broad view of the need.

- Have a written process for interviewing stakeholders and confirming the goals of your project.

Listen to your stakeholders.

- Categorize stakeholders based on influence and/or need.
- Prioritize the overall list of requirements based on stakeholder importance.
- Prioritize your design elements based on the requirements.
- Consider using a House of Quality approach to tie design elements to requirements.

If one person or group is giving you difficulty, build support elsewhere.

- Don't waste time trying to sell ideas to a skeptic.
- Read *Crossing the Chasm*, by Geoffrey Moore, for information on how to build mass support. When you gain mass support, your "opponent" either joins you or loses influence and becomes irrelevant.

Relationships take work. Communicate constantly to all levels.

- Communication is 90 percent of a project manager's job.
- Address potential conflict situations promptly, directly, and diplomatically; use "I" messages; state the problem; let the other person talk first; and work together to solve the problem.
- Always consult others when making diplomatic decisions.

RUN MEETINGS EFFECTIVELY

Engage the right people at the right time.

- Don't involve a cast of thousands if they don't all need to be involved at once.

Engage people in the right way.

- Some people may need to be invited to a meeting; others can simply be updated via e-mail.

- Consider having a communication plan to list all types of communication, the audience for each type, the frequency, and the method.
- Consider a RACI Roles and Responsibilities chart, which can help provide input to a communication plan. For each major deliverable, this details who is responsible (the doers), who is accountable (the owners), who needs to be consulted (for input), and who needs to be informed.

Use best practices when running meetings.
- Prepare in advance; learn about the topics at hand.
- Have a set agenda, distributed in advance.
- Include the right people—only those who will have input or some role in the meeting.
- Let others talk first to hear all sides; then offer your input.
- Don't be afraid to ask questions.
- Try to go with the majority, but don't hesitate to make your case if you disagree, especially if you understand the issues at hand. Ultimately, you own the final decision.

CHAPTER 4

Lessons from the Great Campaigns

My son should often read and meditate on history; it is the only real philosophy. And he should read and meditate on the campaigns of the Great Captains. This is the only way to learn the art of war. —NAPOLEON

We have seen Napoleon rise to glory on a solid set of ideals, hard work, and exhaustive diplomacy. Now we will explore Napoleon on the battlefield—and preparing for battle. We can learn much from Napoleon's battle preparations, strategies, and motivation techniques, all applicable to modern-day project management. This is especially true of his greatest campaigns, particularly the 1805 campaigns in Ulm and Austerlitz against the Third Coalition.

There were seven coalitions against France, from the French Revolution through the Napoleonic era. The First Coalition (1792–1797) began toward the end of the French Revolution, when Napoleon was still an artillery major fighting the English in the Mediterranean port of Toulon (the battle in which he was first recognized), and continued during the Italian campaign, when he was promoted to general. Toward the end of the Revolution, France's neighbors, led by a privileged royal class, were not about to allow revolutionary activity to spread to their countries, and thus formed a coalition against France—later referred to as the First Coalition. Napoleon was instrumental in turning things around, both at Toulon and during the Italian campaign, and the coalition ended with the Treaty of Campo Formio with Austria.

The Second Coalition (1798–1801) formed while Napoleon was in Egypt, when the new French government neglected to maintain adequate diplomatic relations during this crucial postrevolutionary period. Once again Napoleon saved the day: returning to France, taking over as First Consul, organizing successful campaigns to put down the coalition, rebuilding France's infrastructure, and establishing relations with England and the Church. Peace lasted for a while, but soon there would be a Third Coalition. This led to the two greatest campaigns of Napoleon's career.

THE THIRD COALITION

In 1803, Napoleon discovered that England had no intention of fulfilling its obligations tied to the Treaty of Amiens, particularly its promises to return Alexandria to Turkey and to return Malta, a recent English capture, to France. Even worse, England was now encouraging antirepublican sentiment throughout Europe. England's King George III began preparing for war, justifying his actions based on reports of massive French military preparations— reports that were false and meant to stir up fear throughout England and rally the public's support for a war. From the English perspective, Napoleon's expanding realm was a threat, and they were still reeling from recently losing the colonies to America. Napoleon tried to negotiate with England several times to no avail, even offering to have Russia, one of England's allies, mediate. In May 1803, England declared war on France, and the period of peace officially ended.

The Causes of the Third Coalition

There were two events that led Austria and Russia to join the British in the war against France. First, when Napoleon discovered that a Bourbon prince, the Duke of Enghien, was involved in a royalist plot to assassinate him, he had the prince kidnapped and brought to trial in a military court, where he was found guilty and executed. This event angered many people in Europe, as they deemed the evidence circumstantial—a matter still debated today.

Second, there was Napoleon's appointment as emperor. When the people of France became concerned about continued plots against Napoleon's life, they called on him to establish a hereditary monarchy. Napoleon accepted the idea, but with the caveat that his rule would be supported by a senate and a constitution, so as to be more of a republic. He consulted his generals and his Council of State. All were in favor. He then put the vote to the people. The vote came back in favor by more than 3.5 million to three thousand. Supported by an overwhelming majority, Napoleon was proclaimed emperor of the French on May 18, 1804. Between the Duke of Enghien affair, Napoleon's designation as emperor, and misinformation, Russia and Austria were convinced of the need to stop Napoleon. By August 1805, the campaigns of the Third Coalition and the period commonly known as the Napoleonic Wars had begun.

THE ULM CAMPAIGN

In August 1805, Napoleon was in Boulogne, a coastal town in northern France, waiting for his squadrons at sea to clear the way for his huge invasion force to cross the Channel into England. Through his sources in Italy, he was also aware that Austria was preparing for war. He wrote to his foreign minister, Talleyrand:

The more I reflect on the situation, the more I feel it urgent to take deci-
sive action. By April, I shall find 100,000 Russians in Poland, paid by
England, 15 or 20 thousand English in Malta, and 15,000 Russians in
Corfu. I should then be in a critical situation.

The Plans Begin

Austria's plan was to attack the French army in Italy, simultaneously invade French-controlled Bavaria, and wait there for the Russians to arrive from the east to assist. With the combined forces of Austria and Russia, and full control of Italy and Bavaria, they could invade France.

Napoleon knew he needed to act at once. He decided to pull his entire army of nearly two hundred thousand men from Boulogne, go east across France and Germany, and defeat the Austrians before Russia could arrive. Thus, the French were approaching from the west and the Russians from the east, both trying to get to Austria in the middle.

Setting the Objectives

Napoleon set two objectives. His primary objective would be to invade the Austrians in the Danube Valley before the Russians could arrive, which is where he would focus his two hundred thousand troops. A secondary objective would be to simultaneously attack the Austrian troops who were farther south in Italy to prevent them from joining the main forces to the north. To accomplish this, he would have Marshal Massena command the fifty thousand troops in the French-infused army of Italy. Also, Napoleon would use reserves to support this secondary objective, so as to make use of all possible troops. This would help ensure the success of this secondary objective, and thus protect the primary objective to the north.

ENGAGING KEY STAKEHOLDERS

The first thing Napoleon did after determining the objectives was to engage the support of key stakeholders. He negotiated agreements with the southern German territories, including Bavaria, to allow use of their land as a battleground and to secure their assistance. He also negotiated secret treaties with the Prussians to the north, to assure that they remained neutral.

DOING THE RESEARCH

Napoleon then issued orders for an advance guard to march to the Rhine and sent his brother-in-law, Marshal Joachim Murat, to perform reconnaissance missions around Bavaria, reporting on the topology of the roads and rivers. He sent yet others to inspect bridges, riverbanks, and surrounding territories. Napoleon paid so much attention to detail that he instructed Marshal Berthier, the director of his Imperial General Staff, to create an index of each of the Austrian army's units and current location, to be reported on a daily basis.

SETTING PROTOCOLS

Napoleon laid out an initial plan, identifying which troops were to be in which regions by specific dates (some of his troops were already in the northern German states waiting to meet up with the rest of his army) and establishing communication protocols. His army would march in parallel lines—seven corps across a one-hundred-mile front—with each corps commander regularly updated via messages from Napoleon's Imperial General Staff as to the position and current directives of the other corps. Likewise, each commander had to keep the Imperial General Staff updated. This was truly an integrated army.

Equipped for Success

Napoleon's *Grande Armée*, as it was now called, marched 375 miles from the Channel coast to the Rhine, which ran along the French/German border, in less than six weeks, at a rate of fifteen miles per day—an unprecedented feat. Napoleon made sure his troops understood the importance of the mission, were well trained to live off the land, and had their basic needs met—especially good walking shoes, although some rode in wagons. What also helped was that the French had reengineered their artillery to use lighter material, making the trek less burdensome than with traditional equipment.

Staying Flexible

During the march, Napoleon learned from his ally, the Bavarian elector, who fled to a nearby town and was able to keep in touch with Napoleon's officers, that the Austrians had indeed crossed the Inn River and invaded Bavaria. A week later, Murat informed Napoleon that the Austrians had pushed farther ahead into Ulm, a nearby Bavarian town, under the command of General Karl Mack, an old warhorse. Napoleon immediately redirected his troops to loop around and surround Ulm from the east.

An Easy Victory

The rapid march of his *Grande Armée*, the extensive reconnaissance, the keen diplomacy, and, above all, the up-to-the-minute reports, all paid off. By late September, Napoleon's troops had General Mack's armies surrounded, and the battle was practically won before any fighting began. Mack was facing west, from which direction he expected the French to appear, but they surprised him by arriving behind him from the east, the direction from which he expected the Russian reinforcements to appear. For added effect, Napoleon had some troops appear from the west as a ploy. Furthermore, by arriving from the east, Napoleon cut off Mack's line of communication with Vienna, the Austrian capital, and separated Mack from the oncoming Russians.

Where were the Russians during all of this? Unfortunately for the Austrians, the Russians were running eleven days behind because of a communication problem. As it turned out, they were still using the Julian calendar. They had not yet switched over to the Gregorian calendar that the rest of Europe was following (and the Western world uses today). They were still a hundred miles away.

FINISHING THE JOB

With Ulm under imminent control, Napoleon needed to address the threat of the approaching Russians. His objective would be to proceed east to take Vienna. Napoleon immediately reorganized his army. He left Murat in charge of finishing the job at Ulm, with detailed instructions as usual. Unfortunately, although Murat was a heroic officer and soldier, he was far from a strategic thinker. He decided to improvise and didn't follow Napoleon's orders—something Napoleon routinely chided him for. As a result, some Austrians escaped and took a bridge just northeast of Ulm, and others escaped southward into Italy. Napoleon shortly returned, bombarded Ulm, and forced Mack to surrender.

In a few days at Ulm, Napoleon defeated Mack's army, which represented half of the Austrian army. Napoleon accomplished this victory with minimal losses—and those were only because of Murat's errors.

LESSONS FROM THE ULM CAMPAIGN

Let's examine the lessons the Ulm campaign carries for us, such as the importance that awareness and speed played in Napoleon's success; the flexible but unified structure of his *Grande Armée*; and his pioneering use of Economy of Force—a concept still valued today in both military and, yes, project management circles.

THE IMPORTANCE OF AWARENESS AND SPEED

Napoleon quickly became aware of Austria's intent while his army was in Boulogne. He was able to do this because of his network of spies that kept him abreast of the ever-changing situation in Europe. While engaging spies is not appropriate in business, there are other ways we can stay in touch with events that could impact our projects, whether through informal networking or relying on input from our teams and/or colleagues, which, in essence, is not unlike the use of spies. With this knowledge, we are then in a position to take action when needed, assuming we're astute enough to realize the dangers of inaction.

> It is in this vital balance of awareness and speed that success is to be found, as speed alone can be dangerous, and knowledge doesn't do much good unless we have the good sense to know when to act.

Consider Napoleon's letter to Tallyrand about the need to take action. Napoleon thought about what would occur if he did not act. He knew that if he did not act, it could have broad implications with the Russians in Poland and Corfu as well as the English in Malta. We, too, must consider the risk of not acting when contemplating a project. Ideally, we would do this during early planning, as part of risk analysis, or by building the cost of not doing the project into a business case for the project. If the cost of not acting can be quantified, it is even better.

In addition, let's bear in mind that after Napoleon did think about the risk of inaction, he moved quickly. He knew the importance of speed, and that wars can be won or lost based on a matter of minutes. The same is true for projects. As we'll explore in detail later, many things can go wrong with just the slightest delay. In this case, Napoleon's speed enabled him to both surprise the Austrians and take advantage of the Russians' tardiness.

It is in this vital balance of awareness and speed that success is to be found, as speed alone can be dangerous, and knowledge doesn't do much good unless we have the good sense to know when to act. Most importantly, we need to recognize the risks of delay. We'll examine this in more detail in Part 2.

FLEXIBLE AND UNIFIED: LESSONS FROM THE GRANDE ARMÉE

In addition to awareness and speed, there were many other factors that led to the success of the Ulm campaign, some from the way Napoleon structured his *Grande Armée*. Never before was an army structured for such flexibility, yet still kept unified by a common high-level goal. Today, we refer to this alignment of activities with high-level goals as "strategic management." While there were others in revolutionary France who began developing this concept, Napoleon was the first to execute it on such a grand scale, which required orchestrating all of his forces to operate in concert with one another. His forces needed to operate as separate, self-contained units with the ability to make decisions on the fly, yet they needed to work in harmony with one another. How was this accomplished?

DECENTRALIZED COMMAND AND CONTROL

First, in addition to infantry (foot soldiers), cavalry (soldiers on horseback), and artillery reserves (weapons specialists), each corps had its own commander and full staff, including a chief of staff, intelligence officers, and engineering, logistics, and other staff-level officers. In this way, each team was a self-contained unit, capable of caring for itself. Also, Napoleon made sure to convey the project's concept in detail before actions commenced, which meant that throughout the campaign his communications were able to be brief and to the point. As a result, his teams were empowered for decentralized decision making through this combination of up-front clarification of purpose and principles, and ongoing broad directives.

For this to work, all groups and leaders needed to follow a common set of goals and objectives as well as common guidelines, and there needed to be some central body managing the whole affair. Napoleon's central body was his high command, which consisted of a cabinet with three bureaus: the Intelligence Bureau, the Topographic Bureau, and the Secretariat, which dispatched all orders. Furthermore, he had an Imperial General Staff, directed by Marshal Berthier, which managed the day-to-day operations of the army and served as a central communications point. Today we refer to this combination of decentralized decision making and centralized planning and administration as "decentralized command and control"—and the Ulm campaign was the first use of this concept.

CENTRALIZED PLANNING
AND ADMINISTRATION

The construction of Napoleon's *Grande Armée* could correlate to several things in project management. First, let's look at centralized planning and administration. For multiple major efforts within a large project, various project leaders could be assigned, reporting to a single project manager. They would all follow a common policy manual and a common set of goals and objectives. For example, if we have a project to develop two new products that will be released together, we could have a project leader for each product, both reporting to the overall project manager. The guidelines and policies would be the same for both efforts, and the project manager would track the combined efforts in one project plan.

The project manager could also establish a core team, which would conduct unified planning, communications, quality, research, administration, or any other items that make sense to consolidate. This is much like Napoleon's cabinet, which managed planning efforts; and his Imperial General Staff, which managed operations. The core team could keep each of the project leaders up-to-date on progress and current directives of the other teams, assuring that all efforts are being done in harmony—much as Napoleon's Imperial General Staff kept the corps commanders up-to-date. In addition, a member of the core team could be responsible for centralized project control, including managing the project schedule, risks, issues list, and other items that could alleviate the burden for the project manager.

Another thing to consider is whether or not to manage multiple projects as a "program," which is a group of separate but related projects. Often, it's a toss-up whether to manage the overall effort as a large project with multiple subprojects or as a program with multiple projects, and generally the same rules apply. A program typically works best when there needs to be some facility to launch and end multiple projects throughout the life cycle of the effort. An example would be an annual program of multiple newsletter issues, each one representing a project.

A program also works well if the individual projects require heavy leadership and planning within themselves and have only minor touch points between them. Ultimately, it often comes down to the culture of an organization. The key point is that related efforts in an organization should be grouped together in some way and administered centrally.

In addition to centralized planning and administration of a project or program, in many organizations a PMO (Program Management Office or Project Management Office) will serve as the unit responsible for setting policy and ensuring that a common methodology is used for managing projects across the organization. In this way, not only will multiple projects within a program share common planning and administration, but all programs and projects in the organization will share a common doctrine. PMOs often serve other functions as well, such as training, auditing, mentoring, resource management, or even centralized management of projects.

DECENTRALIZED DECISION MAKING

As for "decentralized decision making," various project leaders—or project managers, in the case of a program—would be given high-level deliverables to achieve and would be responsible for leading their staff accordingly. Of course, the clearer the deliverables, the more chance of success, but the key is that the project manager cannot be micromanaging all efforts, so instructions must be clear and simple up front. Most importantly, we need to communicate the goals, objectives, and guiding values and principles. This enables decision making on the fly by the respective project leaders. Finally, to make all this work, we need to be sure that the various teams are not operating in isolation, and that a mechanism is in place for sharing frequent updates on status and changes in events.

These methods, when used in concert with centralized planning and administration, can provide us with a proven, scalable way to successfully lead our projects without getting bogged down in micromanagement.

ECONOMY OF FORCE:
THE NAPOLEON/GOLDRATT CONNECTION

So far, the Ulm campaign has brought us some valuable things to consider, including the importance of awareness and speed, centralized planning and administration, and decentralized decision making. Now, let's examine one more crucial lesson from the Ulm campaign—the use of Economy of Force.

Napoleon took his entire *Grande Armée* with him when he left Boulogne for the long march to the Rhine. He chose not to leave half his army in Boulogne because he knew that concentration of forces is critical in war; otherwise, efforts are diluted. He focused most of his forces (two hundred thousand troops) on the primary objective—invading the Austrians via the Danube Valley in the north. And he invested the minimal effective number of forces (fifty thousand troops) in the secondary objective—to prevent the Austrians to the south in Italy from joining the others. This was a strategy Napoleon often used: concentrating his forces on the most important objectives at the strategic point of impact and giving only the minimal effective number of forces to secondary objectives.

Napoleon didn't waste his reserves, but studied the situation and used them strategically. He committed all of his reserves, but at the points where they would be needed most; for example, to support a secondary objective to prevent it from impeding the associated primary objective, or for some strategic need later on. At Ulm, either to use his reserves as part of the main body of troops—or not to use them at all—would have been wasting them.

Napoleon's strategic use of his forces was admired and studied by many, including the Prussian general Karl von Clausewitz, whose book *On War* is still considered the leading book on military strategy.[1] The French general Antoine Henri de Jomini's classic book, *The Art of War*, expanded on these concepts to include the importance of diplomacy.[2] These works exposed Napoleon's principles to the world for the first time, especially the principle known in military circles as "Economy of Force."

Economy of Force consists of using all available resources, but giving secondary objectives only the minimal amount needed. This preserves the majority of resources for the most important work. In other words, the secondary objectives can bear some risk in favor of focusing on the primary objective. "Concentration of Force," which involves focusing the majority of resources on the primary objective, goes hand in hand with Economy of Force. The one remaining variable is the use of reserves, which, while they shouldn't be wasted, should be strategically used, often to supplement the secondary objectives or held for some strategic planned activity. The key point is that we don't want the secondary objectives to become so critical that they impede the primary objective.

ECONOMY OF FORCE
AND PROJECT MANAGEMENT

What does this have to do with project management? Everything. Not only are the concepts of Economy of Force, Concentration of Force, and the associated strategic use of reserves relevant to project management; indeed, there is an entire movement dedicated to the project management field that takes fundamentally the same approach. The methodology is called "Critical Chain Project Management" (CCPM), which is part of Dr. Eliyahu Goldratt's Theory of Constraints management philosophy. Its applicability to managing projects is documented in his landmark book, *Critical Chain*.[3] Critical Chain Project Management carries the promise of nearly doubling the throughput of projects and greatly improving on-time accuracy, and has been proven to do so by a wide variety of government and Fortune 500 organizations.

The basic concept of Critical Chain Project Management is to focus your key resources on the critical tasks, removing all other interruptions, while adding a protective time buffer (reserves) to the end of each chain of noncritical work to prevent it from impeding the flow of the critical work. A buffer is also added at the end of the project, where it is most likely to be needed. Sound familiar?

All of these buffers necessitate removing any hidden padding that people inherently put into each task estimate to accommodate unpredictability—padding that typically gets wasted because of procrastination or other reasons. In this way, by considering the psychological issues involved and by acknowledging that uncertainty is a given, we achieve a more holistic plan. Even Clausewitz recognized the dangers of any formula that doesn't take into account people and uncertainty, when he said the following about traditional war plans:

> They aim at fixed values; but in war everything is uncertain, and calculations have to be made with variable quantities. They direct the inquiry exclusively towards physical quantities, whereas all military action is intertwined with psychological forces and effects. They consider only unilateral action, whereas war consists of a continuous interaction of opposites.[4]

Certainly, the same can be said for traditional project management.

THE AUSTERLITZ CAMPAIGN

After Napoleon's army defeated General Mack at Ulm, it then headed east to face the Russians. Meanwhile, the Russians had gathered in Moravia—northeast of Vienna, in what is now the Czech Republic—along with the remaining Austrian army. The

Austro-Russian army was ninety thousand strong. Since Napoleon had to leave troops to hold Vienna and protect the army's rear, he had only seventy-five thousand troops at his disposal.

By now Napoleon was in Vienna, where he established his head-quarters. Again, he sized up the situation and knew he needed to act quickly. He decided to march his troops to Moravia. Much like his preparations for Ulm, Napoleon had spies survey the situation. Then Napoleon surveyed the area personally and determined an ideal battle spot from which he would have good visibility. It was near the village of Austerlitz, now called Slavkov, which was situated just to the east of a large plateau known as the Pratzen Plateau. Napoleon could see everything from atop the plateau.

Napoleon had Berthier's Imperial General Staff issue instructions to the corps commanders. The plan was to give the appearance of weakness on the right flank, luring the Austro-Russian army into attacking this supposedly weak spot to the south. Then reserves from Vienna would arrive to attack the enemy from the south, while Napoleon's massive army to the north would loop around and attack their center.

The Austro-Russian army situated itself just east of the plateau. Napoleon's army, initially located on the plateau for observation, backed down to a nearby river. Napoleon would give the impression that he was retreating by moving down from the plateau. Always on top of things, Napoleon then received word that the Austro-Russian army was gathering a bit farther south than he expected, so he sent revised instructions to his reserves in the south. Otherwise, every-thing was going as planned.

MOTIVATING THE TROOPS

On December 1, 1805, Napoleon made a rousing speech to his troops, a speech that would later be published, illustrating Napoleon's keen foresight to the world.

Soldiers! The Russian army is facing you to avenge the Austrian army of Ulm . . . The position we occupy is a formidable one; while the enemy marches to turn my right, he will expose his flank to me. Soldiers! I will command your battalions in person, and I shall not expose myself if, with your usual courage, you throw the enemy's ranks into disorder and confusion. But should victory be for one moment uncertain, you would see your Emperor expose himself in the front rank, for there must be no question of victory on an occasion when the honor of the French infantry is at stake . . . This victory will end our campaign, and we can go into winter quarters where we shall be reinforced by the new armies forming in France. Then the peace that I shall make will be worthy of my people, of you and of me.

Later that night, around nine o'clock, Napoleon did something that was unheard of for a commander of his stature. He rode up and down the entire six-mile front along his line of seventy-five thousand soldiers. He didn't want to take any chances, and wanted to be sure everyone was ready and knew the plan. As he rode past them, the troops went crazy with enthusiasm, waving their torches and shouting, *"Vive l'Empereur!"*

THE BATTLE BEGINS

That night was freezing cold, and both parties set fires to stay warm. The next morning there was a tremendous fog from the mist and from the campfires. The Austro-Russian army began its attack. They were confused from the start, as they had a complex plan that was much too detailed for such a large army to follow effectively. Besides, their instructions had to be delivered in Russian and German, and they were marching in thick fog. The day before, Napoleon had his army mostly grouped to the north, intentionally exposing his southern right flank. The Austro-Russian army took the bait and set their plan in motion. They ordered their troops to begin descending from the plateau to attack Napoleon's right from the south.

The fog worked in Napoleon's favor. Many of his troops to the north kept on low ground, disguised by the fog. By the time the Austro-Russian army committed themselves and attacked his right, he had made his move and sent his left onto the Pratzen Plateau to attack the enemy's center. As the sun came up, Napoleon's troops rose magically out of the mist and took the plateau, much to the Russians' surprise. Within a few hours, the French had total control of the plateau, and the enemy's center was completely destroyed. Napoleon's armies then looped around as planned and took the enemy from behind.

Intense fighting ensued, and even though Napoleon's troops were outnumbered, they appeared to be everywhere at once because they used their infantry and cavalry strategically, and because they had divisions of troops that moved rapidly from one scene of action to the next. This unified army made full use of its troops and gave the impression of superior numbers against a disorganized larger army. By four o'clock that afternoon, it was all over. What was left of the Austro-Russian army fled south across an icy lake, where many perished.

The Aftermath

Napoleon wandered among his victorious army, tending to the wounded. That night, he drafted a proclamation to his army:

Well done, soldiers! In the battle of Austerlitz you have accomplished all I expected of your valor: you have crowned your eagles with immortal glory. An army of 100,000 men commanded by the Emperors of Russia and of Austria has been dispersed or captured in less than four hours. What escaped your arms was drowned in the lakes. Forty flags, the stan-

dards of the Russian Imperial Guard, 120 guns, 20 generals, more than 30,000 prisoners are the result of this eternally glorious battle. This famous infantry, that outnumbered you, was unable to resist your attack, and henceforth you have no rivals to fear.

Soldiers! When we have completed all that is necessary to secure the happiness and prosperity of our country, I will lead you back to France; there you will be the constant objects of my loving care. My people will hail your return with joy, and you will have but to say, "I was at the battle of Austerlitz," to hear the reply, "He is one of the brave!"

The morning after the battle, a meeting was arranged between Napoleon; Alexander I, czar of Russia; and Francis I, emperor of Austria. At the meeting, it was agreed that the Russians would withdraw to Poland and Napoleon would negotiate a settlement with Francis I. These negotiations led to the Treaty of Pressburg, under which Austria would lose territory to Italy, Bavaria, and the southern German states. Also, Napoleon would give Hanover to Prussia in order to pacify them—provided they agreed to close their ports to England. The settlements of the Treaty of Pressburg guaranteed that Austria would not remain a threat to France and, more important, that France would be secure from the east, surrounded by friendly states.

As for France, Napoleon wasn't kidding when he said in his proclamation that his soldiers would be the constant objects of his loving care. He more than lived up to his promise. He distributed fifteen million francs among his soldiers. In addition, he gave all wounded soldiers a bonus equal to three months' pay. He arranged for the wives of those killed in battle to receive substantial lifetime annual pensions and declared an annual memorial service to be held in the Notre Dame cathedral. Most unusually, he literally adopted the children of the dead—paying for their education and living expenses and allowing them to add the name of Napoleon to their own. Finally, he issued numerous bulletins recounting brave deeds of people and army units, including those of his allies in Bavaria. Napoleon assured that this was an accomplishment that would not be forgotten, nor would the efforts of his soldiers go unnoticed.

LESSONS FROM THE AUSTERLITZ CAMPAIGN

As we can see, many of the lessons from the Ulm campaign were repeated in the Austerlitz campaign. Once again, Napoleon had a primary objective: attacking the Austro-Russian army at Austerlitz. And he had just a few related secondary objectives, such as protecting his rear and flanks, and securing his headquarters back in Vienna. Again, speed saved the day and allowed for the element of surprise. From Napoleon's march along the front, we were able to see the power of being visible to our teams, something we discussed in Chapter 1. There are two additional lessons here worthy of exploring in more detail. First, we'll see how Napoleon inspired moral force through his preparatory speech to his troops; then we'll see how his *Grande Armée* was able to appear superior, even against an army that was larger in numbers.

MORAL FORCE:
THE IMPORTANCE OF THE KICKOFF SPEECH

Let's look more closely at Napoleon's rousing speech to his troops before the action began. He was able to accomplish the following with that one brief speech:

- He made sure his army understood the concept of the mission and that the plan was sound: *"Soldiers! The Russian army is facing you to avenge the Austrian army of Ulm . . . The position we occupy is a formidable one; while the enemy marches to turn my right, he will expose his flank to me."*

- He declared his personal leadership role in the mission, but asked for their help in keeping him safe, expressing his confidence in them in the process: *"Soldiers! I will command your battalions in person, and I shall not expose myself if, with your usual courage, you throw the enemy's ranks into disorder and confusion."*

- He stressed the importance of the mission by committing himself to do all that was necessary to make it successful: *"But should victory be for one moment uncertain, you would see your Emperor expose himself in the front rank."*

- He painted an uplifting picture of the future: *"This victory will end our campaign, and we can go into winter quarters where we shall be reinforced by the new armies forming in France."*

- He talked about what would follow: *"Then the peace that I shall make will be worthy of my people, of you and of me."*

This brief, simple speech carries many lessons that we can use when communicating with our team before or during the formal kickoff of our project—ideally, after planning, but before execution. We can get our team's buy-in and inspire confidence by communicating the project's concept, declaring our commitment as leaders, asking for the team's help in making the project successful, stressing the importance of the project, painting a picture of success, and discussing what is to follow. Through this, we can avoid the usual skepticism and apathy that so often accompany projects, especially large ones. Most importantly, we can get off on the right foot.

Moral force is critical in business, just as it is in war. People who are inspired with a sense of purpose, and have the confidence that they are working in an environment of order and not chaos, will go out of their way to help make the project a success. Those who are merely given tasks to do, without knowledge of why or how the tasks fit in with the big picture, are not only less inspired but less capable, as they are operating with blinders on.

MAXIMIZING RESOURCES

Another key lesson from the Austerlitz campaign was that once the battle began, Napoleon's army, although outnumbered, appeared to be everywhere at once. This was mainly because of their strategic and coordinated use of cavalry and infantry, and their rapid reassignment of important forces. In other words, Napoleon maximized the use of his resources.

How can we apply this to project management? To begin with, let's assume that rather than cavalry and infantry, we have other targeted skill sets that we need on multiple efforts, such as business analysts, software architects, or computer programmers, and that we need these people for multiple software development projects. Now, let's assume we have a limited number of these resources, and not enough as may be required for each project. Of course, some of these skill sets may be more constrained than others—that is, the demand exceeds the availability.

Adopting Eli Goldratt's Theory of Constraints model, we would begin by determining what our biggest constraints are—ideally no more than one or two at a time—and scheduling our projects around the availability of that constraint. For example, let's say we have enough computer programmers, but only a few architects and business analysts. We would schedule our projects around the availability of the architects and business analysts and have those resources do their part on one project at a time. They'd jump to each project in sequence—ideally in the order of earliest project due date first—and loop around between these projects as needed. The key is that everything would be scheduled sequentially, so they are not spread so thin that nothing gets done. Some attempt should be taken to group their tasks together within any given project where possible, to minimize the mental setup time that occurs when switching back and forth between projects.

This assumes that we're sharing our resources across the organization and not hoarding them in one specific department. In this way, by using a combination of shared resources and the "mobile unit" approach, each project then has the types of resources it needs—via strategic use of "combined arms"—and it appears there are enough architects and business analysts to go around.

This approach also requires that an organization have a broad view of all projects in the pipeline, otherwise any efforts to coordinate things in harmony would be fruitless, much like the Austro-Russian army's misguided attempts. We cannot hope to rapidly redirect our forces when needed without this broad visibility. But with broad visibility, identification of our critical resources, avoidance of multitasking, better sharing, and rapid redeployment of targeted key people, we can truly maximize our resources and enjoy the same advantages Napoleon had at Austerlitz.

EXECUTIVE SUMMARY

We've witnessed the creation of the Third Coalition, Napoleon's rise to emperor, the structure of his *Grande Armée*, and his greatest achievements at Ulm and Austerlitz, all of which have brought us lessons to use in our daily lives. In particular, from Ulm, we've seen how a combination of awareness and speed, flexible but unified teams, and resources focused on the most critical work can lead to remarkable success. From Austerlitz, we've learned how effective up-front communication to our team can get things off on the right foot and how assembling our key resources into mobile teams can give the impression that we have more people than we do. Certainly, these lessons apply as equally to us today as they did in Napoleon's time, and indeed, many of them are already encapsulated in current movements, such as Eli Goldratt's Theory of Constraints and Critical Chain Project Management. Yet, there are even more lessons to be learned from these campaigns—and from everything we've seen so far.

In Part 2, we will explore Napoleon's Six Winning Principles—a basic set of guidelines and tools that we can use as a daily compass while managing our projects. When exploring the six principles, which are based on Napoleon's own maxims, we will refer back to the events we've studied in Part 1 and clearly see how they led to Napoleon's unprecedented success—and how they can help us as well.

MARCHING ORDERS

LESSONS FROM THE ULM CAMPAIGN
Stay aware—act quickly.
- Make use of your team and/or colleagues for input on current events that could impact your project.
- Quickly determine the risk or cost of not doing the project. This can be used in the business case.
- Decide quickly if action is needed, as even minor delays can have broad implications.

Enable centralized planning and administration.
- Assure centralized planning and administration and a single doctrine across all related efforts.
- Group related efforts under one project where possible.

- Consider a core team to handle central communications, planning, operations, risk and issue management, and overall leadership across the related efforts.
- Consider managing the related efforts as individual projects within a program, especially when there needs to be some facility to launch and end multiple projects throughout the life cycle of the effort, or if the individual projects require heavy leadership and planning within themselves and only have minor touch points between them.
- Consider using a PMO for a common project management methodology and doctrine across the entire organization.

Enable decentralized decision making.
- Give broad but clear directives.
- Communicate the goals, objectives, and guiding values and principles.
- Enable frequent communication to ensure teams are up-to-date on changing events.

Focus your resources on what is important.
- Concentrate your resources on the most critical work—the maximum effective amount to guarantee success—and give secondary objectives only the minimal effective amount of resources.
- Commit all your resources, but use excess resources strategically, either to supplement noncritical work or for some strategic need later in the project.

LESSONS FROM THE AUSTERLITZ CAMPAIGN
Make your kickoff speech inspiring.
- Convey the project's approach and the reliability of the approach.

- Express confidence in the team.
- Don't be afraid to ask for the team's help.
- Stress the importance of the project and your commitment to its success.
- Paint a picture of a successful to-be state.
- Discuss the aftermath of the project—what will follow once the project is complete in terms of follow-up items, anything that will be of benefit to the team members, and so forth.

Maximize your resources.
- Identify your key resources, especially those in short supply.
- Share key resources across all projects.
- Don't attempt to have key resources multitask—schedule project tasks around their availability.
- Use the key resources as mobile units, marching from project to project for tasks that require their services.
- Address the projects with the earliest target completion dates first.
- Develop or purchase a system to provide broad visibility across all projects in the pipeline.

PART 2

~

Napoleon's

Six Winning Principles

CHAPTER 5

Introduction to the Six Winning Principles

*Get your principles straight. The rest
is a matter of detail.* —NAPOLEON

In Part 1, we observed many factors that led to Napoleon's success, including the right foundation of raw skills, the ability to develop a compelling vision, astute diplomacy and networking, and a wealth of other dynamics that led to his achievements on the battlefield. We've seen Napoleon's rise to emperor, the structure of his *Grande Armée*, and his greatest achievements at Ulm and Austerlitz. The relevance to us today is plain to see, especially given that many of the lessons parallel those of modern-day leadership and management gurus, such as Eli Goldratt, Tom Peters, and others. Now, in Part 2, we will explore Napoleon's Six Winning Principles that made him so successful. But first, let's take note that a principle is not a hard-and-fast rule to be obeyed religiously, as Napoleon cautioned us:

It is true that Jomini always argues for fixed principles. Genius works by inspiration. What is good in certain circumstances may be bad in others; but one ought to consider principles as an axis, which holds certain relations to a curve. It may be good to recognize that on this or that occasion, one has swerved from fixed principles of war.

Although it is critical to explore lessons learned from past projects, what will eventually make us successful is to habitually use the fundamental, timeless principles that apply to our art, with the caveat that we may intentionally stray from them if circumstances dictate. And nowhere are these principles better explained than in an exploration of Napoleon's rise to power.

The good news is that the many lessons we have explored all boil down to six primary principles that are universally applicable to anyone who leads people—principles that can serve as a compass for us to consistently steer our projects safely into port.

Napoleon's Six Winning Principles

- EXACTITUDE—awareness, research, and continuous planning
- SPEED—reducing resistance, increasing urgency, and providing focus
- FLEXIBILITY—building teams that are adaptable, empowered, and unified
- SIMPLICITY—clear, simple objectives, messages, and processes
- CHARACTER—integrity, calmness, and responsibility
- MORAL FORCE—providing order, purpose, recognition, and rewards

---

These principles work together and feed off one another like interlocking gears. A lack of any one of them will impede success. We can have a highly motivated team, but without the proper planning and adequate, simple systems and processes, they can fail. We can do extensive planning, but without the flexibility and speed to sustain the effort, the project can sink under its own weight. Thus, we need to consider all six principles to be truly effective.

We need to keep in mind, however, that even being well versed in all six principles is not a guarantee of success. Knowledge of principles is just theory. To be truly successful, we must use the principles in practice and build experience, to the point where it becomes second nature. Only then can we hope to develop what is known as *coup d'oeil* (pronounced koo-doy, literally "strike to the eye," a French expression for "glance"). *Coup d'oeil* refers to the ability to instantly analyze a situation and make correct judgment calls. Even Jomini, a passionate advocate for principles, acknowledged these limitations, as evidenced by his statement below:

> A general thoroughly instructed in the theory of war, but not possessed of military coup d'oeil, coolness, and skill, may make an excellent strategic plan and be entirely unable to apply the rules of tactics in the presence of an enemy; his projects will not be successfully carried out, and his defeat will be probable.[1]

Jomini also pointed out that principles alone—even without the requisite experience—will help identify errors to be avoided, and thus increase the chances of success.

> It is true that theories cannot teach men with mathematical precision what they can and should do in every possible case; but it is also certain that they will always point out the errors which should be avoided; and this is a highly important consideration, for these rules thus become, in the hands of skillful generals commanding brave troops, means of almost certain success.[2]

So, knowing that the use of principles can serve as a general compass to guide our paths, that sometimes we may need to stray from them, and that experience using them can help us make correct judgment calls, let's proceed to examine the six principles that worked so well for Napoleon time and time again. Then we can begin using them as our guides to build experience and reach our maximum potential as leaders and project managers.

CHAPTER 6

———◇———

Exactitude

*If I always appear to be prepared, it is
because before entering on an undertaking,
I have meditated for long and have foreseen
what may occur. It is not genius which reveals
to me suddenly and secretly what I should do
in circumstances unexpected by others, it is
thought and meditation.*—NAPOLEON

Napoleon often spoke of the importance of exactitude. By exactitude, he meant pinpoint precision through constant situational awareness, extensive research, and continuous planning—not just once, but throughout the entire initiative. He knew that if such precision were to be reached, it would be dependent on a combination of preliminary investigation and up-to-the-minute knowledge of events. In this way, he could increase the chances of zeroing in on the right target at the right time.

It should go without saying that these same concepts can bring exactitude to our projects as well, so it is worth further examination to find out just how Napoleon accomplished this. Discovering that, we will learn how to build the awareness that made Napoleon so successful and how to conduct the level of research at which he excelled. Both of these elements can give us the knowledge we need to make the right decisions. We'll also see how Napoleon planned his objectives in a progressive fashion, not just once at the beginning of his initiative. This ensured that his plans were always aligned with the most recent events. And so, with these lessons awaiting us, let's begin our journey with an exploration of how awareness, research, and continuous planning can lead to exactitude—the first of Napoleon's Six Winning Principles.

AWARENESS

We have seen how Napoleon's awareness led him to recognize the need to act quickly when required, to sense the spirit of his troops or the needs of his people, or to instantaneously sum up a situation with a glance through his telescope—the coveted ability of *coup d'oeil.* We have probably seen others in our work environment who always seem to be "in the know," raising issues in meetings that we may never have thought of. But how do we, too, build that awareness, which helps us zero in on the accuracy we need? The answer is that it is like climbing a ladder. The rungs are *visibility, observation and analysis,* and *experience,* and the ultimate goal is *situational awareness.* We will now examine each of these in more detail.

VISIBILITY

Napoleon began his financial reform of France by asking for a spreadsheet showing the financial information for each region. Similarly, before each battle he made sure he would have a good position from which he could see all actions, and he asked for reports on the positions of all opposing troops. Napoleon knew that in order to be aware of events, he needed to begin with a foundation of good visibility. We, too, need good visibility—but in our case that means visibility of projects, organizational events, people, and any external information that could be relevant to our needs. There are various ways to obtain each of these types of visibility.

For example, for visibility of projects, we first need to be sure there is some central repository where all projects can be viewed and ideally arranged into strategic portfolios. There are numerous enterprise project management and portfolio management tools on the market that can help accomplish this.

For visibility of organizational events, we can increase our networking activities by simply wandering around more, joining certain groups, or talking to colleagues or people on our teams about organizational activities going on—especially those that could impact or be impacted by our projects. Some organizations have regular seminars or intranet sites for each department. Some even provide Web-based seminars called "webinars" that advertise or explain certain departmental or functional initiatives. These are all excellent sources of information. And while corporate espionage is a touchy subject matter and to be avoided, some well-placed contacts can also be of assistance, provided information is passed on in an ethical manner.

The best method for obtaining visibility of people is simply to be present among them as much as possible—the classic "management by wandering around" or MBWA approach, popularized by Tom Peters.[1] Certainly, project management software—specifically, resource management software—can help identify who is doing what, provided this information is being kept current. Communication, however, is critical as well. Napoleon was able to redirect his troops immediately upon hearing that the Austrians had entered Ulm. He also was able to redirect his reserves at Austerlitz upon hearing that the Austro-Russian army was positioned farther south than expected. Without constant communication, he would not have had visibility of those events, and corrective actions would not have been possible.

As for visibility of external information, the best thing is to read the trade magazines or any other publications related to your field of endeavor. Anyone in the project management field would benefit from joining the Project Management Institute (PMI), which issues a regular magazine and offers additional specific-interest-group (SIG) membership for a variety of industries. General business publications also offer input as to what is happening in various industries and can bring a wealth of ideas.

> Visibility is one thing; the ability to observe and analyze what you are seeing is another. As Sherlock Holmes said ... "You see, but you do not observe."

The combination of all these avenues mentioned will help provide visibility of projects, organizational events, people, and external information, and with that we have the foundation for the ability to become fully aware. But this is just the beginning. Visibility is one thing; the ability to observe and analyze what you are seeing is another. As Sherlock Holmes said through the magical pen of Sir Arthur Conan Doyle in *A Scandal in Bohemia*, "You see, but you do not observe."[2]

OBSERVATION AND ANALYSIS

Napoleon once said, "In war, everything is perception—perception about the enemy, perception about one's own soldiers." And perception goes beyond just seeing; it implies a certain insight and forming of an opinion. That is the difference between seeing and observing. We can *see* a list of projects or a bunch of activities going on in the organization, but unless we process that and are able to digest what it means to us, it is useless.

The key is that we need to be able to make decisions based on what we see. The U.S. Navy describes effective decision making as "the ability to use logical and sound judgment to make decisions based on available information." *Company Performance at the National Training Center: Battle Planning and Execution,* by Brian W. Hallmark and James C. Crowley—a study done by RAND for the U.S. Department of Defense—goes further to caution us that these decisions should not be based solely on some signal that gives a vague idea of the situation—what it refers to as "the bat signal approach," for those familiar with Batman. Rather, it suggests using a "searchlight" approach, scanning over the data to look for relevance.[3]

Edward Tufte, the world's leading expert on presenting data and information, suggests that we avoid the overuse of signals, such as red, yellow, and green lights, in favor of indices that mean something and give a bit more detail about the real situation. Reliance on red, yellow, and green lights alone can mask potentially important information. That's not to say that these should be eliminated. On the contrary, they can give a quick view of certain problem areas. Rather, they should be used in conjunction with more meaningful indices.

Napoleon was well familiar with the use of indices as well, as we saw how he was able to measure the progress of his financial reforms by using the price of wheat as an index. In this way, he was able to quickly compare how well each region was doing. We can use the same approach when observing and analyzing information about our projects. For example, the Critical Chain methodology uses a flow index to measure how much buffer has been used versus how far along the project is. The Earned Value method for tracking cost and schedule uses a Cost Performance Index (CPI) and a Schedule Performance Index (SPI) to indicate how well the project is doing versus where it should be. Critical Chain and Earned Value are not mutually exclusive. Some organizations use both, with Earned Value being used to satisfy required reporting of time and cost progress, while operational decisions and project "health-checks" are based on Critical Chain's buffer and flow indices.

The intent here is not to explain everything there is to know about these methodologies—that alone would take an entire book. The aim is merely to show that tools such as these provide effective indices for making sense out of a large amount of information. Of course, we must be able to observe more than projects alone; we must do the same with organizational events, people, and external information. With those elements, however, we are not so lucky as to have automated indices to use as a guide; we must rely on experience.

The ability to recognize which organizational events are relevant to our projects, which people-related issues may impact us, or which external information is significant, is proportional to the amount of our experience. Even project indices won't be of much use unless we can comprehend what to do afterward, and that, too, takes experience—the next rung on our awareness ladder.

EXPERIENCE

It is a common cliché that there is no teacher like experience. As much as we read and study theory, the only way to achieve success consistently is to learn from mistakes and practice firsthand what we have read about. Perhaps Napoleon put it best when he said:

> One may teach tactics, military engineering, artillery work, about as one teaches geometry. But knowledge of the higher branches of war is only acquired by experience and by a study of history of the wars of the great generals. It is not in learning grammar that one learns to compose a great poem, to write a tragedy.

Thus, we can conclude that theory is to practice what grammar is to poetry, or any other written art form. Theory is a good guide for what to avoid, but ultimately we must observe others who have done it successfully, practice a great deal, and learn from mistakes. Then we can create our own "poetry."

Even Napoleon wasn't able to fully exploit his knack for grasping the whole situation at a glance, his *coup d'oeil*, without having been through the wringer a few times. As he said, "On the field of battle, the happiest inspiration [*coup d'oeil*] is often only a recollection." What seems to be a sudden insight is often based on some memory from a past experience, whether consciously or subconsciously.

For example, when Napoleon was given command of the Italian campaign and his superiors wanted to split efforts between another general and him, Napoleon balked, declaring, "One bad general is better than two good ones." This wasn't a sudden insight. He remembered that during his first major battle as a captain during the French Revolution, the mission failed because the other senior officer—in charge of providing cover—refused to proceed in bad weather. Not only did Napoleon learn the perils of lost opportunity, but he also learned the dangers of combined operations. And by the time of the Italian campaign, he was able to benefit from the value of experience. We can deduce from this that not only is experience the best teacher, but failure is often the best experience to learn from.

Success or failure aside, we can increase the chances that we will learn from experience by working from a sound set of principles, such as those listed here, and having periodic "principle checks" throughout our projects. As my old boss, Lou Ockey, used to say, "There's a difference between someone with twenty years of experience and someone with one year of experience twenty times." Principle checks can help ensure that we do not become the latter.

Experience really becomes essential when we need to make a judgment call without having the benefit of full visibility. Clausewitz said, "Whatever is hidden from full view . . . must be guessed at by talent, or simply left to chance."[4] While some things indeed must be left to chance—although uncertainties in general should be prepared for via strategic buffers or contingency budgets—there are times when we need to make decisions on the fly without having all the facts. Only the combination of principles and experience can help us then.

The ultimate level of experience is to have been through the details involved in our projects. Napoleon had hands-on experience with everything he oversaw, whether making gunpowder, constructing gun carriages, using a cannon, or applying various tactics. We can be successful without such hands-on experience, and many successful project managers have only surface knowledge of the specific technology or business involved in their projects, but hands-on knowledge certainly helps.

Let's say there's a certain area, be it project management, leadership, or some business or technical area, in which we just don't have the right experience to be successful on a given project—or our team lacks experience. What can we do in that case? With a lack of experience in any endeavor, the best thing we can do is to receive training—ideally, instruction that includes drills to mimic real-life situations. This is a technique that has worked for armies for thousands of years, and, while not a substitute for experience, it is indeed helpful. Although principles, theory, and training can help us become successful, it is the practice of those principles combined with the various experiences we've been exposed to that makes us continuously successful. As Napoleon said:

The knowledge of higher leadership can only be acquired by the study of military history and actual experience. There are no hard and fast rules; everything depends on the plans of the general, the condition of his troops, the season of the year, and a thousand other circumstances, which have the effect that no one case will ever resemble another.

So, with adequate visibility of projects, events, people, and information; the ability to process and analyze that information; and
experience using the principles of project management, we are now
ready to proceed to the ultimate rung on our ladder—situational
awareness.

Situational Awareness (Coup d'Oeil)

Situational awareness, or *coup d'oeil*, refers to the ability to quickly
digest and classify information, so as to make a correct decision on
the fly. This can also be referred to as "strategic intuition" and
assumes a broad view of events at any given time—the pinnacle of
true awareness. It was Napoleon who first referred to this intuition
as *coup d'oeil*, and in military and business circles, the term became
synonymous with "Napoleon's glance." Clausewitz, in his book *On
War*, credited this rare ability as a key enabler to Napoleon's success.[5] But can *coup d'oeil* be learned, or is it inherent only in certain
people? Let's consider Napoleon's view:

> *My great talent, the one that distinguishes me the most, is to see the
> entire picture distinctly . . . There is a gift of being able to see at a glance
> the possibilities offered by the terrain . . . One can call it the coup d'oeil
> and it is inborn in great generals.*

Alas, from Napoleon's standpoint, and from much literature on
the subject, it seems that *coup d'oeil* is a combination of learned
habits and inborn talent. Yet, all is not lost. We can greatly improve
our chances of achieving this lofty goal—mimicking it, as it were—
by building the foundation that we've covered thus far: namely,
broad visibility, observation and analysis, and experience. But there
is one more ingredient we need that holds it all together like glue—
frequent communication.

Let's recall from the Ulm campaign that Berthier's Imperial General Staff kept all corps commanders up-to-date with the position and current directives of adjacent troops. Just as important, they kept Napoleon aware of all activities through regular updates from the corps commanders. This gave Napoleon and his corps commanders the situational awareness they needed to be successful. They didn't have the benefit of e-mail and cell phones, so dispatches had to be delivered on horseback. Maintaining close lines of communication was key, especially since the *Grande Armée* consisted of seven corps spread out over a one-hundred-mile front.

Not wanting to take any chances, Napoleon asked for frequent updates, with instructions to report details listing the time, not just the date. He needed to know about tomorrow's problems today. This was not micromanagement. On the contrary, he gave simple, clear orders—not the endless minute details that were typical of generals of his day. He knew that things in war were unpredictable, and that—even though extensive research was critical—extremely complex, rigid plans early on would be a waste of time. Better to have broader directions and more frequent communication.

Certainly, it was frequent communication that allowed Napoleon to redirect his troops when hearing that the Austrians had entered Ulm. Likewise, it was the knowledge that "communication is power" that led him to circle his troops around Ulm, cutting off the Austrians' line of communication with Vienna to the east—not to mention adding the element of surprise. And it was miscommunication that caused the Russians to arrive eleven days late because they were using a different calendar.

To obtain the *coup d'oeil* that Napoleon possessed, or at least get close to it, we need to ensure frequent communication, and this means communication to and by all parties. This not only guarantees *us* situational awareness, but our team as well. Following are some examples of this type of communication:

- Receiving work completion updates from project team members
- Receiving status updates from project leaders and subteam leads
- Receiving news of related current events
- Issuing new or changed work orders
- Communicating status to customers, management, and other stakeholders
- Issuing marketing materials or news dispatches to the public

Any or all of these items can lead to greater awareness by all parties and increase the chances that course corrections can be made when needed. Thus we can see that project management is not about getting people to adhere to some rigid plan set forth before all details are known, but about situational awareness and making the plan follow reality. Projects are by nature fluid and uncertain, and communication is the key to keeping everything on track. It is no wonder that the Project Management Institute views communication as 90 percent of a project manager's job.

> Communication is the key to keeping everything on track. It is no wonder that the Project Management Institute views communication as 90 percent of a project manager's job.

As for the frequency of updates from our project teams, remember that Napoleon asked people to report details to the hour level. This may be overkill in most project environments, but we can greatly improve our planning ability by asking for daily updates, and certainly no less frequently than weekly. Our teams should, for their active tasks, communicate hours spent to date (for cost reporting purposes), time remaining or percentage

complete (for planning purposes), and any issues they've encountered (for exception and risk handling). Frequent reporting of time
remaining or percentage complete is critical, as it enables us to look
at our project plans in real time and see the impact on the remaining schedule.

We can come very close to mastering the art of *coup d'oeil,* or
maintaining situational awareness, by obtaining good visibility of
projects, events, people, and information; using proper indices to
identify status and problem areas; building experience to be able to
identify what is relevant; and establishing frequent two-way communication. This is our first step toward achieving exactitude. The next
step, after ensuring we have a good foundation of awareness, is to
improve our chances even more through specific, targeted research.
Thus we come to our next enabler for exactitude—research.

RESEARCH

Napoleon once said, "Intelligent and intrepid generals assure the
success of actions. One must be slow in deliberation and quick in
execution." We can see the extent to which Napoleon prepared for
a campaign, whether researching the subject matter in detail, as he
did with the Egyptian campaign, or extensively investigating the
terrain, as he did with all his campaigns. He also read at length
about past battles in the area or against the same generals. All of this
information tipped the scales in his favor. One can talk about
awareness and intuition, but without the proper research on a given
endeavor, these general abilities are diluted. Indeed, awareness and
research are indelibly linked, and each relies on the other.

Napoleon knew this better than anyone. Although he spoke of
the innate ability to see the whole playing field, he still spared no
expense researching the territory in advance. "There is no greater
coward than I when I am drawing up a plan of campaign," he

said. "I magnify every danger, every disadvantage that can be conceived." It becomes obvious, then, that he was able to do this through a keen insight—awareness—into what might ensue, aided by the extensive research he typically conducted of the terrain and of past projects. And during his research he always kept an eye out for risks that could come back to haunt him later. With this combination of awareness and research, we can conduct the kind of risk assessment Napoleon spoke of, and thus improve our chances for ascertaining a situation correctly—and obtaining *coup d'oeil.*

The elements that contribute to effective research are study of the terrain, study of past projects, and preliminary risk identification.

Study of the Terrain

Before the Ulm campaign, Napoleon sent Marshal Murat to inspect the topology of the land and others to inspect bridges and riverbanks. Likewise, he had Berthier gather an index on the locations of the Austrian troops. At Austerlitz he sent spies to the Austro-Russian camp to inspect what they were up to. And even then, he personally inspected the territory, looking for a suitable place for battle. These are all examples of the ways in which Napoleon studied the territory before battle.

In project management, we must also study the territory in advance. This does not necessarily apply to the physical territory—although it could be relevant, depending on the nature of the project. More broadly, this refers to getting familiar with the subject matter of the project, the players involved, and the nature of the people we'll be dealing with. This may mean reading up on a certain business area we're not familiar with, a specific technology, the organizational structure, or the nature of certain types of people, depending on their functional or geographical culture. This could include finding out specific individuals' likes and dislikes, if this can be done discreetly. Some project managers even create a "political plan," which outlines the organizational culture, stakeholder roles, potential issues, approaches to take, and any other information that will help manage the political arena. It can also be helpful to talk to others familiar with the territory or with the key stakeholders we'll be working with.

We can learn quite a lot by investigating past projects in addition to inspecting the political, business, and technical landscape. Thus, our next area of research is the study of past projects.

THE STUDY OF PAST PROJECTS

Before every battle, Napoleon did an exhaustive study of other battles that had been fought in the same area or against the same armies. He didn't want any surprises, and valued the opportunity to learn from others' mistakes—or successes. We can use the same approach by studying relevant past projects before undertaking ours. Much like Napoleon, our study of past projects may include researching similar projects that were undertaken or projects that dealt with the same players. Both can provide unique, relevant information from different perspectives. The ideal situation is to have a searchable database of archived projects, preferably categorized by various topics. Many Enterprise Project Management (EPM) tools offer categorization of lessons learned by subject area, such as plant start-ups, staffing, communication, or any number of other relevant topics. This enables a knowledge base that can be quickly mined for information when beginning a project.

We might also talk to people who were involved in these projects, especially the project manager, to see if there were any issues that could impact our project as well. Or maybe the project had some lessons regarding how best to work with specific departments or people. Much can be learned from a brief conversation with a project manager who has managed projects dealing with the same topic or audience.

Along with any data we've gathered on our own regarding the territory, this information can be used to assemble a list of risks that could pose a threat to our project. This takes us to our third and final area of research—the identification of preliminary risks.

PRELIMINARY RISK IDENTIFICATION

Once we've done the prerequisite reading and have examined past projects, we are now ready to identify possible risks, which is necessary if our plans are to be effective. This will be based mostly on the input we collect from our research; much the same way that Napoleon gathered information before a battle and spent hours and sometimes weeks meditating on what dangers could occur. Preliminary risk identification is a natural next step after research.

Some organizations use a risk checklist with categories such as schedule, cost, or quality risks; technology risks; project management risks; external risks, for example, vendors, consultants, and weather; and organizational risks. Industry-specific risks can also be considered. Fortunately, some good risk questionnaires and checklists are available for free via the Internet, so there's no need to create one from scratch. Rita Mulcahy's book *Risk Management: Tricks of the Trade® for Project Managers,* also contains some valuable templates and checklists.[6] The bottom line is that a risk checklist or questionnaire can save an enormous amount of time and can generate ideas that otherwise may go unnoticed.

Remember Napoleon's maxim of being "slow in deliberation and quick in execution"? Let's not forget that it is possible to get caught up in "analysis paralysis," spending so much time analyzing things that we delay execution and miss a potential window of opportunity—or run into other dangers that delay can bring. A good rule of thumb is to invest time up front for research and planning, but to go forward once you have 60 to 80 percent of the information you need, and certainly don't wait until you have 100 percent.

Some experts, such as former U.S. Secretary of State Colin Powell, suggest that even 40 to 70 percent knowledge is adequate to begin moving ahead. Much depends on the industry, the risk tolerance of an organization, and the time available. It is important to understand that if we spend too much time on risk analysis, the delay itself becomes a risk. Napoleon recognized this when he said, "The torment of precautions often exceeds the dangers to be avoided. It is sometimes better to abandon one's self to destiny."

> A good rule of thumb is to invest time up front for research and planning, but to go forward once you have 60 to 80 percent of the information you need, and certainly don't wait until you have 100 percent.

Besides, planning is not a onetime activity; it should be done throughout a project, as planning in detail closer to the point of action gives us the benefit of greater accuracy. That doesn't mean all phases of a project shouldn't be examined at a high level early on as part of an initial risk assessment, merely that finer details can be considered as events get closer.

All in all, by taking some time up front to conduct adequate research—of the terrain, past projects, and preliminary risks—we can greatly improve our chances of success and be much more capable when dealing with uncertainties, which are bound to happen. Having done that, we are ready to do further planning, which takes us to our next enabler for exactitude—continuous planning.

CONTINUOUS PLANNING

As much as Napoleon spoke of extensive planning, even he didn't plan every detail in advance, only as far out as he could see. He did, however, think about the ultimate goal from a broad perspective. For example, when planning the Ulm campaign, his initial plan—after doing some quick but extensive research—was to invade the Austrians before the Russians could arrive. Only as he got closer did he find out that the Austrians had entered Bavaria and then Ulm. Then he was able to refine his plan. More importantly, he didn't even think about planning the details for addressing the Russians, as he didn't know for sure where he'd be facing them. Certainly he had it in the back of his mind, as his broad plan was to address the Russians next, but he didn't worry about those details early on.

It is the same with projects. If we maintain awareness and do the proper research, our initial project plan should contain enough detail to get a rough timeline and cost estimate, but with much more detail about the early phases of the project than phases that are farther out into the future. This requires that planning be an ongoing process, with a fluid project plan, constantly changing to match current circumstances—as opposed to the wishful thinking that circumstances will somehow magically conform to our plan. Plans should not be created and etched in stone to be followed verbatim. Napoleon knew this instinctively. So did Dwight D. Eisenhower, who said, "Plans are nothing—planning is everything." PMI also endorses this logic, referring to the evolutionary project plan approach as "progressive elaboration."

For example, I laid out the entire table of contents and outlined each chapter when I was preparing this book—I needed to anyway for the book proposal. I set a schedule to follow, knowing that it would probably change as the book progressed. Sure enough, as I wrote, I found better ways to structure it. I removed chapters, added chapters, and merged contents into other chapters. As I began each of the three sections of the book, I outlined the upcoming part in finer detail, which made the writing effort much easier. I knew more about what I wanted to say, based on what I had written so far. One might call it "just-in-time planning." This is much different from "winging it." The entire project should be laid out up front. It would be foolish, however, to assume that it would not need refinement as things progress.

There is actually a technique that has become common practice in project management circles, called "rolling wave scheduling," that uses this same approach.

ROLLING WAVE SCHEDULING

The idea behind rolling wave scheduling is that a project will be broken into phases—typically ninety days but sometimes as long as six months. The first phase will initially be much more detailed than future phases. Midway into each phase, the next phase will be refined in greater detail, such that it resembles a rolling wave, with a new wave forming before the current wave fades into the sea. This is similar to the way Napoleon planned and executed the Ulm campaign before addressing the details of the Austerlitz campaign.

A rolling wave schedule offers the benefit of having later tasks planned closer to the point of activity, when estimates will be more accurate. It is often difficult to plan and estimate future phases in fine detail up front, as we can't always know what the circumstances will be. As the saying goes, "The map is not the territory." We can have a plan or a map, but once we get into the territory, that's when we'll really know what we're facing. To make this approach successful, however, there are some guidelines we should follow.

First, we should start with a Work Breakdown Structure (WBS). This is a hierarchical list or picture of all the deliverables of our project, including the management of the project, all major categories of work, and the major deliverables for each category. The WBS, typically noun-oriented, represents the entire scope of the project and should be created with the collective minds of the project team. After the WBS is created, we then create a master plan, which outlines the major events that must happen throughout our project in order to accomplish the deliverables. Often, it is in the form of a high-level timeline or milestones list. This should be relatively easy to do for the entire project, and enough to get a rough time and cost estimate. Then—assuming our project is approved— we proceed to develop a detailed master schedule. This is where rolling wave scheduling comes in.

The first thing we need to consider is how many phases our project should have. The number of phases in a project can vary, but generally each phase should be ninety days. That's about as far as we can see into the horizon with any level of certainty, although for some projects the horizon could be shorter or longer. There is a standard guideline for how much detail to include for the nearest horizon (the first phase): tasks should be no less than eight hours in length and no more than eighty. The idea is that smaller tasks can be managed offline and larger ones should be broken into chunks. Phases that are farther out on the horizon can be at a higher level, until that horizon approaches.

That is not to say we cannot provide an "order-of-magnitude" estimate early on (typically in a range of –25 percent to +75 percent accuracy), when we create our master plan, or even a "definitive estimate" (typically in a range of –5 percent to +10 percent accuracy), when creating our full master schedule. We can even commit to a hard due date, which we'll often be required to do. We might find ourselves needing to reforecast the project, however, as each phase approaches and we refine the details for that upcoming phase. In a perfect world, a rolling wave refinement would just involve refining the details and not changing the overall time, cost, or deliverables. Since we have project sponsors to satisfy, we should first try to resolve any issues, perhaps by overlapping some tasks (which can add risk), or by using more resources (which can also add risk and increase the cost). As a last resort, we may need to negotiate trade-offs in scope, time, or cost—known as the "triple constraint"—and submit a project change request accordingly.

The rolling wave approach is a major factor in continuous planning. It provides a more realistic approach to project scheduling and it increases exactitude as well, since the details are planned closer to the point of action. As a side benefit, it also serves to keep the project manager involved throughout the length of the project, not just during the early phases. All too often, a project manager will focus on assembling the perfect project plan and then become complacent during the all-important execution phase. Then, as the project winds to a close, he or she gets a second wind, scurrying to resolve last-minute issues to at least give the illusion of success. By using a rolling wave approach, we manage efforts throughout the project and avoid that fate.

If a rolling wave schedule is also set up to provide interim deliverables with each phase, further fine-tuning can be done when planning subsequent phases, based on the lessons learned. This brings even more exactitude. This takes us to another important element of continuous planning—phased deliverables.

PHASED DELIVERABLES

Whether planning a series of objectives for a battle campaign or scheduling construction projects, such as creating a museum or building a road or canal, Napoleon always insisted on tangible, piecemeal results, instead of waiting for the entire project to be completed to yield benefits. As his secretary, Baron Fain, noted in

his memoirs, Napoleon was often frustrated when he saw preparations being made on too large a scale, which would result in a
bunch of wasted effort if the project were somehow interrupted pre-
maturely. Fain noted that if Napoleon were to build a fortification,
he would have each phase result in some deliverable, beginning with
a defensive ditch, then a high wall, and so on.[7] Napoleon said:

> *By beginning everything, we risk finishing nothing . . . It is better to
> achieve a canal of ten leagues every ten years, than to have to wait a cen-
> tury for a canal of a hundred leagues to be finished.*

Likewise, when adding a gallery to the Louvre, although Napoleon
planned the whole project from a high level, he instructed the architect to complete sections in phases, and said: "If I cannot complete
it, at least I don't want to leave behind me a long line of unfinished
pillars, waiting sadly upright to be crowned by their vault and the
rest of the buildings."

We should consider the same approach when managing projects.
How many times have we begun a project so broad in scope that
after a year passed, nothing was delivered? Then, with the cost soar-
ing, the project was canceled. It is fine to think broadly, but it is better to plan in phases, with each phase providing tangible deliverables.

This can also be used as a way to measure the progress of a project. According to Baron Fain, Napoleon had a system by which he
monitored the ratio of money spent versus how much work was
accomplished. Fain explained that if a project were planned to take
ten years, Napoleon would check to be sure that each year would use
one-tenth of the total funds and deliver one-tenth of the total work.[8]
This is an excellent way to measure project success. It not only shows
how much you've spent, it shows how much you've received for what
you've spent. With traditional "planned versus actual" methods, it
could look as if you are on schedule (the right number of hours

logged) and on budget (the right amount of money spent), but it's not clear how much work was actually accomplished. Napoleon focused on deliverables versus money spent, as opposed to just tracking money planned versus money spent. The same approach could be used to track schedule progress by looking at deliverables versus time spent.

How can we adopt this method for monitoring our projects? It just so happens there is a modern-day method that mirrors this formula, giving evidence that there is nothing new under the sun. This method is called "Earned Value Management," originally developed for the U.S. Department of Defense, and now an international standard for project management. The concept behind Earned Value is that it measures how much work has been accomplished based on the planned value at that point in time. This can be made easier by having phased milestones, each offering at least one deliverable that has some defined value—either a fixed value or weighted percentage of the overall funds.

To build on Baron Fain's example, let's say we have a ten-month project, and we plan to complete one deliverable each month, each taking one hundred hours and costing one thousand dollars. The total project budget is ten thousand dollars. By the end of two months, we should have spent two hundred hours and two thousand dollars, and completed two deliverables. But let's say we did spend two hundred hours (right on schedule) and two thousand dollars (right on budget), but completed only one deliverable. Is the project in good shape? Is it really on schedule or on budget? Alas, it is neither. This is where Earned Value Management comes in.

Earned Value represents the value of what was accomplished to date—measured by the percentage of work completed multiplied by the total funds of the project. In this case, the Earned Value would be one thousand dollars—10 percent of the work completed multiplied by the total budget of ten thousand dollars. This can be compared with the Planned Value—cost that should have been incurred by this time—to determine if a project is really on schedule. Since the Planned Value after two months is two thousand dollars, we are indeed behind schedule by one hundred hours, using a rate of ten dollars an hour. Likewise, since our actual cost is two thousand dollars, we are one thousand dollars over budget, since we delivered only one thousand dollars worth of product but spent two thousand dollars. Traditional methods would have shown us to be on schedule and on budget.

There are quite a few books that offer more details on implementing Earned Value Management, including the definitive book on the subject, *Earned Value Project Management*, by Quentin W. Fleming and Joel M. Koppelman.[9] This method, which mirrors Napoleon's, is an effective tool for reporting budget and schedule status to management, and phased deliverables are a key way to make this work.

By having phased deliverables, we can achieve early wins, begin realizing benefits sooner, and allow for measuring completion of work, which gives us a true picture of our project's health. And by combining phased deliverables with rolling wave scheduling, we can exercise continuous planning, which gets us closer to the exactitude we need. But there is one final element of continuous planning to consider—ongoing risk management.

ONGOING RISK MANAGEMENT

Let's examine Napoleon's view on the importance of risk analysis:

Military science consists in calculating all the chances accurately in the first place, and then in giving accident exactly, almost mathematically, its place in one's calculations. It is upon this point that one must not deceive oneself, and yet a decimal more or less may change all. Now this apportioning of accident and science cannot get into any head except

that of a genius . . . Accident, hazard, chance, call it what you may, a
mystery to ordinary minds, becomes a reality to superior men.

We can conclude that we must not only spend as much effort as possible identifying and responding to risks, but we must also plan for those risks we cannot identify, which Napoleon refers to as "accident." We can address unidentifiable risks only by having strategic buffers or some sort of management reserve, which is different from a contingency budget that is to be used only for identified risks. We can greatly improve the chances of our project's success, however, by at least keeping a close eye on those risks we *can* identify. And this should not be a onetime activity. Just as we've seen the benefit of planning throughout the life of our project—not just once as an up-front endeavor—we need to extend the same approach to management of risks.

We can do this by scheduling periodic times throughout a project to identify and assess risks. Some experts suggest doing this at every status meeting, which is ideal, but the next best thing is to build it into the schedule, even if it is at the beginning of each phase or during each "stage gate"—periodic checkpoints inserted into a project schedule. Often, project managers, if they identify risks at all, never develop a plan to respond to them; develop a response plan but never execute it; or develop a response plan and execute it, but never check to see if new risks have surfaced or if other risks have been caused by resolving the initial risks. Unless risk management is inherent in the culture of the organization, we can avoid these typical bad habits by scheduling periodic "risk-checks."

How do we actually conduct a risk assessment? Fortunately, there is a proven process for this, and it is simple. We take the risks we identified during our research and then assign probability and impact to each one: the likelihood that each will happen and the level of impact if it does. We can simply use high, medium, and low ratings, although numbers may work better since they can be scored more easily. Then we can decide, based on how tolerant our organization is for risk, for which ones we need to develop responses. We then develop our responses. This is straightforward, as there are only five possible responses to any risk:

1. Avoidance—do something to avoid the risk completely; change your plan so that the risk won't happen.
2. Mitigation—do something to reduce the probability or the impact of the risk.
3. Transference—transfer the risk to someone else, for example, purchasing insurance or outsourcing, provided the contractor bears the risk.
4. Active Acceptance—accept the risk, but develop a contingency plan for if it happens or put aside a contingency budget.
5. Passive Acceptance—accept the risk, but decide what to do only if and when it happens.

The response we choose for each risk will depend on the risk's probability and impact and the risk tolerance of the organization. For example, passive acceptance may be a perfectly acceptable solution for something with low probability and impact, depending on the organization's risk tolerance level. Once we've chosen the risks to address, we can then decide what actions to take or determine if any actions need to be included in our plan.

Some industries take things a step further and perform detailed quantitative analysis by investigating numerous "what-if" scenarios—typically using simulation software—and performing decision-tree analysis to determine the courses to take. What we covered is quite adequate for most industries and a good step forward from what's typically being done—nothing.

We can assure that we're planning continuously throughout our project and staying on course by performing ongoing risk analysis in combination with a rolling wave schedule and phased deliverables. And this, combined with the knowledge that awareness and research offer, can provide the exactitude valued by Napoleon.

EXECUTIVE SUMMARY

At the beginning of this chapter, we determined to show how we can achieve exactitude—pinpoint precision—through increased awareness, extensive research, and continuous planning, which includes risk management. It is evident that these combined elements make up a powerful toolbox for keeping our projects on target. Before we move on to our next principle, let's recap these elements.

First, by *awareness*, we mean visibility of projects, organizational events, people, and external information; observation and analysis of that information; adequate experience to know what is relevant; and, via all of that, the strategic intuition to be able to make decisions on the fly—what we call situational awareness or *coup d'oeil.*

In addition to this broad awareness, we need to conduct specific and targeted research for the project in question. This moves us closer to our goal of pinpoint precision. By *research*, we mean a detailed study of the "terrain"—the terminology, people, and cultures we'll be dealing with—a study of past projects, and identification of preliminary risks. Yet, we also need to avoid getting stuck in "analysis-paralysis," so we should be prepared to go forward with 60 to 80 percent of the information we need, depending on the time available.

We also need to practice *continuous planning* by adopting a *rolling wave* approach (refining each project phase as its horizon approaches), providing interim deliverables with each phase, and identifying and assessing risks throughout the project life cycle. And if things look as though they might deviate from what we've told stakeholders, we can take corrective action and, as a last resort, negotiate trade-offs in scope, time, or cost—the *triple constraint.* This should be kept to a minimum, however, if we've done the proper research, allowed for risks and uncertainty, and are monitoring the progress of our deliverables (not just time and cost).

In summary, we can achieve better accuracy and thus exactitude by increasing our awareness, conducting adequate research, and taking a continuous planning approach. Let's keep in mind, however, that many projects begin with all the tools necessary for exactitude and still fail. This is why we have six principles and not just one. The next principle we'll discuss, and one that must be considered in order for exactitude to achieve its full potential, is *speed.*

MARCHING ORDERS

BUILD AWARENESS

Visibility—maintain visibility of projects, organizational events, people, and external events.

- For projects, use a common repository and enterprise project management/portfolio management software.
- For organizational events, view intranet sites and increase networking.
- For people, use resource management software in addition to more face-to-face contact.
- For external events, subscribe to trade magazines, business publications, and join PMI.

Observation and Analysis
- For projects, use meaningful indices, not just red, yellow, and green indicators.
- For organizational events, people issues, and external

information, experience is needed to be able to separate what is relevant and/or what needs to be addressed.

Experience—build experience, as only experience can tell us what information is relevant. And only experience can enable true awareness—strategic intuition.
- Use the principles. Consider doing a periodic "principle check" to be sure they're being used.

Situational Awareness *(coup d'oeil)*—gain the strategic intuition necessary for making correct decisions on the fly. Do this through broad visibility, keen observation and analysis, experience, and frequent two-way communication.
- Stay aware of current related events.
- Keep your team and stakeholders aware of changing events.
- Ask for frequent task updates from team members.
- Frequency of team reporting depends on the nature of the project and the culture of the organization, but should be at least weekly.
- For each task, ask your team to report time spent to date (for budget tracking), time remaining or percent complete (for planning), and issues (for exception and risk handling).

CONDUCT EXTENSIVE RESEARCH
Study the terrain.
- Read up on the business area and/or technology as appropriate.
- Find out who the stakeholders will be and their likes and dislikes.
- Consider creating a political plan, outlining the organization's culture, stakeholder roles, issues to address, and approaches to take.

- Read up on the functional or geographical culture of the people you'll be dealing with.

Study past projects.
- Study similar projects and those that involved the same players. Both can bring unique lessons.
- Consider building a lessons-learned database, searchable by category.

Identify preliminary risks.
- Consider using a risk checklist or questionnaire.
- Beware of analysis-paralysis. Don't aim to know everything; go forward with 60 to 80 percent of the information you need.

PRACTICE CONTINUOUS PLANNING

Use the rolling wave scheduling method by planning each horizon as it approaches.
- Begin with a Work Breakdown Structure—a hierarchical list of all the work that makes up the project—and a master plan—a high-level timeline and milestones. Then create the master schedule.
- Break your project into phases (typically ninety days each).
- Early on, plan the first phase in detail and future phases at a higher level.
- Midway into each phase, refine the next phase in greater detail.
- If refinement causes a deviation from the promised time, cost, or scope, try to resolve the problem by overlapping tasks or adding resources.
- If that seems too risky, negotiate trade-offs in scope, time, or cost with the project sponsor.

Include phased deliverables in your project plan.

- This allows benefits to be achieved earlier and reduces the risk of ending up with nothing if the project is canceled unexpectedly.
- Consider using Earned Value Management to measure the value of the work performed (deliverables achieved) versus the time and money spent. This gives a more accurate picture of the project's health.

Practice ongoing risk management.

- Use predetermined checkpoints throughout your project.
- Identify new risks, assess probability and impact, and develop appropriate responses—avoid, mitigate, transfer, accept with contingency, accept without contingency.

CHAPTER 7

Speed

The loss of time is irreparable in war. The reasons that one gives are always poor, because operations misfire only through delays. The art consists simply in gaining time when one has inferior forces.—NAPOLEON

It is clear that Napoleon always kept a broad awareness of events, which, combined with targeted research and ongoing planning and risk management, enabled him to make correct decisions and thus achieve the exactitude he often spoke of. But exactitude is only part of the equation. Napoleon was able to surprise General Mack at Ulm because of the speed with which the *Grande Armée* acted and moved across Western Europe. It was this same speed that allowed Napoleon's army to take advantage of the Russians' tardiness. Likewise, it was a rapid march to Austerlitz by Napoleon's reserves that became an essential part of Napoleon's plan.

Speed means much more than just surprising the competition, as Napoleon was well aware. Many things can go wrong because of project delays, in warfare or in business:

- The political, economic, or organizational environment can change.
- A window of opportunity can be lost.

- The team can lose focus.
- Opposition can build.
- Stakeholder interest can fade.
- New risks can evolve.
- An important deadline can be missed, causing a domino effect.

Any or all of these can lead to project disaster. In addition, we must remember that speed begets speed. Once momentum takes hold, barriers and distractions have less impact. As the Borg said in *Star Trek*, "Resistance is futile." Napoleon knew this instinctively:

The strength of an army, like the power in mechanics, is estimated by multiplying the mass times the rapidity; a rapid march augments the morale of an army, and increases all the chances of victory.

Napoleon recognized that the scientific definition of momentum—mass times velocity—applies to achieving goals with people as well. And he knew that without adequate mass, velocity becomes even more critical. Mass and velocity alone do not complete the picture, because regardless of the mass and velocity, there is always some sort of resistance that will cause the momentum to fade—unless there is quite a bit of mass.

A Wiffle ball, familiar to most Americans, is a light plastic hollow ball with holes in it, used for backyard baseball games in close quarters. It sails slowly through the air when thrown or hit with a plastic bat, and it won't break anything or hurt anyone since the material is light. The holes in the ball are there for air resistance, which serves to slow down the ball. Of course, the ball must be thrown or hit for it to go anywhere.

Let's say we want the ball to go faster. Throwing a Wiffle ball faster can increase the speed, but because of air resistance, not by much. If we want the ball to go significantly faster, we need to either remove the holes (reduce resistance) or use heavier material (more mass), since mass can help overcome resistance. A combination of both would be ideal.

We can deduce that to achieve and maintain speed, we need to reduce resistance, create a catalyst for inspiring movement (thus increasing our velocity), and increase mass. The same is true when managing a project. We must find ways to reduce resistance, whether the resistance is coming from our stakeholders, the use of inadequate tools, or any other barriers that may stand in the way of our team. We must also provide a catalyst for movement by increasing the urgency level of our project. And finally, we must increase our mass by focusing all of our resources on the critical work to be done.

Before we explore how to do this, let's take note of the dangers of concentrating on speed alone. Going back to our Wiffle ball example, adding more speed to the ball won't do much good if our aim isn't true and if we don't use proper technique. Thus, speed must be balanced with exactitude. Applying this to managing projects, if we ignore the up-front research and planning we need to be successful, we end up with haste and not speed. And, as General George S. Patton once said, "Haste is speed without planning."[1] While the "go forward with 60 to 80 percent" guideline we discussed can help with achieving speed and not haste, this is only a guideline. Ultimately, the decision is an art more than a science and depends on the circumstances. This fine balance is the secret to success in both war and project management.

Meanwhile, with those cautions, let's examine further how to

> "Haste is speed without planning."
> —GENERAL GEORGE S. PATTON

achieve the speed that made Napoleon so successful. We'll do this by exploring the three areas we've mentioned—reducing resistance, increasing urgency, and providing focus for our projects.

REDUCING RESISTANCE

The *Grande Armée* marched at a rate of fifteen miles per day to reach the Rhine in less than six weeks during the Ulm campaign. They were able to do so because Napoleon worked hard to reduce any resistance they might have encountered. He did this in two ways. First, he negotiated agreements with important stakeholders, like Bavaria and Prussia, to be sure they would be partners and not obstacles. Second, he ensured that his troops had every advantage in their favor, whether this meant better training, superior equipment, adequate clothing, or the removal of anything else that might serve as a barrier to success. When leading projects, we, too, need to reduce resistance by managing stakeholders and removing barriers for our teams. Let's learn how we can best do that.

MANAGING STAKEHOLDERS

One of the first things we must do when undertaking a project is to identify our stakeholders and make sure they're on board with our goals, and, if possible, modify our goals to accommodate their needs—just as Napoleon secured agreements with Bavaria and Prussia before undertaking the Ulm campaign. We spoke earlier of the need for a communication plan—to identify who needs to know what, when, and how—and possibly even a political plan—to outline the political structure and potential issues. Certainly, these tools, as well as the ability to speak the stakeholders' language, as we discussed in Chapter 3, can help pave the way. After we've done that preparatory work, we must, however, take the next step and meet with our stakeholders, ideally as a group, to discuss the rationale for doing the project, address their concerns, and try to create a shared vision for the project.

We are making stakeholders partners and increasing our chances for success by including them in the up-front goal setting and requirements definition of the project. Likewise, we can design our project around these collective needs, which may be prioritized according to stakeholder need or importance. This goes back to the House of Quality approach we discussed in Chapter 3, where we use stakeholder requirements to determine the design priorities of our project.

Sometimes, though, even this isn't enough. If our project introduces major cultural changes or a paradigm shift in an organization's way of thinking, we need to have a full plan for addressing the people-change aspects of our project, along with a designated "change champion"—someone responsible for influencing the change throughout the organization. Targeted and ongoing communication is key.

This is where Dean Anderson and Linda Ackerman-Anderson's Transformational Change approach can come in handy. In their book *Beyond Change Management* and its related workbook, *The Change Leader's Roadmap*, they offer a systematic approach to addressing the resistance that typically accompanies such massive change. Their approach includes conducting readiness-assessment, building change management skills, resolving barriers, mapping design requirements to stakeholder needs, and many other items that we've discussed here.[2] Anyone implementing a major change in an organization would be wise to use the Andersons' system, or something similar.

With stakeholders on board, the next way we can reduce resistance for our project is to assure there are no remaining barriers facing our team.

REMOVING BARRIERS

Napoleon made sure his troops were well provided for before embarking on a campaign. He made sure they had the knowledge they needed to complete their assignments and ensured that they had good shoes, excellent training, and knowledge of how to live off the land. And because they could live off the land and had lighter artillery than most, they were able to travel lighter and faster. He ensured that his troops had the tools and training they needed to be successful, had their basic needs met, and would be unencumbered. Well equipped, well trained, well informed of the mission's need, and assured that stakeholders were on their side, Napoleon's army was motivated to take the unprecedented journey and cross 375 miles in fifteen days. This demonstrates the power of removing barriers for your team.

> A word of caution is needed concerning the perception that a new software package will be a cure-all for what ails an organization. The tool won't necessarily help if the underlying processes aren't resolved first.

As project managers, we must find out what barriers stand in the way of our teams' success. Barriers can take many forms, including inadequate training, lack of the right tools for the job (equipment, clothing, software, etc.), political barriers (conflict among superiors or peers, mixed messages, uncommitted stakeholders, etc.), or process barriers (excessive bureaucracy, interruptions, multitasking, etc.). A word of caution is needed concerning the perception that a new software package will be a cure-all for what ails an organization. The tool won't necessarily help if the underlying processes aren't resolved first. We must first remove the barriers of ineffective processes and excessive bureaucracy, and then we can choose a tool that best suits our new way of working. By removing barriers up front, we can tip the scales in our favor before we even begin.

Although removing barriers up front can help, resistance can return very quickly as the project proceeds. We must constantly keep an eye out for things that are impacting our team: conflicts, difficulty solving a problem, constant interruptions, or any other barriers. A significant part of a project manager's job is removing barriers—another reason that it is a good idea to have a Project Control Specialist who can maintain the project schedule, manage the issues list and risk plan, and perform other functions that can weigh down the project manager.

In summary, by getting stakeholders on board; having the right training, processes, and tools in place; and continuously removing any other barriers for our team (political or otherwise), we can reduce resistance for our project. We can now examine another element to consider when trying to achieve speed: increasing urgency.

INCREASING URGENCY

When Napoleon wanted to increase his troops' sense of urgency, he first ensured that they understood the importance of the mission, then made sure they were focused on the objectives at hand, and, finally, he provided specific dates by which certain deliverables or objectives were to be met. The first two items are certainly relevant today, but recent thinking has offered new perspectives on the third item—managing by target interim dates.

Consider Eli Goldratt's Critical Chain Project Management (CCPM) approach. According to Goldratt, focusing on target dates for each task doesn't work and indeed can be counterproductive, unless, of course, the task happens to be time-critical. This is because of two related tendencies inherent in human nature—Parkinson's Law and what Goldratt calls "Student Syndrome."

"Parkinson's Law," coined by British historian Cyril Northcote Parkinson, states that "work expands to fill the time available for its completion." In other words, when people commit to a deadline for a task, they will, by nature, spread the work out accordingly. They sometimes even add additional "bells and whistles" just because there's time. Similarly, the "Student Syndrome" dictates that they'll often wait as late as possible to begin, much like college students cramming at the last minute for an exam.

Goldratt also pointed out that people tend to add padding to their estimates to assure that they will meet whatever date they commit to. Unfortunately, in the case of either Parkinson's Law, where they spread out their work, or the Student Syndrome, where they procrastinate, this padding gets wasted, and thus we end up with longer project durations. Goldratt suggested that by removing the padding from the control of the resources and putting it in the hands of the project manager, we would encourage the resources to focus more on the task at hand. His suggestion is that we do this by asking for aggressive but possible estimates—defined as those with a 50 percent probability of success—and by isolating any padding in the form of "strategic buffers." We achieve project control by asking resources to frequently report time remaining on their tasks, and by measuring the consumption of the buffers.

We need to be aware that this is a theory—albeit one that has proved successful for those organizations brave enough to attempt it—and, like all theories, there are real-life exceptions. One such exception is that not all task estimates can be reduced. Some tasks simply take what they take. We obviously should not ask for reduced estimates for these tasks. There are some tasks that absolutely must have specific deadline dates. We need to make people aware of the deadlines for these. Finally, not all people add padding to their estimates, spread out work to fill the time, add bells and whistles, or procrastinate. Reducing those people's estimates by half would not be appropriate.

Considering these exceptions, it may be best to implement these changes on a limited basis, pinpointing only those resources and tasks for which the changes are appropriate. For now, suffice it to say that we can significantly increase the sense of urgency on our projects if we ask for frequent updates of time remaining or percentage complete, in addition to time spent and any issues encountered; and if we try to get better control of the hidden padding that many people include, asking instead for realistic estimates. And by combining this with clarifying the importance of the project up front—stating why, not just that it is important—and allowing resources to focus on the tasks at hand, we can almost guarantee an increased sense of urgency.

To learn more about implementing the full Critical Chain methodology, I suggest Eli Goldratt's book *Critical Chain* and/or searching the Web for the numerous consultants and software vendors that support this approach.[3] Now that we've seen how to reduce resistance and increase urgency, let's examine the final ingredient necessary for achieving and maintaining speed: providing focus.

PROVIDING FOCUS

As discussed in Chapter 4, one of the most important things Napoleon did to allow his *Grande Armée* to achieve its legendary speed was to provide unrelenting focus on the primary objective at hand, giving only the minimal resources necessary to secondary objectives. In this way, he could achieve the mass he needed at the critical point of contact. This concept became known as "Economy of Force," which enables Concentration of Force, and is still the most important principle in military strategy today. The key point is to centralize your forces on the most critical work and not dilute the effort by scattering resources over a million initiatives.

Goldratt's Critical Chain model echoes this approach in the project management arena by scheduling projects around the availability of the key resources that tend to be bottlenecks—constraints—and not attempting to have those resources multitask. In this way, the critical tasks can be focused on—one at a time and uninterrupted. This model is based on Goldratt's "Theory of Constraints," which suggests that we initially focus on the top one or two resource constraints, making sure the most critical work will be focused on in sequential order, and then progressing to do the same for the next most frequently used resources, and so on.

It is imperative not to activate more projects than we have the capacity to handle, since we're staggering our projects around the availability of our resources—known in the project management field as "cross-project resource leveling." Also, when activating projects, we should consider grouping related efforts under a common goal wherever possible, as either one large project or a program. But still, the same rules of resource contention apply. For example, Napoleon had a primary objective to attack the Austrians at Ulm, yet the ultimate goal was to defeat the Austrians and Russians. In this case, he ran the Ulm and Austerlitz campaigns as part of an overall "program." The ultimate goal of defeating the Austrians and Russians never left his mind. He focused on that goal and attacked each objective piecemeal. Most importantly, he didn't dilute his efforts by trying to attack England as well.

Another example is the way in which Napoleon addressed rejuvenating France after becoming First Consul. He addressed France's financial issues, created a civil code, reformed education, and ultimately rebuilt France, all in a few short years. Each of these was a small victory, giving further confidence to his stakeholders, yet each was a major effort in its own right. Therefore, Napoleon did not try to address all of them together. He knew that interest would be diluted across the multiple efforts and resource conflicts would occur—many of the same people were required for all of those efforts. As Napoleon knew from the battlefield, major initiatives are best done one at a time.

Napoleon said:

> *It is the same with strategy as with the siege of a fortress: concentrate your fire against a single point, and once the wall is breached all of the rest becomes worthless and the fortress is captured. It is Germany that must be crushed; once this is accomplished Spain and Italy will fall by themselves. Therefore it is essential not to scatter our attacks but to concentrate them.*

The same is true today. Simultaneously attacking too many major efforts leads to a lack of focus, not only by the resources involved, but by stakeholders as well. Energy is scattered, and we lose momentum. We need to activate fewer projects, focus on the critical ones, group related ones together where appropriate, and have key resources focus on one task at a time—moving across projects as scheduled.

Perhaps of most importance, we should never simultaneously attempt two major goals—which could be likened to taking on two major wars at the same time. This was not only one of Napoleon's maxims—one he was later forced to violate with dire consequences—but this was also a well-known axiom of the Romans, as Jomini pointed out in his book *The Art of War.*[4] An exception, as Jomini noted, is when a major goal is addressed by bringing in additional resources—either separate resources in the organization that are not needed for the first objective or an outside contractor that provides the capacity to do both. If both major initiatives are un-

> We should never simultaneously attempt two major goals—which could be likened to taking on two major wars at the same time.

related and involve the same stakeholders, however, we run into the same trouble—loss of focus.

This concept of centralizing your resources toward one strategic initiative at a time is not unique to the military strategies of Economy of Force and Concentration of Force or to the project management Critical Chain method. Geoffrey Moore's popular book on high-tech marketing, *Crossing the Chasm*, supports the same approach for trying to "attack" a mass audience with a disruptive technology. His method is to concentrate an overwhelming amount of force on the smallest strategic audience within a specific niche, capture that audience, move to broader audiences, then to adjacent niches,[5] which is fundamentally the same concept.

Now that we've discussed the need to focus our resources on the most important work, let's not forget that there also can be too many resources. In our attempts to focus attention on the critical tasks, what we need to do is focus the right number of resources to absolutely ensure success, but not so many that we reach the point of diminishing returns. Jomini explained that if you are facing three separately led armies of thirty thousand to thirty-five thousand each (totaling around one hundred thousand), it is better to have a central army of one hundred thousand attacking those armies in succession than an army of four hundred thousand stumbling over themselves.[6] Having too many resources raises issues with logistics, mobility, communication, and more. The key is that your forces are central, united, and have the right number of troops to guarantee success.

Frederick Brooks pointed out the same phenomenon in his timeless book *The Mythical Man Month*.[7] Adding resources does not always solve a problem and often makes it worse by increasing communication channels, adding learning curve issues, and generally compounding complexity. So, the key for critical tasks is to find the maximum effective amount of resources, while the key for

noncritical tasks is to find the minimum effective amount of resources. This is Economy of Force.

This leads to the question: What do we do with excess resources
after the critical tasks are adequately staffed? In that case, we can
either supplement the noncritical work up to the maximum effective level (but no more), reserve the excess resources for some strategic need, or use them for some unrelated, but still important, need.
The key is not to waste them, as this causes poor morale and wastes
money. If we look hard enough, there is always some need.

EXECUTIVE SUMMARY

We began the chapter by discussing the importance of speed and
the fact that many things can go wrong as a result of even the smallest delays. We also used a Wiffle ball example to illustrate the three
elements that contribute to achieving and maintaining speed:
reducing resistance; increasing urgency, which acts as a catalyst and
helps increase velocity; and providing focus (mass).

We can use the same concepts when managing projects. We can
reduce resistance by proactively managing stakeholders and removing barriers for our teams, such as ineffective processes, inadequate
tools, and interruptions. We can increase the sense of urgency on
our projects by asking our resources for frequent updates of time
remaining and by getting better control over the hidden padding
that many people inherently put in their estimates. Finally, we can
provide focus by adopting the Economy of Force principle, which
states that we dedicate the maximum effective amount of resources
to the primary objective and assign only the minimum effective
amount of resources to secondary objectives. Excess resources can
be used to supplement noncritical work, for some targeted strategic
need, or for some unrelated, but still important, need. The key is to
make use of all resources and to use them wisely.

Understanding Eli Goldratt's Critical Chain Project Management (CCPM) methodology can help, since it endorses many of these same principles, including frequent updates, control over hidden padding, and the Economy of Force approach. The primary selling point of the CCPM model is that it has been proven to greatly increase project throughput—or speed. We need to observe caution when using it, as there are always exceptions to any rule.

Let's not forget that speed needs to be balanced with exactitude; otherwise, we get haste. And even with speed and exactitude, we need to remember that we're dealing with the organization, coordination, and motivation of people. To assure that we're successful from a holistic standpoint, the remaining four principles—flexibility, simplicity, character, and moral force—deal with just that.

For example, flexibility assures that our resources are organized to meet varying needs across multiple projects. Flexibility also assures that our teams are empowered to adapt to ever-changing circumstances, yet still held together by common doctrine and leadership. With that in mind, let's explore the principle of flexibility in more detail and see just how we can accomplish these important goals.

MARCHING ORDERS

REDUCE RESISTANCE
Ensure stakeholders are on board.
- Start with a good communication plan, a political plan, and an understanding of the stakeholders' perspectives.
- Meet with the stakeholders to clarify the rationale for the project, hear their concerns, and jointly fine-tune the goals and requirements.
- If the project introduces a cultural change, appoint a change champion.

- Consider Dean Anderson and Linda Ackerman-Anderson's Transformational Change approach.

Remove barriers.
- Eliminate process barriers first—ineffective processes, excessive bureaucracy, interruptions, multitasking, etc.
- Give people the right tools for the job, including software and equipment.
- Make sure people are well trained.
- Resolve political barriers—conflict among superiors or peers, mixed messages, etc.
- Assist with troubleshooting.
- Consider assigning a project control specialist to handle specialized duties—maintaining the project schedule, managing issues and risks, etc.—allowing the project manager to focus on execution.

INCREASE URGENCY
- Ask for frequent updates of time remaining or percentage completed on tasks.
- Try to get better control over hidden padding that people inherently put in their estimates; ask for realistic estimates.
- Clarify the rationale and importance of the objectives up front.

PROVIDE FOCUS
Practice Economy of Force.
- Concentrate your resources—the maximum effective amount to ensure success—on the most critical work, and give secondary objectives only the minimal effective amount of resources.
- Commit all your resources, but use them strategically, either

to supplement noncritical work, to serve some strategic need later in the project, or to serve some unrelated, but still important, need.

- Activate fewer projects and focus on the most critical ones.
- Group related efforts as a single project or program.
- Focus on a single primary objective at a time.
- Don't attempt two major goals at the same time, unless one of them is addressed by separate resources not needed for the other. Even then, if that separate initiative is unrelated but shares the same stakeholders, loss of focus can occur.

CHAPTER 8

Flexibility

Plans of campaign may be modified ad
infinitum according to circumstances, the genius
of the general, the character of the troops, and
the features of the country. —NAPOLEON

John Lennon said, "Life is what happens to you while you're busy making other plans."[1] Napoleon knew this all too well and made it a point to always be prepared for changing situations. Knowing that plans are worthless unless kept fluid, he planned continuously and remained aware of the situation at all times. We've seen evidence of this. But just as important, he made sure his army was structured for maximum flexibility. He made certain they were able to quickly react to a variety of situations, yet still operate according to a strategic plan. There were three ways he accomplished this.

First, he made sure his troops were adaptable. For example, at Austerlitz, he organized his soldiers into mobile units. This allowed them to jump from one area of need to the next (as opposed to staying within their own division), which gave the illusion they were everywhere at once. They were also ready for change at a moment's notice and were well trained in the ability to swiftly regroup to meet any given situation.

Second, he made sure they were empowered. By arming them

with knowledge of the mission's concept and structuring them so they could operate independently, he was able to give brief, simple instructions to his commanders and know that the mission would be followed through. And by receiving regular communications from his commanders as to any variations, he made his army contributors to the plan, not just followers of a rigid process that didn't take reality into account.

Finally, he made sure they were unified. His armies operated under a common doctrine and were integrated through centralized planning and administration. Most importantly, they served under one ultimate leader—Napoleon.

Let's examine these three elements in more detail and see how we, too, can gain maximum flexibility by ensuring that our teams are adaptable, empowered, and unified. In doing this, we'll apply the same approaches that worked for Napoleon.

ADAPTABLE TEAMS

Adaptable teams are those that have access to shared resources and are ready and trained to handle a variety of situations as they arise. Mobility and readiness are key to adaptability, and both enabled Napoleon's *Grande Armée* to succeed at Austerlitz and completely overwhelm the Austro-Russian army on the Pratzen Plateau. Let's now see how we, too, can make maximum use of our resources and ensure that they're ready for a variety of circumstances.

SHARED RESOURCES

We must first make sure we are able to shift our resources quickly across multiple areas of need, if we want to achieve the same adaptability Napoleon did at Austerlitz. This requires a pool of resources that are shared across the organization and not dedicated to one specific department. Once we've established that, we also need to make sure that these resources are used strategically and not just assigned to projects and tasks in a scattershot, impromptu manner. For example, if we need a certain role fulfilled across multiple key projects, we would determine which resources we have that can fill the role and where in those projects they'll be needed. We would also determine the importance of each project with relation to other work. The key, as we discussed earlier, is to stagger the project schedules around the availability of these key resources and to not activate more projects than we can accommodate.

Here is a more specific example: we have three projects that require someone who can write technical instructions, but we have only two people in the organization who can adequately do that. We need to plan the project schedules around the availability of those resources. Ideally, these people would be freed up from their other work to serve on these important projects, but if the other work is also important, the project may need to wait until they're available. It all depends on what is most important to the organization, and some negotiation or governance may need to take place. The same might apply to a group of resources that combine their roles to serve a specific purpose. This group could be moved from one project to the next as a mobile unit, much like Napoleon did at Austerlitz. This gives each project the true resources it needs, instead of using anyone who is available, regardless of qualifications.

Fortunately, most enterprise project management software allows this to be done easily. To make it work effectively, we need to have our resources regularly update the time remaining or percentage complete for their current task, so we know what they're really allocated to; and we need to avoid multitasking wherever possible, which only serves to extend everything and make forecasts unpredictable. Unfortunately, many organizations identify all the roles they'll need in a given project, and then solicit all of those people for the entire length of the project instead of only where they're needed. Then they have these same people booked on ten other projects at the same time. The results are that all of the projects end up taking longer; the resource finds it more difficult to predict how much time is left on any given task because of all the interruptions; and enterprise resource management becomes impossible.

We can simultaneously gain more control and more flexibility by thinking of resources as shared, mobile units. We gain more control because we are using our resources strategically and not haphazardly. And we gain more flexibility because we then have the right kind of people for our projects when we need them. That is the power of mobility. But, to really be adaptable, we need to go beyond just making sure our resources are shared and mobile. We need also to ensure that they are trained in a variety of situations and ready for change at a moment's notice.

READY FOR CHANGE

Napoleon spared no expense in training his army for a variety of situations and terrains. At one minute they could be in one formation, and at the next minute they could completely reorganize to adapt to a different terrain or opposing formation. This quick switch was one of the ways in which they could continually surprise the enemy. Extensive situational training and the fact that they were well equipped for decision making enabled them to do this. As project managers, our teams must also be ready for change and able to adapt to a variety of situations. We can create the greatest plan in the world, but if our people can't recognize when a situation calls for the need to vary from the plan, or if they aren't trained to handle various circumstances, we're sunk. This is why the greatest type of training is simulation training, which mimics various conditions and truly tests people's ability to adapt. This has worked for years in the military, and the same approach can work anywhere else.

Our people will be much better equipped to deal with change by being trained in various conditions through effective simulations. This doesn't have to be fancy; a simple walk-through of various hypothetical scenarios can be quite effective. There are organizations that offer simulation training based on a wide variety of circumstances for various industries, and this can be well worthwhile because it brings some outside perspectives to the table that might otherwise be overlooked.

Training is only one element of being ready for change. Napoleon's troops were able to re-form into different configurations, depending on the need at hand. We can do the same. We do not need to have people permanently assigned to positions or need to be stuck with the same team we began with. If the needs of a project suddenly change and call for a different team configuration, by all means, we should reconfigure accordingly. Maybe people can be brought in as "guest" members as needed, or perhaps we can ease up in a particular area and move those team members to a greater area of need. We can even plan these configuration changes in advance if certain phases of a project call for a different team structure. We should always be on the lookout to see that our team configuration is appropriate for the situation at hand.

The bottom line is that we can be ready for change at a moment's notice by assuring that our people have had extensive simulation training and that our teams can be reconfigured as needed. A team that is ready for change and built from shared, mobile units can give us the ultimate in adaptability.

Adaptability is only one of the three elements of flexibility. To be truly flexible, we also need our teams to be empowered. We need unity as well, because empowerment without cohesion breeds chaos. When all three elements of adaptability, empowerment, and unity are in place, then we can say we've obtained maximum flexibility. We've learned how to make our teams adaptable. Now let's learn how to be certain they are empowered.

EMPOWERED TEAMS

Napoleon's commanders, as we saw from the structure of the *Grande Armée*, were given both the authority and the ability to operate independently when needed. Each corps had a full staff of officers and support personnel, and their commanders were well briefed in the purpose of the mission with guiding principles to observe and warning signs to look out for. In the case of Austerlitz, all the soldiers were also briefed, as Napoleon didn't want to take any chances. He was able to coordinate his armies over a broad territory by arming his troops with the knowledge needed to be successful and empowering them to make decisions on the fly. He knew he couldn't be everywhere at once and that empowering his troops would enable him to manage a large force more effectively. In addition, since his troops reported their progress and position back to Napoleon with great frequency through Berthier's Imperial General Staff, he was able to adjust his plans accordingly. His plans could be fluid, based on reports from the field.

To make this work, Napoleon made sure they were all unified and working under a common strategy, but the point is that his teams were equipped for decision making and treated as contributors to the plan, and this empowerment led to greater flexibility for the army as a whole. Let's consider both of these elements in more detail.

EQUIPPED FOR DECISION MAKING

In order to equip his teams with the ability to make effective decisions, Napoleon fully briefed his teams on their mission's concept and gave them guiding principles to follow. Following is an example of this in a message that Napoleon had Berthier deliver to a general just before the Ulm campaign:

> *I have no faith in waiting until the last moment to inform you of the plan of campaign adopted by the Emperor: it is advantageous that you be instructed fifteen days in advance in order that you can make all of your preparations . . . so that when I transmit the Emperor's orders to commence hostilities you will be prepared to play the important role that His Majesty, in his vast plans from the Baltic as far as Naples, has entrusted to you . . . The intention of the Emperor is that you will enter Naples at the same time that he crosses the Rhine, which will occur in late September.*

The note went on to explain how many men the general would have, what he could expect under various alternate possibilities, and what he should do in each condition. The letter closed with this statement:

> *This letter is the principal instruction for your plan of campaign, and if unforeseen events should occur, you will be guided in your conduct by the spirit of this instruction.*

By arming the general early on with all he needed to be successful, Napoleon greatly improved the chances that the general would be well equipped to make the right decisions when needed. We can do the same and let our teams be guided by the spirit of our instruction. To learn how to accomplish this, let's refer to a study done for the United States Department of Defense by RAND's National Defense Research Institute: *Command Concepts: A Theory Derived from the Practice of Command and Control.*[2] The study applied to military C2 (Command and Control) systems, but the principle applies equally to project management in general.

In essence, the study recommended the use of a "command concept" approach, which we can adapt to the project management world as the "project concept approach." The idea is that after planning but before execution, it is critical for a project manager to convey the whole concept of the project to the team, not just the tasks that they must do. Studies have shown that this approach enables better cross talk, greater accuracy, and better decision making by team members and staff. A general guideline is that when conveying the concept to the team before execution, the project manager should act as if it is the last time he or she will get to address the team—much the same as Napoleon issued his instructions to his general. What would a project concept look like for us? Ideally, it would include the following:

- The situation
  - The problem or needs being addressed
  - What to expect from unfolding events (anticipatory)

- The solution and plan
  - Purpose (the mission)
  - Approach (how this will be achieved, from a high level)
  - Strategic goals and tactical objectives
  - Important checkpoints (stage gates)
  - Measures (What is considered success? What expectations need to be met?)
  - Alternatives reviewed and why this approach was chosen
  - Guiding principles/priorities/constraints
  - Communication protocols (how to communicate and handle risk events and emergencies)

- Enabling factors (words of wisdom)
  - Timing considerations

- What-if scenarios
- Priorities if faced with tough decisions

These are the types of details Napoleon shared with his commanders before the execution of a campaign was about to begin. Then, once activities began, he just needed simple, concise messages to keep things on track. And since his commanders would update him with any details that might change the overall plan, they were able to be contributors to the plan instead of being subservient to it. Let's examine this in more detail.

Contributors to the Plan

We saw how conveying the project's concept up front can help equip our teams to make proper decisions on short notice. Now let's see how we can subsequently issue broad directives and not feel that we have to micromanage our teams. At the same time, we'll see how we can collect the right feedback to engage our teams in keeping our overall plans fluid. Fortunately, we have a proven tool for this, called a "work package."

A work package is a broad directive that states a final deliverable, along with general instructions, objectives, and guidelines to follow. The project manager needs to be concerned about only the final deliverable as far as the overall project plan goes. The work package is then assigned to a team leader or an individual, who is responsible for managing the work package and establishing an independent plan to complete the work. Then, the work package owner needs to report only whether anything in carrying out the work package will cause a need to change the overall plan—if it changes a major deliverable or milestone. In this way, we gain flexibility and lose the constraints of a rigid plan. More importantly, we make our team contributors to our plan.

To take this one step further, we can even solicit input from the work-package owner before issuing the authorization to begin. Consider Napoleon's statement when issuing a directive to Vice Admiral Latouche-Tréville during the failed attempt to invade England, just before the Ulm campaign: "Think over carefully the great enterprise you are about to carry out; and let me know, before I sign your final orders, your own views as to the best way of carrying it out." Napoleon valued his people's input, as he knew they were closest to the action and could have much to offer. Likewise, he favored broad, simple directives, since he knew he couldn't be everywhere at once and that micromanagement would be futile.

Unfortunately, in this case, his admirals weren't up to the task, and the mission was botched, similar to how Murat's foolishness almost undid the great efforts of the Ulm campaign. This should serve as a caution to us that broad directives work only if we have reliable people managing them. If we don't have people we can delegate work to without heavy intervention, we're behind from the start. So, before attempting to use work packages, we need to weigh the ability of our people to independently manage the work we need them to do—or at least make the work package instructions appropriate to the level of the person executing the work package. Then, we need to make sure we brief them effectively so that they can be successful.

We are enabling our team to thrive with broad directives by equipping them with a better understanding of the project's concept. And we are relaxing the need to have an overly detailed project schedule by keeping their directives broad through the use of work packages. Better yet, we are off-loading much of the detailed planning to the work-package owners, who are most capable of planning at that level of detail. Furthermore, when they update us with a need to change our overall plan, they become valued contributors to the plan and thus reduce our need to feel as if we must be everywhere at once.

This combination of decentralized decision making and participative planning makes a team fully empowered. A team that is adaptable and empowered is flexible indeed. But let's not forget that an adaptable, empowered team can also become unmanageable unless held together in some way. We can end up with chaos instead of flexibility. So, to achieve true flexibility, we also need our people to be unified.

UNIFIED TEAMS

One of Napoleon's most well-known maxims was Maxim 64, quoted in David Chandler's book *The Military Maxims of Napoleon*: "Nothing is so important in war as undivided command: for this reason, when war is carried on against a single power, there should be only one army, acting upon one base, and conducted by one chief."[3] Napoleon was speaking from experience. Having seen a former mission fail when his co-commander refused to proceed in bad weather, he later insisted on sole command during the Italian campaign, saying:

> *Kellerman would command the army quite as well as I do; for I am certain that our victories are due to the bravery and the daring of the men. But I am convinced that to combine Kellerman and myself in Italy would be to court disaster . . . In any case, I am certain that one bad general is better than two good ones.*

We would be wise to follow the same advice, as many projects have failed due to mixed messages from multiple chiefs and having related projects driven separately and operating under separate rules and strategies. Consider the scientific concept of entropy, which refers to the level of disorder in any system. While some disorder or freedom is needed to increase the probability of good things happening—thus the energy and creativeness we get from having empowered teams—without some sort of immobilizing force to keep things together, chaos will ensue. Whatever isn't held together will ultimately break apart. This would seem to be common sense, but many organizations attempt to address a multitude of interconnected projects in dissimilar and often conflicting ways. Or they have several leaders responsible for a single project, which serves to generate the same conflicts. Clearly, this is not flexibility—it is confusion.

We need to do two things to avoid this confusion. First, we need to ensure that all parties are operating under a common set of guidelines and protocols—shared doctrine. Second, we need to avoid having related initiatives driven by different leaders, unless those leaders report to one overall leader who can resolve conflicts and define strategy.

OPERATE UNDER A SHARED DOCTRINE

A shared doctrine can be established in different ways. A PMO (project or program management office) can institute a common methodology, along with templates and principles, for managing all projects in the organization. A particular program might require a set of standards that apply to the projects in that specific program. A specific project might also benefit from additional guidelines or templates appropriate to that project, including common terminology.

For example, the Russians didn't arrive at Ulm on time because they were still operating on the Julian calendar. Something similar happened in 1999 when NASA lost a $125 million Mars orbiter because their contractors used the English unit of measurement while NASA's team used the metric system. The bottom line is this: for projects that deal with multiple countries or that span several organizations, it is especially important to establish a common set of terminology and protocols.

UNITY OF COMMAND

We can avoid the confusion that goes with mixed messages by doing all we can to determine who is ultimately in charge of related projects, even if that means bringing several superiors together to facilitate some sort of agreement. We owe it to them to make sure our projects are successful. And if we are asked to co-lead a project, we need to politely ask that one person be given the ultimate responsibility for resolving conflicts and leading the overall effort. Even a core leadership team needs one person at its helm. We can offset any risks that go with empowerment by ensuring that our teams are operating under a common doctrine and under one ultimate leader. And then, we have true flexibility.

EXECUTIVE SUMMARY

In this chapter, we have seen how to build a more flexible force by ensuring that our teams are adaptable, empowered, and unified. First, there is no doubt that we gain the ability to take on broader initiatives by assuring that our teams are adaptable and empowered. We are ensuring that our teams have the same adaptability that the *Grande Armée* did at Austerlitz by strategically assigning our resources across multiple projects, restructuring our project teams when needed, and providing training in a variety of situations. We are ensuring that they are empowered by conveying the projects' concepts to our teams in advance and using a work-package approach to make them contributors to our plans. Finally, we need to balance this freedom by providing a common doctrine and unity of command, which keeps things from getting out of control. This balance of freedom and unity that Napoleon managed so well can give us the flexibility we need to be successful.

So far, we have examined three of Napoleon's Six Winning Principles: exactitude, speed, and flexibility. Surely, it is a powerful combination to have pinpoint precision through awareness, research, and continuous planning; increased speed through reduced resistance, heightened urgency, and better focus; and true flexibility through teams that are adaptable, empowered, and unified. Yet, it is possible to have all three of these elements in abundance and still fail. The history books are peppered with such examples. To be truly successful, we need to add the principles of simplicity, character, and moral force. In the next chapter, we'll discuss the need for simplicity, and that means straightforward objectives, concise messages, and uncomplicated processes.

MARCHING ORDERS

MAKE SURE YOUR TEAMS ARE ADAPTABLE

Assure that your resources are shared and mobile.

- Begin with a shared resource pool—as opposed to having resources fully dedicated to specific departments.
- Plan out the roles needed across key projects.
- Determine the importance of the projects in relation to other work—this may require some level of governance.
- Negotiate for the resources you need, and schedule the projects around their availability; free them up as their work completes.
- Consider using related groups of resources as mobile units, moving from project to project sequentially to do their piece of the work.

Ensure that your team is ready for a variety of situations.
- Consider simulation training or at least prepare walk-throughs of various scenarios.
- Don't be afraid to restructure your team as needed, or even plan for different team configurations for certain phases of the project.

MAKE SURE YOUR TEAMS ARE EMPOWERED

Convey the project's concept early on in the project.
- Include the situation or problem being addressed, what to expect from unfolding events, the mission's objectives and approach, how to handle various possible scenarios, and guiding principles to go by.

Issue broad directives, not detailed how-to instructions.
- Consider the use of work-packages—high-level deliverables, where a work-package owner manages the detailed tasks outside of the master schedule.
- Be sure the work-package owner can comprehend the overall concept and requirements and is capable of driving the work package to completion.
- Be sure the work-package has guidelines and instructions as needed to complete the deliverable accurately.
- Ask the work-package owner for input on how to carry out the deliverable.
- Ask the work-package owner for progress updates and warnings when a change will affect the overall project plan, milestones, or deliverables.

MAKE SURE YOUR TEAMS ARE UNIFIED

Establish a common set of processes and guidelines at the organizational, program, and project levels as appropriate.

- Consider using a PMO to establish a common project management methodology.
- For multiple related projects, consider grouping them as a program with common principles across all projects in the program.
- For projects that span geographical or organizational boundaries, be sure to establish common terminology and protocols, including time zones, units of measure, and so forth.

Ensure unity of command.
- Determine who is ultimately in charge of multiple related projects, and if necessary, bring the parties together to facilitate agreement on one owner.
- If asked to co-lead a project, politely ask for one person to be given responsibility for conflict resolution and ultimate accountability.

CHAPTER 9

Simplicity

The art of war does not require complicated maneuvers; the simplest are the best, and common sense is fundamental. From which one might wonder how it is generals make blunders; it is because they try to be clever.—NAPOLEON

From Napoleon to Patton to Jack Welch, great leaders have often cited simplicity as a key element of success. Simplicity can take various forms when it comes to managing projects and people. It can mean straightforward objectives, as opposed to trying to get overly complicated; or it can mean concise, clear, and focused messages, something that top leaders and marketing people have stressed for years. It can also mean simple processes for managing and executing our plans. In all of its forms, simplicity is a way to reduce confusion and misunderstanding. Napoleon knew this better than anyone, as things were confusing enough in battle without the added complications of intricate maneuvers and unclear messages.

Throughout his career, Napoleon focused on achieving simplicity in three major areas. First, he made sure his objectives were simple. He knew that complicated objectives carried many risks and were often unnecessary, so he always planned for the most straightforward, basic path wherever possible.

Second, to support these objectives, Napoleon made sure that his messages were simple. Napoleon knew that cluttered or vague messages could undermine even the most straightforward objectives. Before any battle, he conveyed clearly and concisely what the objectives were, why they were important, and how they were to be achieved. He didn't confuse things by talking about future details or other topics. Once the mission commenced, he simply offered frequent, brief communications to keep things on track. It was the same during his administration years, when he issued a series of clear, simple messages to the public upon establishment of the new government. He knew that people need clarity and focus, not long-winded messages that say a lot but communicate nothing.

Finally, Napoleon's processes were simple. He realized that even if the objectives were straightforward and well communicated, confusion could still arise if the underlying processes to achieve them were overly complicated. This simplicity was evident in his uncomplicated battle plans, his effective organization of the *Grande Armée*, and his efficient administrative policies and laws.

Napoleon was able to greatly diminish the chances of confusion among all parties, including the *Grande Armée* and the people of France, with straightforward objectives, concise messages, and uncomplicated processes. We can bring needed clarity to our stakeholders and project teams using the same techniques. What worked for Napoleon, Patton, and Jack Welch can work for us as well.

Let's explore how we do this by assuring simplicity in all of our objectives, messages, and processes.

SIMPLE OBJECTIVES

Napoleon knew that the more complicated an objective was, the more likely it was to go wrong. Therefore he always favored the most straightforward objectives. For example, at Ulm his goal was to defeat the Austrians before the Russians arrived. To reach that goal, he devised clear, simple objectives—to get there fast and invade via the Danube Valley to the north. Then, upon hearing that the Austrians had taken Ulm, his objective was to loop around and surround General Mack from behind before he knew what had hit him. All of the underlying plans would be geared toward these objectives.

At Austerlitz, Napoleon knew he needed to lure the Austro-Russian army into attacking on his terms so he could split their center. To accomplish this, his objective was to feign weakness to lure the enemy into attacking his right. Once they committed, he would attack them with the bulk of his troops to the left, which were hidden from view. He would supplement this with surprise reinforcements from the south. Again, all plans were supportive of these objectives.

Napoleon had other secondary objectives during both of these campaigns, but they, too, were supportive of these primary objectives. The key point is that his primary objectives were simple to the core, especially as compared with what other leaders were doing at the time; and therein lay the beauty. Consider this statement by Napoleon:

> *The art of war is like everything that is beautiful and simple. The simplest moves are the best. If MacDonald, instead of doing whatever he did, had asked a peasant for the way to Genoa, the peasant would have answered, "Through Bobbio"—and that would have been a superb move.*

Napoleon was referring to his marshal, Jacques MacDonald, who was routed at Trebbia, Italy, by the Austro-Russian army in 1799. As he pointed out with this example, the most straightforward objectives are usually the best, and sometimes this just means asking someone who has done it before. Unfortunately, this often eludes people, and they try to get fancy. When developing objectives, we must consciously ask ourselves, *Why build a complex system when we might have an alternate, simpler way to solve a problem? Why spin our wheels looking for a solution when we can simply ask someone who's been there and done that?* It often goes back to the need to identify what the root problem is that we are trying to solve and then determine the simplest way to go about solving it. The minimalist approach is often best and more likely to be achieved.

> Why spin our wheels looking for a solution when we can simply ask someone who's been there and done that? ... The minimalist approach is often best and more likely to be achieved.

Once we've assured that our objectives are as straightforward as possible, the next step is to communicate them effectively. Again, the principle of simplicity applies.

SIMPLE MESSAGES

Napoleon said, "Any order that can be misunderstood will be misunderstood." He made sure that his orders were clear and focused, as he knew that messages too vague or too expansive could cause confusion.

Let's examine the issue of clarity. We spoke of the need for straightforward objectives, and certainly we want to communicate those in a concise manner. But sometimes, in an attempt to be concise, a manager will communicate an extremely simple objective in a manner that's so vague that it isn't obvious to anyone what it actually means.

For example, let's say you asked someone to bring you some large rocks. That's a seemingly simple request. Yet, since you haven't clarified what you mean by large rocks or how you intend to use them, they may bring rocks the size of golf balls or they may bring boulders. Jaclyn Kostner used a similar example in her enlightening book *Virtual Leadership: Secrets from the Round Table for the Multi-Site Manager,* in which King Arthur called upon his knights to bring large rocks, but didn't indicate that the purpose was to build Camelot.[1] You can guess the results. So, even though our objectives may be simple and straightforward, we also need to communicate them clearly.

Let's take a look at an order by Napoleon to Marshal Soult when the *Grande Armée* was preparing to embark on the journey from Boulogne to the Rhine for the Ulm campaign:

Let me know whether the horses, the supplies, the men, will all be ready for embarkation in two weeks. Don't reply in terms of metaphysics, but inspect your magazines and depots.

This was a brief, clear communication that was not cluttered with unnecessary details. From this communication, Marshal Soult knew that he needed to conduct an inspection and ensure that horses, supplies, and men would be ready for departure. An unclear communication might have been, "Please make sure everything is ready for us to depart in two weeks." Certainly, this would have been brief, but could have been misinterpreted. Likewise, Napoleon could have cluttered this message by adding unrelated information. The primary request might have been lost, buried in a sea of details.

This takes us to the next key factor for simple communications: they must be focused. As service marketing guru Harry Beckwith stated in his book *Selling the Invisible,* "Saying many things usually communicates nothing."[2] Beckwith suggests that all communications focus on one clear message, and that any details included should be concise and supportive of that one message. Indeed, this mirrors our Economy of Force philosophy of focusing on one primary objective and just a few supporting secondary objectives.

Napoleon subscribed to this communication philosophy, as evidenced by the previous example and by his messages and orders in general. When he had established the new consulate in France, he first issued a brief statement announcing the republic and its principles. Then, in a separate communication, he announced the constitution and its benefits. Subsequently, he announced other items as they were developed. By focusing on one message at a time without a lot of noise, he ensured that the people were able to digest it and savor it. We must strive to do the same thing wherever possible.

We have discussed the need for simplicity in our objectives and messages. Certainly this can go a long way toward avoiding unnecessary confusion. But there is one more area where simplicity can help us avoid confusion: our processes. And that can mean making sure our plans are easy to maintain, our administrative procedures are easy to understand, and our personal organizational systems are efficient.

SIMPLE PROCESSES

If our objectives are simple and understandable, and we've clearly communicated them to our team, the next step is to ensure that our underlying processes are uncomplicated as well. Napoleon excelled at developing efficient processes that were ingenious in their simplicity. First, he made sure his plans of campaign were kept at a high level; he merely issued broad directives to his commanders. He had a simple system of frequent communication with his commanders to facilitate this, via Berthier's Imperial General Staff. This was simplicity at its finest. We, too, can use this approach by keeping our master schedule at a high level and using the work package approach to off-load the fine details to a work-package owner, as discussed in Chapter 8.

Napoleon also established efficient and easy-to-follow administrative systems. Although some bureaucracy is needed to assure order, excessive bureaucracy is not. Napoleon once astutely said,

"The ancients had a great advantage over us in that their armies were not trailed by a second army of pen-pushers." He understood the importance of order better than anyone, but also recognized the need to move quickly. The trick is to have enough administration to avoid chaos, yet not have it hinder progress. And this fine balance is truly an art. One of Napoleon's dreams was to simplify the legal system. He felt there were simply too many laws, as echoed in his statement "Why should one-third of the population live well off of the quarrels of the other two-thirds?" His civil code is notable for its simplicity, and is still the code used in France today and is the basis for codes in many other countries. Napoleon said:

> In the discussions over the drawing up of the Civil Code the objections chiefly made were that it did not give the judge sufficient scope. Extreme exactness in the laws has been found unpleasant and oppressive by all nations since ancient times, and they have therefore introduced into their laws only main features of an obvious and productive character . . . One would try in vain to introduce a definite application of the laws to all offences, and one would soon be forced to see that the laws made in this spirit and with this kind of exactness would be incomplete . . . When a law does not . . . make its intentions clear, a judge will often give a decision against his own will through acting on the strict letter of the law.

In other words, if we declared policy based on only the most obvious and productive rules needed, then we would allow people to make more decisions based on sound judgment. And if we focused on building people's cognitive skills and ensuring the right principles are in place instead of trying to make everything dummy-proof, which would be a futile exercise, we'd have a simpler, more flexible, and more effective system. The same goes for our processes and methodologies. As much as possible, we need to try to avoid bureaucracy in our processes, and we can limit this by focusing on only the most important things to assure success.

In Chapter 4, we saw how Napoleon's system of running the *Grande Armée* worked: the Intelligence Bureau, Topographic Bureau, and Secretariat made up his cabinet; and the Imperial General Staff provided centralized communication and control. His administrative affairs were equally well organized, as documented by Baron Fain.

Every other week, Napoleon's ministers would send him records for their respective areas: war, interior, or finance. The war records included marching orders and troop movements by day, health status of each regiment, soldiers and divisions that distinguished themselves in some way, and updated personnel records. There was a common record book listing all branches of the service and separate books for each area; yet they all followed the same format. Fain said, "Napoleon's consistency of method and simplicity of organization were remarkable; the same procedure served for all uses, like a master key that opens all locks."[3] Finance records showed the price of wheat in each region of France, with color-coded references to the maximum, minimum, and average prices for each region. At a glance, Napoleon could make decisions based on those areas with immediate need.

In addition to the records submitted by his ministers, which were supplemented by Napoleon's regular brief communications with his commanders, Napoleon held weekly operational meetings with the administrative councils for each area—war, interior, and finance, each held on different days—to review needs and make decisions. He held monthly fund allocation meetings, always making sure to have subject-matter experts present as needed. Project engineers would present their plans and estimates, and justify their projects at these meetings. Only the most important projects were accepted, as Napoleon was cautious about starting too many endeavors at once.

Napoleon's personal organizational systems were just as simple. Again, Fain gives us a clear picture of the way he worked. Each morning, Napoleon would answer his mail, which he first sorted into three categories: *current* (mail he needed to address that day), *pending* (mail he needed to look at in the near future), and *answered* (mail he had replied to or that needed no reply). Letters that were delusional or written by lunatics were simply disposed of—even Napoleon had spam. He would then peruse issues that were reported by the various factions of the government. He'd prioritize these issues as high-profile/urgent, to be delegated, or irrelevant. Following that, he held a daily "doctor's in" session—called a "small levee"—with his servants, assistants, and those who needed to see him about some matter. He also held a "great levee" weekly, which anyone could attend. After lunch, which was usually held with his family and friends, Napoleon would spend time reviewing the record books and status reports and taking appropriate actions.

Napoleon said, "The craft of emperor has its tools like all others." This craft comes very close to the way in which most businesses would operate. It is simply a matter of good time management. Napoleon's typical day of checking mail, reviewing issues, holding a "doctor's in" session, reviewing records and status reports, and taking actions is not unlike the typical day of a project manager, and certainly it is a good model to follow. His monthly fund allocation meetings, similar to portfolio reviews, and his weekly operational meetings with his various councils, which were used to review actions and make decisions, were an efficient way to manage multiple projects.

The bottom line is this: we can greatly avoid the confusion that goes with complex structures by ensuring that our processes are simple, including streamlined policies, undemanding methodologies, and well-organized administrative and personal systems.

EXECUTIVE SUMMARY

The power of simplicity is exponential. It eliminates confusion, increases morale, and generally promotes progress. Napoleon's tendency toward straightforward objectives, clear and focused messages, and efficient processes made life easier, not only for his armies and staff, but for himself. We, too, can reap many rewards by applying simplicity to our objectives, messages, and processes.

We can achieve simple objectives by focusing on the root of the problem and aiming for the easiest way to solve it, which often means speaking to those who have done it before. We can simplify communications by assuring that our messages are clear, concise, and focused on one thing at a time. And finally, we can simplify our processes by keeping our plans at a high level, focusing on only the rules and principles that matter, streamlining our methodologies, and practicing good time management with well-organized administrative and personal systems.

Thus far, we've covered four of Napoleon's Six Winning Principles: exactitude, speed, flexibility, and simplicity. These principles work together like an intricate clock. If one piece is missing, things can't function properly. We may get lucky and succeed once or twice, but not consistently. But there are two more crucial pieces to this "clock": character and moral force. Together, these will give us the "soft skills" we need to be consistently successful. In the next chapter, we'll see how character traits, such as integrity, calmness, and responsibility, can build trust—a vital element of success.

MARCHING ORDERS

SIMPLE OBJECTIVES
Aim for the most straightforward approach.
- Remember the problem you are trying to solve, and meditate on the simplest way to go about solving it.
- Don't forget to ask others who have "been there and done that."

SIMPLE MESSAGES

Make sure the message is clear.
- If it can be misunderstood, it probably will be.
- Don't confuse conciseness with vagueness. Be brief but clear.

Focus on one message at a time.
- Supporting details are okay, but not extraneous details.
- Remember the Beckwith principle: Saying many things usually communicates nothing.

SIMPLE PROCESSES

Keep plans at a high level.
- Use work packages to off-load the details to other task owners or leaders.

Simplify administrative systems.
- Use the "less is more" approach when it comes to rules. Not everything needs to be dictated by policy. Leave room for good judgment. Enable this with training in cognitive skills and sound principles.
- Aim for simple processes and methodologies: only implement that which is crucial to success.
- Practice good time management: try to organize activities into weekly or daily events, such as daily e-mail and issues reviews, "doctor's in" sessions, afternoon project record reviews and actions, and weekly operational meetings.

CHAPTER 10

Character

A military leader must possess as much character as intellect. Men who have a great deal of intellect and little character are the least suited . . . It is preferable to have much character and little intellect. —NAPOLEON

Traits such as integrity, calmness, and responsibility are often associated with the greatest leaders throughout history. Napoleon was no exception. Driven by his ambition to leave a positive mark on the world, he always maintained his honor and integrity. He knew that any looting or pillaging by his troops would leave a permanent stain on his image, and he went out of his way to encourage respect for different cultural backgrounds. Equality was always foremost in his mind and the guiding value of his administration. Any persecution of individuals or groups based on their heritage would have been out of harmony with that value—it would have displayed a lack of integrity. He always stuck to his principles, doing the right thing even when pressured to do otherwise. He was open-minded enough to solicit the opinions of others in general, but he was unbendable when it came to actions that violated the core principle of equality.

Although prone to minor outbursts on occasion, Napoleon generally kept a cool head, especially when faced with danger and, above all, when among his troops. He knew that a leader who didn't maintain composure could quickly demoralize people and cause general concern among the masses. Another key to his success was his sense of responsibility. He assumed full responsibility for his actions, bearing the weight of France and its citizens—especially his troops—on his shoulders. Integrity, calmness, and responsibility are central to good character, and there is no doubt that Napoleon had these traits in abundance.

The Project Management Institute also recognizes the importance of such traits, and has added Professional Ethics and Responsibility as a key component of its project management certification exams. As made evident by the exam questions, this can be particularly tricky when leading projects across multiple countries and cultures, as Napoleon certainly had to deal with. But whether we're leading a major international project or just a handful of people, the same general principles apply. Let's explore further how we can build the three essential character traits of integrity, calmness, and responsibility.

INTEGRITY

When we speak of integrity, we are referring to the need to be integrated or whole. This means that our values, actions, and words must be in complete harmony. Napoleon demonstrated this in three ways. First, he made sure that his actions and the actions of his troops adhered to his core values. We need to do the same, as our integrity depends not only on *our* actions, but on the actions of our teams as well. Second, he made sure that his words and actions were aligned. He knew that to say one thing and do another would display a lack of integrity and break people's trust. We need to do this as well, as it is very easy to say the right thing, but often difficult to avoid old habits. Finally, Napoleon made sure that this integrity extended to any promises he made, implied or otherwise. Let's examine, through Napoleon's example, how we can align our actions with our values, integrate our words with our actions, and reinforce this by sticking to our promises.

Let's begin with Napoleon's key value of equality. Of his well-received civil code, Napoleon said, "The Civil Code is the code of the century; its provisions not only preach toleration, but organize it—toleration is the greatest privilege of man." Of religion he said, "Faith is beyond the reach of the law. It is the most personal possession of man, and no one has the right to demand an accounting for it." These were not merely words. Napoleon lived these words. He fostered an environment of equality, and this meant tolerance and respect for all people and cultures. Wherever he went, he freed Jews and Muslims, protecting their heritage despite cries of objection from the French people.

Napoleon also made sure that his army's actions were in line with his values. For example, during the Italian campaign, he reprimanded a division of soldiers who were conducting atrocities in Mantua:

> *Soldiers of Victor's division, I am not pleased with you! The only glory you can reap in our present expedition is that which comes of good conduct. I therefore order: every soldier convicted of any injury to persons or property of the conquered shall be shot at the head of his battalion.*

Soon after, he wrote a letter to the Genoese after they toppled a statue of Genoese Admiral Andrea Doria simply because he was an aristocrat. In the letter, he pleaded with them to rebuild it and even offered to pay the expense. He later issued another reprimand to the Genoese when he found out that they were excluding members of the aristocracy from public affairs: "To exclude all the nobles from public functions would be a shocking piece of injustice: You would be doing what they did themselves in the past." Remember that before the Egyptian campaign he announced to his soldiers the importance of respecting the culture of the Egyptians (see Chapter 3). These were but a few of the many ways Napoleon's actions were in line with his belief in equality.

There are several lessons for us to learn from this. First, we need to determine what our core values are—and certainly, tolerance and respect should be among them. Second, we need to send a clear message to our teams that these values must be adhered to. Our integrity depends on it. If we involve our teams up front in determining those values, this becomes less of a challenge. Then, to sustain this harmony, we need to repeat our values frequently and take corrective action if we see our teams straying from those values—this doesn't have to go so far as shooting them, as Napoleon's example was an extreme case.

For example, if respect is among our core values and we berate one of our team members in front of others, we are blatantly demonstrating that these values mean nothing and we are not to be trusted. If one of our team members does the same, and we do nothing, it makes our values impotent and damages our reputation. In that case, we need to remind the team member of our core values in an even-tempered but straightforward way.

We've discussed making sure that our actions are in harmony with our values; now let's recall that Napoleon also made sure his words and actions were aligned. For instance, he always said that his sole aim was for the glory of France, not himself. As examples show, his actions supported this. When a small arch was built in front of the Tuileries garden to celebrate Austerlitz—the Arc de Triomphe du Carousel, not to be confused with the larger Arc de Triomphe—the architect added a statue of Napoleon. Napoleon immediately had it removed, saying that the arch was to represent the armies of France, not himself. When he heard of plans to change the name Place de la Concorde to "Place Napoleon," he vetoed it, saying, "*Concorde* is what makes France invincible." Even becoming emperor was not out of harmony with his declaration of his love of France, contrary to what some believe. Indeed, becoming emperor was a means to solidify France's security.

Just as Napoleon backed up his statements with appropriate actions, so must we. When we make statements to our teams or stakeholders, we are declaring that our actions will follow suit. People expect that what we say is an indication of who we are, so it is important that our actions do not stray from our declarations. We must make a conscious effort to double-check ourselves, as it is very easy to fall victim to the temptations of glory or the heat of the moment. For instance, if we are managing a construction project and we tell our team that safety is first but then cut corners to come in under budget, we are showing a lack of integrity and breaking trust with our team. Whether our decision was based on glory or panic doesn't matter, as the distrust lingers on long after the event has faded.

Napoleon also demonstrated integrity by living up to his promises. Sometimes, he had to fight to do this, but he knew it was important for integrity's sake. For example, at the end of the Italian campaign, Napoleon offered a lenient proposal to the pope despite his directors' wishes to the contrary (see Chapter 3). In addition, he offered a moderate treaty with the Piedmontese rather than gouging them, as his corrupt directors would have liked. Finally, he lobbied for the funds needed to rebuild the country, employing local artisans wherever possible. He promised liberty in his proclamation to the people of Italy; he knew that not to perform these actions would have broken that promise and thus destroyed trust. If we make a promise to our team or our stakeholders, we need to live up to that promise or they won't believe us the next time around. And if we get pressure from our superiors to do something that stands in the way of keeping that promise, we need to speak up or risk damaging our reputations.

Sticking to our promises also implies an unwritten—or sometimes even written—oath to those we work for. For example, Napoleon gained respect in his first major battle for the French army by dislodging England and her allies from the Mediterranean port of Toulon. Also, this respect was boosted when Napoleon was offered a chance to take command over his superior officer, who was floundering—hesitant to proceed in bad weather, as discussed in Chapter 2. Napoleon could have taken advantage of that opportunity—if his ego were half what he's been accused of over the years, he would have. But he didn't. He declined the opportunity and instead offered to convince the superior officer of the need to proceed. He did convince the senior officer and the battle was a resounding success. This was integrity at its finest. We can apply this lesson by observing the proper chain of command, and instead of running around a problem with a senior manager, addressing it head-on. This is often the harder route but the correct one. Nobody said integrity was easy.

We, too, can display integrity and build the trust of our teams and stakeholders by sticking to sound principles, aligning our words and actions, and living up to our promises. But integrity is only one part of character. We also need to be calm in the face of danger and responsible for our actions and commitments.

CALMNESS

We discussed in Chapter 1 the need to keep a cool head, something Napoleon felt was a critical skill for any leader. We display predictability by remaining calm in the face of danger and not getting overly excited at the first sign of good news. Predictability, as much as integrity, generates trust. But the point is not merely to be predictable; it is to be calm. Otherwise, one could panic in the face of danger and get overly confident upon any hint of success, and be entirely predictable in both cases.

We inspire hope in those around us by remaining predictably composed and thinking through the true situation and impact when faced with news. We send a message that all is well and that things will be resolved in due course. Napoleon had moments when he'd go into a tirade about one thing or another, but with his staff and his troops, he remained calm—especially on the battlefield. It was Napoleon's calm demeanor before the Austerlitz campaign that gave his troops the confidence they needed for the big battle ahead. During that campaign, upon hearing that the Austro-Russian army was headed farther south than expected, he merely redirected his troops accordingly. And during the Ulm campaign, when he'd heard that the Austrians had taken Ulm, he didn't panic. Instead, he thought through the situation and realized that it would allow him to circle around behind them and cut off their line of communication with Vienna. He turned seemingly bad news into an advantage.

There are many times when we're faced with news and immediately assume the worst, especially when it involves change. Often, after we think it through, it turns out not to be so bad, and indeed may not impact us at all. So, being calm not only offers hope to others; it also helps us to make wise decisions—we're not making judgments or overreacting in the heat of passion. There are also many distractions that could end up being irrelevant in the great scheme of things, and a calm, logical perspective helps us avoid getting sidetracked. We can support this by having a big-picture view, and fortunately we will have that view if we've taken the time to build our awareness and conduct adequate research (see Chapter 6). This allows us to first examine the facts before we begin to develop misguided theories. As Sherlock Holmes said in *A Scandal in Bohemia*, "It is a capital mistake to theorize before one has data. Insensibly, one begins to twist facts to suit theories, instead of theories to suit facts."[1]

Many "major" problems turn out to be less critical than originally thought. Therefore, it's better to think through a situation logically—

even if it means practicing some deep-breathing techniques—if that's what will help us slow down and examine things in proper context. We must also keep in mind, however, that the same principle is true when receiving good news. To become overly confident upon hearing of a short-term accomplishment is to risk becoming complacent and erasing all of the good gains achieved to date. We must take all news in stride, with the same sense of composure.

There is no doubt that calmness, and the predictability and wisdom it offers, is an essential ingredient of good character. Another essential ingredient is responsibility. By responsibility, we mean full ownership of our work, accountability for our actions, and dedication to self-improvement.

RESPONSIBILITY

Responsibility is a central part of good character. As project managers and leaders, we are responsible not only for our commitments, but for the people who are counting on us to lead them safely to victory. We owe it to them to look out for their interests by taking full ownership of our projects and assuring that we take our jobs as leaders seriously. Sometimes this requires us to stand up for what is right.

A good example of this is found in the Italian campaign, when Napoleon, knowing full well the dangers of combined operations, insisted on retaining full command (see Chapter 3). It took guts to convince the French government, but he knew that to proceed on a course of certain failure would not be doing his country or his troops justice. Napoleon said:

> *A commander is not protected by an order from a minister or prince who is absent from the theater of operations and has little or no knowledge of the most recent turn of events. Every commander responsible for executing a plan that he considers bad or disastrous is criminal: he must point*

out the flaws, insist that it be changed, and at last resort resign rather than be the instrument of the destruction of his own men. Every commander in chief who, as a result of superior orders, delivers a battle convinced that he will lose it, is likewise criminal.

But does this mean that we should revolt every time we're given instructions that we do not agree with? Absolutely not, as Napoleon goes on to say:

It does not follow that a commander in chief must not obey a minister who orders him to give battle. On the contrary, he must do it every time that, in his judgment, the chances and probabilities are as much for him as against him, for our observation only applies in the case where the chances appear to be entirely against him.

Keep in mind that in Napoleon's case people could lose their lives if things didn't go right, but the general principle remains the same: we are responsible for the outcome of our projects, and with this responsibility comes the need to convince management of the right thing to do.

Responsibility also carries with it the need for self-discipline and thoughtfulness—especially regarding the need to think before we speak. Consider Napoleon's advice to his brother Joseph, soon after Joseph was made king of Naples following the Austerlitz campaign:

I have read your speech, and you must permit me to say that I find some of its sentences bad. You compare the attachment of the Neapolitans to you with that of the French to me; it sounds like an epigram! What affection do you expect from a people for whom you have done nothing, among whom you are by right of conquest, at the head of 40,000 or 50,000 foreigners? As a general rule, the less you speak, directly or indirectly, of me and of France in your documents, the better.

Napoleon offered similar advice to his niece (and adopted daughter), Princess Stephanie of Baden, when he said, "Accustom yourself to the country and think well of everything, for nothing would be more impertinent than constantly to speak of Paris." The point was that to win over these countries, it was important to be empathetic to their points of view. It is the same for us. Responsibility means being accountable for our actions and our words, and this means thinking about the impact before we speak. Many otherwise successful projects have met resistance because of irresponsible communication that simply preached an agenda rather than considering the needs of its audience.

> Many otherwise successful projects have met resistance because of irresponsible communication that simply preached an agenda rather than considering the needs of its audience.

This consideration for people also applies when giving criticism. Napoleon certainly offered his share of criticism, but he always did so privately. Praise, however, was given publicly. For example, when offering constructive criticism to one of his generals, Napoleon said, "I have now made public my approval of your conduct; what I write confidentially is for you alone." This is a good example for us to follow. Without a doubt, public praise and private criticism is a policy that should be adopted by any leader, and indicates a sense of responsibility and good character.

In addition to being responsible to others, we must also be responsible to ourselves. This makes us more capable of being responsible to others. We can do this by staying sharp, and that means being dedicated to our profession and staying on a path of self-improvement. This is also an element of one of Stephen Covey's "7 Habits of Highly Effective People"—what he calls "Sharpening the Saw." In fact,

Covey goes even further to say that this means a constant self-renewal of mind, body, and spirit.[2] This means that—in addition to sharpening our minds—we should eat well, exercise, and generally maintain a sense of balance in our lives. Napoleon would hardly disagree, and certainly he subscribed to this in terms of social needs, spirituality (if not religion), and learning. The only area he fell short in was a sense of balance between work and relaxation, and perhaps this was a leading cause of his downfall, as we shall see later. When it came to dedication to learning, however, he was without peer, acting like a sponge, absorbing knowledge wherever and whenever he could.

We can assume responsibility by taking full ownership of our projects, even if it means convincing management of the right thing to do; being fully accountable for our actions, including the need to think before we speak; and staying sharp by being dedicated to our profession and self-improvement in general. We exude a sense of good character—a key ingredient for any leader—by combining this responsibility with integrity and calmness.

EXECUTIVE SUMMARY

We began the chapter by looking at examples of Napoleon's integrity, especially in areas of equality and tolerance. We saw how he aligned his values, words, and actions, never wavering for a minute. We also witnessed this integrity in the way he kept his promises and made ethically sound decisions, such as when he stood behind his commanders during hard times. In addition, we saw how maintaining a sense of calmness and addressing problems logically helps build trust and ensures wiser and fact-based decisions.

Finally, we examined examples of responsibility, such as when Napoleon insisted on sole command in Italy, or offered advice on the need to be empathetic to people's needs. We also saw how being responsible to ourselves, through dedication to our profession and constant self-improvement and self-care, makes us more capable of being responsible to others. Integrity, calmness, and responsibility are indeed the three primary ingredients of character. Character is one of the most important of our Six Winning Principles. As Napoleon said, it's even more important than intellect, which our first four principles—exactitude, speed, flexibility, and simplicity—are based on.

We have one final principle to discuss: moral force. Moral force is how we *move* people—how we *motivate* them. It goes hand in hand with character. And with highly motivated people, we can surpass all odds. Jerome Jewell, productivity improvement consultant, refers in his leadership class to a study that was performed by Chip Bell on the attributes of high-performance teams. The study involved the American Ballet Theater, the Tom Landry–era Dallas Cowboys, and the U.S. Eighty-second Airborne Division. It was discovered that they all shared four identical attributes: self-confidence, mission commitment, belief in their leadership, and confidence in their teammates. These were motivated teams, rooted in trust and loyalty.

Character provides the foundation for trust, and, as we'll see, moral force inspires fierce loyalty. With the combined principles of character and moral force, we, too, can build such trust and loyalty—and thus help our teams rise to this elite category. And what better high-performance team to learn from than Napoleon's *Grande Armée*?

MARCHING ORDERS

INTEGRITY

Make sure that your actions, and the actions of your team, are aligned with your core values.

- Include your team in the development of core values. Consider making tolerance and respect key parts of those values.
- Repeat your values often, so the right culture spreads through your team.

- Take corrective action if someone on your team strays from the core values; remind that person of the values in an even-tempered but straightforward way.

Make sure that your actions are aligned with your words.
- Don't say one thing and do another.
- Be observant, so as not to be led astray by glory or the heat of the moment.

Always keep your promises.
- If you make a commitment, be sure to follow up.
- Your job is a promise—don't undermine a superior; address your problem head-on.

CALMNESS
Don't overreact to good news or panic at the sight of bad news.
- Logically think through the situation and its impact.
- Don't get sidetracked by irrelevant events. A big-picture view can help keep things in perspective.
- Examine the facts before developing theories.
- Maintain a sense of tranquillity; deep breathing can help.
- Don't become overconfident after short-term accomplishments; complacency can undo all the gains achieved. Take all things in stride.

RESPONSIBILITY
Be responsible for your actions.
- Assume full accountability for the outcomes of your projects.
- Do the right thing; lobby for it if necessary.
- Insist on changing anything that would give your project less than a 50 percent chance of success.
- Look out for your team's welfare.

Be responsible for your words.
- Practice empathy and thoughtfulness when communicating.
- Don't just focus on your agenda; consider the audience's perspective.
- Always deliver public praise and private criticism.

Be responsible for yourself.
- Be committed to your profession; never stop learning.
- Strive for continuous self-improvement; broaden your horizons.
- Take care of yourself—exercise, eat well, and maintain a sense of balance.

CHAPTER 11

———◇———

Moral Force

*In war, everything depends upon morale;
and morale and public opinion comprise
the better part of reality.* —NAPOLEON

M oral force is perhaps the most important of Napoleon's Six Winning Principles. It is what allows teams to surpass expectations and overcome the inevitable obstacles; it is what gets everyone on board with the mission and excited by the potential outcome. People do their best work when they have self-confidence and feel that what they're doing is worthwhile and important—and are recognized accordingly for their efforts. Napoleon understood this when he said, "It is moral force more than numbers that wins victory . . . The moral is to the physical as three is to one."

Although Napoleon noted that a *general* "does not require spirit in war, but exactitude, character, and simplicity," overall, he acknowledged that *teams* need spirit in order to succeed. He said, "There are only two forces in the world, the sword and the spirit. In the long run, the sword will always be conquered by the spirit." In business, we can think of our obstacles as the swords opposing us. Our teams need passion and fortitude to rise above these obstacles. As leaders, we are responsible for instilling this passion and fortitude, and thus providing the ever-powerful moral force. We can do this by providing a sense of order, clear purpose, visible recognition, and coveted rewards.

Napoleon knew this. When he first took command of the French army as a general, he promised his troops "honor, glory, and riches." We can do the same by ensuring that our teams are given work that is worthwhile and in adherence with the right principles (honor), widely recognized (glory), and adequately rewarded (riches). We can give our teams the confidence that they are in good hands by supporting this with a sense of order, much as Napoleon did.

Unfortunately, many leaders ignore this crucial part of their jobs, focusing instead on the mechanics of management or those items that can be measured. Perhaps it is because the moral elements are immeasurable that leaders so often ignore them. Clausewitz said of these incalculable but important elements, "They will not yield to academic wisdom. They cannot be classified or counted. They have to be seen or felt."[1]

To be sure that we do not ignore them, we will explore in more detail how we can inspire moral force by providing order, purpose, recognition, and rewards.

ORDER

One might be surprised to see order listed as an element of moral force. But, just as the French people needed stability after the chaos of the French Revolution, our teams, too, need to know that things are well organized and under control. Pioneering psychologist Abraham Maslow, as part of his Hierarchy of Needs, listed safety as one of the basic needs of human beings, surpassed only by the physiological needs of air, water, food, sleep, and so forth. This referred to the need for stability or structure, much as a child needs limits in order to truly feel secure. Napoleon met this need by providing discipline. Discipline should not be looked at strictly in the context of punishment, as it often is. Rather, discipline implies control or restraint, and this is achieved by regulations, training, and rehearsal. Discipline is what helps people feel prepared, and that gives them self-confidence.

Discipline is not to be found in speeches, however. As Napoleon said:

> *Discipline fixes the troops to their colors. They are not to be rendered brave by harangues [lectures] when the firing begins—the old soldiers scarcely listen to them, the young ones forget them on the first discharge of cannon . . . A gesture by a beloved general, esteemed by his troops, is as good as the finest speech in the world.*

In other words, if we provide order, and people trust that they can be safe under our watch, good discipline will result.

This means that we must be leaders in the most fundamental sense of the word—meaning "to lead." As leaders, we must be ahead of our team, leading the way. As General George S. Patton said, "An army is like a piece of cooked spaghetti. You can't push it, you have to pull it after you."[2] Napoleon's troops were always well prepared and disciplined. They trusted that he was always one step ahead and had them prepared for anything. With that, they were more than happy to follow.

In summary, we can instill a sense of order by providing a set of regulations, ensuring that our teams are trained and well rehearsed, and setting a good example with good character and leadership. Order is the basic foundation of moral force. Once we've established order, we are then ready to provide purpose, recognition, and rewards.

> As leaders, we must be ahead of our team, leading the way. As General George S. Patton once said, "An army is like a piece of cooked spaghetti. You can't push it, you have to pull it after you."

PURPOSE

We discussed earlier the need to convey the project's concept to our team, so that they understand why it is being initiated. This also helps give them a sense of purpose. But understanding the project's concept is only one part of the picture. People must also feel that the mission is worthwhile and important. They must feel a sense of honor at being involved in the project. In fact, many leadership classes teach the acronym MMFI, which stands for "Make Me Feel Important," and this is a valuable tool to remember when leading people.

INTEREST VS. FEAR

Napoleon said, "There are two levers for moving men, interest and fear." It should go without saying that we are always best pursuing the former route, because interest boosts morale and fear destroys it. Jomini said in *The Art of War*: "No system of tactics can lead to victory when the morale of an army is bad."[3] We can gain people's interest and thus boost their morale by giving them a sense of purpose. Sometimes fear can be used to generate interest as well, which Napoleon realized, but this should be done as a secondary resort. Even then, it should be a strategic fear, such as the fear of what might happen if the project is not done. This is the type of fear that Napoleon spoke of. This can be conveyed as "the cost of not doing the project." The intention of this is to "rally the troops," which is different from traditional management-by-fear—"Do this or else." We have to convey purpose.

STIRRING THE MASSES

This effort should not be limited to our teams, as our stakeholders also need to feel a sense of purpose. It is this shared purpose that unites organizations around a cause and gains the critical mass necessary to resist obstacles. We must build this mass from the bottom up. Napoleon knew the importance of this when he said: "Men who have changed the world never achieved their success by winning the chief citizens to their side, but always by stirring the masses." He knew that to sell the top leaders on an endeavor would be minimally effective if the masses weren't sold. Indeed, it becomes less of an effort to sell the top leaders if the masses are stirred.

Geoffrey Moore used the same approach in his book *Crossing the Chasm*. We are better prepared to "cross the chasm" and begin approaching the mainstream market by first getting our "fans" on board and then approaching those influential people who have an agenda that our mission helps—in Moore's words, the "visionaries."[4] This bottom-up approach not only works for marketing products and services, but it also works for selling our endeavor to the stakeholders.

When we speak of selling, let's not forget that the most compelling purpose is a shared purpose. According to Baron Fain, Napoleon would typically open a session with his contemporaries by saying, "Messieurs, it is not to convince you of my opinion, but to have yours that I have called you! Tell me your views; I will then see if what you propose to me is better than what I think." It is important, especially early on, to get the opinions of key stakeholders when determining the goals and purpose of any undertaking.

GIVE AN IMAGE MAKEOVER

Once we have created a shared sense of purpose and stirred the masses, we can solidify this feeling of importance and honor with an "image makeover." People need to feel that they are part of something big and exciting to feel truly important. They need something they can be associated with. This is why organizations spend so much money on branding, and why sports teams have certain colors and logos. It gives team members a sense of common identity—not to mention that it offers a recognizable image to the public. Even Napoleon had a "logo" for his *Grande Armée*—the eagle. He established a commission to determine the proper symbol for the empire. After much deliberation, the eagle was chosen over a host of other alternatives. We, too, should consider giving our projects a brand and our people something to identify with. This institutes pride, and pride goes hand in hand with honor and purpose.

In addition to branding, we can advertise the strength of our teams as part of this image makeover—even magnifying it when appropriate. Napoleon never failed to exaggerate his army's triumphs, through numerous bulletins and proclamations. This served the purpose of magnifying his strength to the enemy, but it gave his people confidence as well. It is a known phenomenon that if we label people as high performers, they'll continue to act that way. Their impressions of themselves will go up significantly—and self-confident people are effective people.

Just as Parkinson's Law dictates that work expands to fill the time allotted, people's efforts expand to fill the labels they've been given. Unfortunately, the opposite is also true. Understating the value of our people demoralizes them and weakens their resolve. This is why we must strive to boost our team's image; within reason, of course—nobody will believe that a college student is a seasoned veteran, least of all the college student.

We can instill a strong sense of purpose and honor by ensuring that our teams feel that their work is important; by stirring the masses from the bottom up—beginning with our wildest enthusiasts; by involving key stakeholders in goal setting; and by giving our teams positive identities through branding and advertising. This, along with order, can go a long way toward infusing our teams with moral force. Two additional elements are needed in order to sustain this force: recognition and rewards.

RECOGNITION

Maslow's Hierarchy of Needs—from the most basic to advanced need—includes: physiological (air, water, food, etc.), safety (security and stability), belonging (social acceptance and love), esteem (self-confidence and attention), and ultimately self-actualization (the intrinsic desire to constantly grow). If providing a sense of order speaks to the basic need for safety, providing recognition speaks to the more advanced need of esteem. Recognition not only addresses the need for attention, but it breeds self-confidence as well—for the same reason we mentioned earlier: people see themselves as they are labeled.

Consider Napoleon's speech to his troops after the battle of Austerlitz. He didn't just say, "Congratulations, well done!" There was much more to this speech. Let's examine the various elements.

- He began by stating in general that they had met the high expectations he had for them and that their accomplishment would have lasting significance: *"Well done, soldiers! In the battle of Austerlitz you have accomplished all I expected of your valor: you have crowned your eagles with immortal glory."*

- Then he proceeded to recite exactly what they had accomplished, so the magnitude did not go unnoticed: *"An army of 100,000 men commanded by the Emperors of Russia and of Austria has been dispersed or captured in less than four hours. What escaped your arms was drowned in the lakes. Forty flags, the standards of the Russian Imperial Guard, 120 guns, 20 generals, more than 30,000 prisoners are the result of this eternally glorious battle."*

- He stated how they exceeded all odds and gave them full credit for the accomplishment: *"This famous infantry, that outnumbered you, was unable to resist your attack, and hence-forth you have no rivals to fear."*

- He confirmed what was to follow, and promised that their work would be rewarded: *"Soldiers! When we have completed all that is necessary to secure the happiness and prosperity of our country, I will lead you back to France; there you will be the constant objects of my loving care."*

- He closed by echoing his opening statement, reiterating the lasting significance this would have: *"My people will hail your return with joy, and you will have but to say, 'I was at the battle of Austerlitz,' to hear the reply, 'He is one of the brave!'"*

While we don't need to promise our people immortal glory, certainly this is a good model for us to follow. People need to be recognized for their efforts and made to feel proud. If they are forgotten, we can be sure they won't be as motivated the next time they are called to action. Napoleon said, "A great reputation is like a great noise: the louder it is proclaimed the further it is heard. The laws, constitutions, monuments, actions—all have their limit, but glory spreads itself through many generations." He made sure with speeches, bulletins, triumphal arches, and annual commemorative events that the glory of his *Grande Armée* would spread though generations—and indeed it has.

We can use this same approach by publicizing our teams' successes and possibly even having an area, either physical or on the Web, to permanently commemorate those projects that have gone exceedingly well. We are giving our people the self-confidence and attention they need and deserve by acknowledging them in this manner. But self-confidence and attention are only two of the benefits of recognition. There is an additional benefit that often goes unnoticed: ambition. Recognizing people for their efforts inspires others to emulate their success. When discussing what he would do if he were in charge of reorganizing the British army, Napoleon said:

> *Ambition is the main driving power of men. A man expends his abilities as long as he hopes to rise; but when he has reached the highest round, he only asks for rest. I have created senatorial appointments and princely titles, in order to promote ambition . . . Instead of the lash, I would lead them by the stimulus of honor. I would instill a degree of emulation into their minds. I would promote every deserving soldier, as I did in France . . . Whatever debases man cannot be serviceable.*

In summary, we instill self-confidence, give our team deserved and needed attention, and inspire ambition in those around us by acknowledging our team publicly and frequently. But is recognition enough? As Napoleon alludes, it is not. Some may say that verbal or written recognition is its own reward. Certainly, a nicely written commendation helps—but to show true commitment to people, more is needed, especially on a major project. This is where rewards come in.

REWARDS

Rewards are a way to express our gratitude for a job well done, while written or verbal recognition addresses people's need for attention and gives them credit for their accomplishments. Combined, they are a powerful source of motivation. A reward does not have to be monetary, but some sort of tangible acknowledgment can go a long way, such as a gift or, better yet, something that benefits the person's family as well. Sometimes a promotion or a role on a coveted project is in order—assuming it is the person who covets the project and not the other way around. A celebration certainly helps, too, but remember to leave the team with something tangible for their efforts. If it is something that will last as a constant reminder, all the better, since this will serve to reinforce performance for years to come—not to mention that they deserve it.

Rewards don't have to be huge; they can and should be commensurate with the size of the project. While a larger project might warrant a substantial monetary award, promotional items with the name of the organization and the project are quite appropriate in many cases. Besides, other people see them, and this serves as inspiration. Napoleon established the Legion of Honor for this purpose: "Show me a republic, ancient or modern, in which there have been no decorations. Some people call them baubles. Well, it is by such baubles that one leads men . . . A soldier will fight long and hard for a bit of colored ribbon."

It is also important to reward everyone who contributed to the success of the project, not just the immediate project team. This sends a message that a project's success depends on the collaborative efforts of various groups, and that such collaboration will not go unrewarded. As the adage says, "Tell me how I'm measured and I'll tell you how I'll behave." Napoleon understood this fully when he established the Legion of Honor. His advisers wanted him to make the award exclusively for soldiers, in order to inspire others to join the service. Others wanted him to establish separate honors for soldiers and civilians. Napoleon vetoed both ideas and said: "If we make a distinction between military and civil honors, we shall be instituting two orders, whereas the nation is one. If we award honors only to soldiers, that will be still worse, for then the nation will cease to exist." He knew that if he wanted the nation to pull together, he needed to treat them as one. And so he did.

The Legion of Honor was established in 1802, with the medal—a five-pointed star with a ribbon—along with a small monetary gift, going to civilians and soldiers who had distinguished themselves. It was, and still is, an extremely coveted award in France, with honors now extended to those outside France as well.

We can learn from this by rewarding all those who helped on our project, not just the immediate project team or one department, as some organizations do. This is especially true if we are trying to inspire collaboration, as it sends the message that it pays to contribute. If we combine a monetary award with a tangible item that will last, people will remember the message long after the money has been spent.

Of course, special projects warrant special rewards. In addition to the Legion of Honor, Napoleon issued great rewards to those involved in major campaigns. Napoleon followed the Austerlitz campaign by providing significant monetary rewards, publicity, annual commemorative events, and other actions that showed he truly cared for his soldiers and their families (see Chapter 4). He did this not only for his soldiers, but for his allies in Bavaria as well.

Finally, let's remember that a reward doesn't have to follow the "big bang" approach, with everything coming at the end of a project. Celebrating frequently during a project is an excellent form of reward as well, and also serves to make the project fun. In the end, there is no greater reward than having fun.

If giving our people a sense of purpose addresses the "make me feel important" (MMFI) requirement, providing rewards addresses another key requirement: an answer to the question "What's in it for me?" (WIIFM). People will clamor to join our projects if we provide visible and lasting rewards and celebrate frequently.

EXECUTIVE SUMMARY

Echoing Napoleon's statement that "the moral is to the physical as three is to one," there is no doubt that even the greatest plan in the world will be for naught unless we have a motivated team behind us. We can provide this motivation by giving our teams a feeling of stability, instilling a sense of purpose and meaningfulness, publicly recognizing their efforts, and providing lasting rewards.

We've seen that we can achieve stability—and thus establish a sense of order—by providing appropriate policies, making sure our teams are fully trained and well-rehearsed, and remaining one step ahead as true leaders. Likewise, we can instill a sense of purpose by ensuring that our teams view their work as worthwhile and important and by providing a feeling of shared identity for everyone involved with the project—ideally through branding and early stakeholder participation. Once our teams have a sense of order and purpose, we can recognize their efforts publicly by stating in writing their specific accomplishments and the magnitude of the results. This also serves to inspire ambition in others. Finally, we've seen how we can reward our teams by providing lasting, tangible tokens of gratitude to go along with any monetary handouts, and by scheduling celebrations throughout and after our projects. We must also remember to reward everyone involved in the project— not just the immediate team or one department—to encourage wide participation.

We can effectively deliver Napoleon's promise of honor, glory, and riches by providing our teams with a sense of purpose (honor), visible recognition (glory), and appropriate rewards (riches), assuming the necessary order is in place to make our teams feel secure. Thus, we can say that we have moral force in our favor by providing order, purpose, recognition, and rewards. And, with exactitude, speed, flexibility, simplicity, and character, and the winds of moral force at our backs, we can fully exercise the power of Napoleon's Six Winning Principles.

We have seen how Napoleon rose from obscurity to become the leader of the world's largest empire, using a solid set of principles and values. We have explored the lessons from this extraordinary rise, and have mapped them to six fundamental but powerful principles that we can use as a guiding compass in our everyday lives. To assist in this, I've included a handy map of the principles and their components on page 257. But first we must see the events that led to Napoleon's extraordinary downfall, for therein lie equally valuable lessons.

In Part 3, we'll explore exactly what went wrong and examine crucial lessons from the failed Russian invasion and Waterloo campaigns, just as we gained insights from Napoleon's greatest triumphs at Ulm and Austerlitz. We will then summarize these lessons in four critical warning signs to watch for, which will help us avoid falling into the same traps that led Napoleon astray. We would be remiss if we didn't learn from Napoleon's mistakes, just as we have benefited from his triumphs.

MARCHING ORDERS

ORDER
Provide an environment of stability.
- Issue a set of regulations, ground rules, policy, etc.
- Be sure your teams are trained and well rehearsed.
- Show good character and lead by example.
- Always stay one step ahead.

PURPOSE
Make sure people feel their work is worthwhile and important.
- Remember MMFI (Make me feel important).
- Only use fear in a "rally the troops" way, for example, to indicate the bleaker alternative if the project is not done, not in a "do it or else" way.

Stir the masses from the bottom up.
- Appeal to the most enthusiastic people first, then those influential people with an agenda that your project supports, and then to the stakeholders at large.

- Read Geoffrey Moore's *Crossing the Chasm* to formalize this approach.

Create a sense of shared purpose.
- Get key stakeholders involved early.
- Ask for their input on the goals of your project.

Give your team an image makeover.
- Consider creating a brand for your project—an image and a possible tagline.
- Advertise the strength of your team, magnifying it within reason; they will live up to that image accordingly.

RECOGNITION
Make your praise effective.
- Address the team in writing, recounting their specific accomplishments and stating the magnitude of the results.
- Give them full credit for the accomplishments.
- Confirm what rewards will follow.
- Announce the accomplishments publicly.
- Remember that recognition instills self-confidence, gives deserved and needed attention, and inspires ambition.

REWARDS
Don't forget to reward your team for a job well done.
- Monetary rewards are good, but should be accompanied by something tangible, visible, and lasting.
- Promotional items with the organization and project name work quite well in most cases.
- Rewards should be commensurate with the size of the project; major projects should be rewarded more significantly.

- Individuals can be rewarded with a promotion or a role on a coveted project, if appropriate.

Make rewards available to all who contribute to your project's success.
- Include key stakeholders as well as other departments and individuals who contributed in some way.
- This encourages future collaboration and contribution, as opposed to the traditional departmental "silo" approach, where each department operates as its own entity as opposed to working collaboratively.

Don't forget to celebrate.
- Celebration makes our projects fun.
- Celebrate frequently—after each milestone, not just at the end of the project.
- Remember WIIFM (What's in it for me?).

PART 3

The Downfall

CHAPTER 12

What Went Wrong?

*The greatest mistake of my career was the
interference in Spanish affairs . . . All my defeats
came from this source.* —Napoleon

Thus far, we have seen Napoleon's rise and have benefited from
the Six Winning Principles that catapulted him to glory. That
he rose to such heights in such a short period of time is amazing,
and, as we've seen, it brings us many lessons. The fact that a charis-
matic leader with such intelligence, strong values, and energy could
lose an entire continent is startling. Surely, the lessons must be
equally valuable. And so they are. Abraham Lincoln said, "Anyone
can overcome adversity, but if you want to test a man, give him
power." For a time, Napoleon handled the challenge quite well; one
does not rule a continent for fifteen years without wide support.
But ultimately, his power, and the very gains that he had accumu-
lated as a result, led to his undoing. One by one, the very principles
that brought him success began to unravel.

There are many theories on what actually triggered Napoleon's
downfall. Some say that it was his kidnapping and execution of the
Duke of Enghien (see Chapter 4), but this is arguable, as there
appeared to be just cause and, after all, it followed several attempts
on Napoleon's life. It is still debated whether or not the evidence was

circumstantial. At any rate, Napoleon's actions caused alarm at the time, but didn't seem to have lasting effect. Some say the catalyst for his downfall was when he became emperor. Again, there was just cause, and it elevated Napoleon to a status from which he could negotiate equally with his peers. No—it seems instead that Napoleon's downfall began after his tremendous victory at Austerlitz, and perhaps even because of it.

Two major stepping-stones triggered Napoleon's ultimate downfall. First, there was the elevation of his power following the success at Austerlitz, which led to the feeling that he could force weaker countries like Prussia and Austria to comply, and also led to increased isolation from his troops. Second, there was the unwise decision to take over Spain when called upon to mediate a local rebellion against its corrupt government—completely misjudging the sentiment of the Spanish people. Not only did this illustrate the wrong way to address a political conflict, but it also highlighted the need to consider the people aspect of any endeavor. This not only applied to the Spanish people, but to his own people as well, as their morale was beginning to decline because of the lack of effective leaders. Let's examine these areas in more detail and see what lessons we can learn.

THE PERILS OF SUCCESS

Following the battle of Austerlitz, Napoleon was at the top of his game. He had defeated Austria and Russia and, with the Third Coalition in tatters, was now the undisputed leader of Western Europe. Even England acknowledged this, although it continued fruitlessly to try to rally support against him. In May 1806, England, still master of the seas, declared a blockade of all French ports, seizing products and even stopping neutral ships. Napoleon responded by establishing a blockade of his own—the Continental

System, whereby all of his allies and countries within his empire would cease trade with Britain. Even Prussia was on board, pacified by receiving Hanover as part of the post-Austerlitz Treaty of Pressburg.

Also around this time, Napoleon solidified his control even further when, upset at hearing that his appointed leaders in Naples and Holland were following their own agendas, he installed his brothers, Joseph and Louis, as kings of those countries, respectively. Joseph and Louis instituted the same reforms Napoleon had brought to Italy, and were generally well received by the populace. Louis even became known to the Dutch as "Good King Louis."

Things went fine for a while. But, nearly a year after Austerlitz, there would be a Fourth Coalition. The Prussians, nervous about Napoleon's gains in southern Germany and rightfully upset upon hearing that Napoleon recently had offered Hanover to Britain in exchange for peace, joined forces with the Russians to declare war on France. Napoleon's *Grande Armée,* however, made quick mincemeat of the Prussians in simultaneous battles at Jena and Auerstadt and then soundly defeated the Russians at Friedland—after fighting them to a draw earlier. Thus ended the Fourth Coalition.

The end of the Fourth Coalition brought the Treaty of Tilsit in July 1807, when the Russian czar Alexander I agreed to join the Continental System if England refused to let Russia mediate in its conflict with France. Russia joined Napoleon's blockade when England made it clear that they still opposed any negotiation with Napoleon. Prussia, having lost land to Napoleon as part of the treaty, was forced to join the embargo as well.

With all of Western Europe aligned with Napoleon in some way, there is general consensus that this was the zenith of Napoleon's career. He was the undisputed leader of Western Europe, had formed an alliance with Russia, and most of Europe was participating in his Continental System. What could be better? But, even with all of that, the seeds of his destruction had already quietly been planted. To be precise, there were two, and they were both a direct result of his increased power following his success at Austerlitz.

First, there was the disregard for Prussia and Austria, in essence forcing them to be allies, which would come back to haunt him later. Second, as his armies grew, Napoleon became more isolated from his associates, which led to poor morale and some bad decisions. Both of these elements, creating forced allies and becoming isolated from associates, bring us valuable lessons.

Forced Allies

While it is to Napoleon's credit that he was able to use a combination of charisma and diplomacy to win over the Russian czar at Tilsit—especially after all the battles they had been through—Prussia and Austria were reduced to mere pawns by now. As mentioned, this would come back to haunt him later. Perhaps this is what led him to declare, "It is better to have a known enemy than a forced ally." In Italy and Egypt, Napoleon had invested time in diplomatic and rebuilding efforts, creating a win-win situation. He won them over diplomatically, although he destroyed them militarily. He didn't make this effort, however, with Prussia and Austria. As a result, he was unable to turn them into true allies, so he kept them as forced allies. Moreover, by offering Hanover to the British, Napoleon betrayed Prussia, which damaged his integrity.

Napoleon left Prussia and Austria weakened and angry, unlike other conquered countries where he had put forth exhaustive effort getting the local populace to embrace his reforms—"stirring the masses" from the bottom up, as he put it. It is possible that with the power he now had, he no longer felt the need to invest in such efforts. Perhaps he felt there was enough momentum and critical mass behind his initiatives that he didn't need to worry about "the little guys." Well, in war—as in business—the little guys can some-times cause more harm than we think.

The more power we gain in our position, the easier it is to ignore this fact. It is easy to force others to adhere to our will, especially those who don't carry much weight. And it is easy to ignore their perspectives, as Napoleon had done with Prussia when he offered Hanover to England. But when we adopt a compliance mental-ity and don't follow up to ensure that people's issues and frustrations are addressed, we run the risk of leaving wounded enemies—a danger pointed out by Machiavelli. This is true whether rolling out a new product, instituting new policies, or intro-ducing any new initiative that requires others to change their habits.

> In war—as in business—the little guys can sometimes cause more harm than we think.

All too often, leaders of an organization will implement a new ini-tiative or policy, and assume that, because they announced it, people will comply. But if our initiative impacts them negatively, and they weren't part of the decision, it can be expected that they'll resist. Soon, as more people become frustrated with their situations, they'll begin to feel hopeless. Unfortunately, negativity spreads like a virus, and before we know it, morale begins to decline. As we've seen, moral force is a vital element of success, so we certainly don't want that.

The way to avoid this scenario is to make sure people's voices are heard, and to follow up to address their concerns appropriately. This may mean modifying our initiative, or it may mean providing a better explanation of the purpose. It may also mean providing additional assistance or support in order to address their needs. But if we ignore them, or assume they'll quietly acquiesce, we risk los-ing them as allies. And to have lasting success, we need people to be on our side—true allies, not forced.

Let's now take a look at the other seed that would germinate and cause problems for Napoleon: increased isolation from his associates.

GOING IT ALONE

As Napoleon's armies grew, he had to rely more on his chief of staff, Berthier, for all communications, and this meant that he had lost personal touch with his troops. Even his generals now had to go through formal processes to be able to speak with him. Not surprisingly, they soon began to get frustrated and began quarreling with one another. Furthermore, because of the separation resulting from his rise to power, Napoleon began to focus more on his ideals than on diplomacy, which led to some bad decisions. If he had involved his close associates more, as he had in the past, some of those tendencies might have been counterbalanced. Instead, whatever humility he had shown before by involving others in decision making had now taken a backseat to his new status.

This isolation extended to the French Senate as well. Indeed, when Napoleon decided to make his brothers kings, he acted alone and didn't consult the Senate. Perhaps they could have convinced him that while it made sense from a military standpoint, it was hazardous from a political standpoint. Although Napoleon had made sure these family members acted fairly, and while his actions would prove successful in those countries, this alarmed his allies, as they wondered what would be next. Of course, they were right to worry. Over time, Napoleon would give his family members increased privileges to secure their status. That subtle departure from the revolutionary value of equality would soon begin to cause alarm in Europe and would further jeopardize Napoleon's integrity. But for now, the seed had just been planted. The point is that he made this decision in isolation.

As we will see, Napoleon's increased separation from his troops and his associates would lead to poor morale and impulsive decisions. And, with similar actions, the same results can befall us. If we're managing a large program or leading a large-scale effort, we, too, need to set up an infrastructure so that we don't get bogged down in details. But we must not lose sight of the fact that we still need to be visible to our teams and, above all, readily available to the immediate leaders reporting to us. The personal touch is critical in leadership, as it keeps morale up and solidifies trust.

Furthermore, we must not become so enamored with our status that we forget we're most effective when relying on the advice of others, not barking out orders. Indeed, it is our reliance on our leadership team and subject-matter experts that will make us successful, not our ability to make decisions in isolation. Of course, we must make snap decisions when needed—sometimes even unpopular ones (see Chapter 1)—but if we consistently isolate ourselves from those around us, we will increasingly make wrong decisions and our reputations will suffer.

The bottom line is that if we adopt a compliance mentality as a result of our power, isolate ourselves from our leaders and subject-matter experts, and forget to involve our stakeholders in major decisions, we will turn around one day and there will be nobody behind us. And with nobody behind us, we can no longer call ourselves leaders.

Now that we've seen the pitfalls of power, as well as the two seeds of Napoleon's eventual destruction, let's explore the next major stepping-stone that led to Napoleon's downfall: the Peninsular War. Without a doubt, this would be the event that would set Napoleon's career into a downward spiral, and, unlike the campaigns he had fought to date, this one would be of his own making. From this, we will learn the dangers of getting involved in political intrigue and then we'll see the domino effect that can be caused by forgetting the people-perspective of our endeavors.

THE TURNING POINT:
THE PENINSULAR WAR

We have seen how Napoleon ignored those countries that he felt carried no weight, and how he began to isolate himself from his associates. Soon, this change of focus from consensus building to isolated decision making would also extend to his relations across Europe. Nowhere was this more evident than in his relentless pursuit of anyone who didn't adhere to his embargo of British trade, the Continental System.

The problem was not necessarily the establishment of that system. Napoleon didn't have many alternatives. After all, England was still trying to bring about his defeat through its own blockade and had declined all of his peace offerings. Furthermore, the system was actually beginning to work. Many countries across Europe were benefiting from increased trade with one another. Anti-British sentiment was spreading; in England itself, peace petitions had begun circulating. If Napoleon had let things go at that, things might have turned out in his favor. Unfortunately for him, he didn't.

Upon hearing that Portugal was still a major source of British trade—the British were large consumers of port wine—Napoleon decided to issue Portugal an ultimatum: either voluntarily join the Continental System or be forced to. The Portuguese responded by stalling Napoleon and secretly asking the British for help. Needless to say, the British were happy to oblige. Meanwhile, Napoleon occupied Portugal.

Adopting a compliance mentality is no way to win friends and influence people (to use Dale Carnegie's term), and this situation was no exception. The invasion of Portugal was the first truly offensive campaign undertaken by Napoleon. All of his campaigns to date had been defensive in nature. Now, fueled by the confidence that he gained at Austerlitz, he felt he could inflict his will by force. With most of Western Europe at his feet and a point to prove,

Napoleon didn't feel a need to take the time to build support among his allies before deciding to invade, and he certainly didn't think about the implications of the invasion. Perhaps he felt the invasion was necessary in order to cripple England or to set an example, but if he had done the research, he would have seen that it was not. This was an aggressive move and would begin to turn European opinion against him.

Occupying Portugal was easy enough (the royal family had already fled to Brazil), but the British were on their way, and Napoleon was about to compound this mistake with an even greater one. A rebellion in Spain brought an opportunity Napoleon couldn't resist. Spain had a weak and unpopular Bourbon king, Charles IV; a treacherous prime minister, Godoy, who was openly sleeping with the queen; and a prince, Ferdinand, who despised his parents to the point that he once considered poisoning them. Moreover, Ferdinand was riling the masses against the oppressive Godoy—and therefore the king and queen.

When Ferdinand wrote a letter seeking Napoleon's protection, the king and queen found out about it, and a local scandal ensued. Charles IV accused Napoleon of plotting with Ferdinand, which led Napoleon to realize that this chaos must stop. Consequently, Napoleon ordered troops into Spain under the guise of protecting Ferdinand, but in reality to conduct reconnaissance on Spain's political and military situations. To add to the chaos, Ferdinand, thinking Napoleon was there to boost him to the throne, stirred the public to even greater passion. This set the stage for Napoleon to be hooked into a political maelstrom that would ruin his career. What lessons can we learn from these tumultuous events?

THE DANGERS OF POLITICS

During the rebellion, Charles and Ferdinand—both claiming rights to the crown—decided with Murat's encouragement to set out for

France to ask Napoleon to mediate. The meeting took place in Bayonne. They didn't make a good impression, arguing constantly throughout the meeting. Napoleon said, "When I saw them at my feet and was able to judge myself of their complete incapacity, an unspeakable compassion filled me for the fate of a great people. I seized the only opportunity offered me by Fortune to cause Spain to rise again, to separate her from England, and to bind her closely to our policy." Napoleon forced Charles and Ferdinand to abdicate their rights to the Spanish throne. He had multiple reasons for doing this.

First, he knew that Spain was the only other European country still accepting British goods. Furthermore, he knew that Godoy had originally planned to attack the *Grande Armée*, should they have come up short against Prussia at Jena, so this government couldn't be trusted. And finally, since he was now unfortunately caught up in the politics of this corrupt government, he figured he could destroy it with the same ease that he had destroyed Prussia and Austria, and create a new, democratic Spain. After all, his agents in Spain assured him that the Spaniards were fed up with the local government and would embrace a change. As Napoleon would learn, nothing comes without a price.

On a lesser scale, this same thing can happen to us in business if we are not careful. It's so easy to get caught up in political intrigue, and even more so if we're asked to take sides. It's tempting to engage in duplicity, making each side think that we're behind them. It's also tempting, especially if we're in a position of power, to simply force the feuding parties to yield to our will. Machiavelli would suggest taking sides with the stronger party—or at least the one that would be of most benefit to us. Any of these solutions can lead to danger if we abandon good principles. But, as leaders, we must make a decision.

Ultimately, the best thing to do, and the thing that will preserve our integrity, is to attempt to facilitate both parties to an agreement

if at all possible—to search for a win-win solution. If the parties
cannot come to agreement and they are within our sphere of influence, then we must stand firmly behind the right principles, which
may mean siding with one party or making an executive decision.
If the parties are outside our sphere of influence and cannot agree,
as was the case with Charles IV and Ferdinand, then it is best to
decline involvement or to refer to a higher authority.

In Napoleon's case, there was no higher authority, so it would
have been best to either ask a third party to mediate or decline getting involved. Even he later said, "My most dignified and safest plan
for Spain would have been a kind of mediation . . . I ought to have
given the Spanish nation a liberal constitution and commissioned
Ferdinand to put it into practice."

At the time, however, seeing the Spanish government as a threat,
Napoleon thought it more important to take advantage of the
opportunity to remove their corrupt government and make Spain
an ally. Consider his reflection on the situation:

> *In the crisis in which France found herself at that time, that is to say,*
> *during the fight for new ideas and the struggle of the century against the*
> *rest of Europe, we could not leave Spain out, and abandon her to our*
> *enemies; we had to bind her to our policy either of her own free will or*
> *by force . . . Moreover the code of laws for the salvation of nations is not*
> *always the same as that for the individual.*

Certainly, the principles seemed sound. As Napoleon later realized, however, he had chosen the wrong methods to carry them out.
As he said in his memoirs, "Circumstances have proved that I erred
in the choice of means, for the mistake lay rather in the means
employed than in the principles."

Most critically, he was greatly mistaken—or at best, misled—
about Spain's readiness to roll over and join the revolution. As a

result, by not giving enough attention to the cultural sentiment in Spain, as he had with Egypt, and by not getting his allies on board, the effort was magnified exponentially. Likewise, his increased isolation from his troops, the need to fight battles on multiple fronts, and a general lack of effective leaders led to morale problems that would increase as time went by. Napoleon had prophetically said, "In war, everything depends upon morale; and morale and public opinion comprise the better part of reality." He would find out the hard way that this is all too true.

THE IMPORTANCE OF PEOPLE

With French troops in Spain, the Spanish people were naturally beginning to get upset. When Murat, who was commanding Napoleon's troops, overreacted to a rebellion by launching vicious attacks on a crowd on May 2, 1808 (the famous revolt of Dos de Mayo), anti-French sentiment began to boil over. Murat, in Spain without any specific instructions, would continue to conduct shows of force to intimidate the Spanish people. Napoleon later said of this recklessness, "Murat spoiled a great deal of my work." After a few months of brutal fighting, Napoleon gave his brother Joseph the Spanish crown and sent Murat to Naples in Joseph's place. Needless to say, the Spaniards didn't take well to their new king.

Napoleon didn't realize that although his contacts from the upper echelon of Spain indicated that most of the country would welcome a new French government, the peasants, and especially those in the northern Navarre region, were vehemently opposed to French philosophies. They viewed apparently forward-thinking concepts, such as "separation of church and state" and "freedom of religion," as a threat to their traditions. Indeed, they were not in favor of any so-called reforms.

Uprisings continued and evolved into what would become the first use of the term "guerrilla war"—meaning "little war." The atrocities that followed—by both sides—were immortalized in the paintings of the Spanish artist Goya. With Napoleon's armies totally unprepared for such a way of fighting, the war continued for six years. To make matters worse, the British sent troops to Portugal, under the command of Arthur Wellesley, the Duke of Wellington, and Napoleon found himself fighting battles on two fronts—Portugal and Spain. Napoleon said, "The unfortunate war in Spain ruined me . . . The Spanish War destroyed my reputation in Europe, increased my embarrassments, and provided the best training ground for the English soldiers. I myself trained the English army in the Peninsula."

Two other things happened around this time that made things even worse for Napoleon. First, because he wasn't readily available, his leaders began quarreling among themselves, which deteriorated morale. He knew he needed one person to lead the affairs in Spain, but he could not find anyone capable of filling the role. Napoleon said, "I cannot appoint a commander-in-chief for all my armies in Spain, because I can find no one fit for the job." Second, because he couldn't find adequate leaders, he began to micromanage, not allowing anything to be done without his approval.

Unfortunately, Napoleon was spread way too thin to effectively resolve the situation. First, he was focused on the situation in Portugal—made more critical by the arrival of the British. At the same time, he was busy trying to negotiate further agreements with Russia. Then, he needed to be in Paris when word came to him that Talleyrand and Fouché, Napoleon's security chief, were plotting against him, anticipating that he would fall. Finally, things became even more complicated when, in 1809, Austria decided to take advantage of Napoleon's entanglements in Spain by declaring an alliance with England, thus forming the Fifth Coalition. Their first action would be to invade Bavaria. While Napoleon suffered his first serious setback in a battle at Aspern-Essling, he ultimately won the campaign with a victory at Wagram, forcing Austria to join his Continental System. It would be his last major victory.

All of these things would distract Napoleon from effectively resolving the situation in Spain. It seemed that wherever Napoleon was personally involved, things would progress, but he couldn't be everywhere at once. Additionally, because he was spread too thin, his diplomatic negotiations began to get sloppy. Thus, the critical success factors of moral force and public opinion suffered.

There are several lessons for us here, and all of them relate to the importance of people. First, we need to be cautious that we don't become so focused on our goal that we forget the need to build support from the bottom up. Napoleon excelled at this in his early days, whether it was appealing to the Italian public, learning the culture of Egypt, or satisfying France's need to restore the churches. But, for several reasons—partly because he was preoccupied with so many things, partly because he was ill advised by his agents, and partly because he was under pressure to seize the opportunity—he didn't do this with Spain. The result was disastrous. We cannot let our ideals, assumptions, or a need to hurry cause us to ignore the people aspects of our endeavors. It will hurt us in the long run.

Second, if we begin taking on many endeavors, we need to rely on effective leaders to manage some of them. We should be building effective leaders anyway as part of a succession plan, but this is critical if we are to scale our efforts across multiple endeavors. Besides, without effective leaders, we tend to begin micromanaging, which leads to other problems, not the least of which is poor morale. Building effective leaders takes work—we need to be sure our leaders are capable of making correct judgment calls and share our general philosophy. Often, people will promote their best performers to a leadership role, only to find out that the best performers do not always make great leaders. Nowhere is this more evident than in the case of Murat.

Murat was certainly heroic, but a hero does not a leader make. A leader needs to have a combination of people skills, analytical and planning ability, an aptitude for strategic thinking, and other things so often written about as attributes of good leadership. Having "been there and done that" is just one element of a good leader, and not always a required one if the other elements are in place. In Murat's case, he was an excellent soldier and good tactical leader of cavalry troops, but he was far from a strategic thinker. Indeed, it was his penchant for heroism and his short-term focus that frequently caused him to go outside the boundaries of Napoleon's broad directives, and it nearly botched the otherwise flawlessly executed Ulm campaign and definitely aggravated situations in Spain.

A third lesson is that not only must we have good leaders, but we must also insist on unity of command from the top down. Otherwise, as with Napoleon and his generals, if we're not readily available, our leaders will begin to develop their own agendas and begin arguing among themselves. The risk of potential problems is lessened with good leadership and unity of command.

The importance of people cannot be underestimated, whether it is the people who will be impacted by our project or the people we need to effectively lead our project. As Napoleon said, "The moral is to the physical as three is to one." Unfortunately for him, this turned out to be true in the case of the Peninsular War. With the people of Spain up in arms and his leaders quarreling, the handwriting was on the wall. Fortunately for us, however, hindsight is 20/20, so we now have the opportunity to benefit from Napoleon's mistakes.

EXECUTIVE SUMMARY

We began the chapter by exploring how Napoleon's power following his tremendous success at Austerlitz ultimately planted the seeds that led to his decline. It led him to adopt a win-lose approach with

Prussia and Austria, which would come back to haunt him later, and soon caused him to isolate himself from his associates. We also studied how he became so caught up in his ideals that he made the shortsighted decision to invade Portugal when the country continued to conduct trade with England. The major turning point, however, was when he decided to take advantage of the turbulence in Spain and uproot the corrupt government, not realizing the intensity of the antirepublican and particularly anti-French sentiment among the general Spanish population.

This underlines the risk of letting our ideals, assumptions, or a need to hurry get in the way of good judgment. It also highlights the dangers of getting involved in political intrigue, and how the best thing to do—if we cannot bring the parties to agreement—is either to bring in a third party to mediate or decline to get involved, something Napoleon acknowledged. In addition, we learned how the lack of effective leaders, combined with Napoleon's overloaded schedule, led to quarreling among his troops, poor morale, and other problems.

We could see how Napoleon's principles became increasingly compromised as he fell into the inevitable traps that accompany such power. One by one, exactitude, speed, flexibility, simplicity, character, and moral force began to dissolve. For example, he didn't have the time to do the exhaustive cultural research that he had done in the past, so exactitude suffered. He then let his ideals cloud his judgment, so speed gave way to haste. The scarcity of effective leaders forced him to micromanage, which took away the flexibility that the *Grande Armée* had in its prime. The sheer number of issues that he was attempting to address—not to mention the uncertainties that accompany guerrilla warfare—hindered his ability to provide simplicity in his plans and objectives. And with his motives beginning to be questioned and his troops quarreling among themselves, both his character and the moral force of his armies suffered.

We can see that although Napoleon's core motives remained sound, circumstances slowly but surely led him astray from his own principles. Fortunately, if we pay attention to the warning signs outlined, we should be able to remain on course and not suffer the same fate.

In the next chapter, we will see how Napoleon, double-crossed by the Russian czar Alexander I, made the ill-fated decision to invade Russia while still embroiled in the Peninsular War. We will also explore the final battle that Napoleon fought at Waterloo after a brief return from exile. Both the Russian invasion and Waterloo will not only reinforce the lessons we've learned thus far, they will also bring us yet additional lessons and warning signs to watch for.

MARCHING ORDERS

BEWARE OF FORCED ALLIES
Don't adopt a compliance mentality.
- Don't ignore the perspectives of those who may not carry much weight; they can come back to haunt you later.
- Once a new change is implemented, follow up to address people's issues and frustrations.
- Invest time in changing the culture so that it sticks; don't feel that it will stick because you said it would.

DON'T GO IT ALONE
Don't isolate yourself from your team and team leads.
- Infrastructure is necessary, especially for large projects, but remain visible to your team and available to your team leads.
- Remember that the personal touch is critical to morale.
- Don't forget the subject-matter experts who got you where you are; the higher you go, the more they're needed.

HEED THE DANGERS OF POLITICS

Beware of getting caught up in political intrigue.

- The best option is to try to facilitate the parties to solve the problem in a win-win fashion.
- If the parties cannot come to an agreement and they are within your sphere of influence, then stand firmly behind the right principles, which may mean siding with one party or making an executive decision.
- If the parties are out of your sphere of influence and cannot come to an agreement, it's best to decline to get involved or to refer to a higher authority.

DON'T UNDERESTIMATE THE IMPORTANCE OF PEOPLE

Don't let your ideals, assumptions, or a need to hurry cause you to ignore the people aspects of your endeavor.

- To be successful, we need to be aware of the impact on people, not just focus on our deliverables.

Don't forget the need to build effective leaders.

- Resist the temptation to make your best performers leaders. Leadership requires people skills, analytical and planning ability, an aptitude for strategic thinking, and other such skills.
- Without effective leaders, we cannot scale to broader endeavors and we must begin micromanaging to keep control.

Make sure the leaders are aligned with your approach.

- Top-down unity of command is critical in order to avoid confusion and bickering among leaders.

CHAPTER 13

Lessons from the Russian Invasion
and Waterloo

*Forethought we may have, undoubtedly,
but not foresight.* —NAPOLEON

We have seen how, to a great degree, Napoleon was a victim of his own success. As his power grew, he fell into the traps that typically accompany such heights. We saw this with his disregard for Prussia and Austria, his increased isolation from his troops, his invasion of Portugal, and his interference in Spanish affairs. Ironically, the Russian invasion, which led to the near decimation of the *Grande Armée*, was a return to form, of sorts, for Napoleon. He employed most, if not all, of his winning principles. And yet he still failed. Indeed, it reads like a riddle. How does one use such sound principles, assemble the largest force in history, win every battle in the campaign, and yet come back with but a fraction of his men?

No doubt, the story of the Russian invasion brings us some valuable lessons, as we, too, can feel we have all odds in our favor and still come out behind if we're not careful. We'll begin by examining the events that led to the Russian invasion. Then we'll see how—little by little, despite exhaustive preparation—things began to go wrong, things that perhaps could have been avoided. Finally, we'll wrap up the chapter, and our exploration of Napoleon's career, with a brief look at the inevitable events that followed, including Napoleon's final battle at Waterloo. Let's explore the situation Napoleon was facing in 1809.

PRELUDE TO AN INVASION

With Austria defeated and his armies still embroiled in the Peninsular War, Napoleon would soon be faced with more challenges. Realizing that the Russian czar Alexander I had been reluctant to help in the recent war with Austria, despite his promise to provide assistance, Napoleon began to grow concerned. Meanwhile, Alexander I was getting pressure from his overbearing mother and his Russian nobles to break the Treaty of Tilsit and go to war against Napoleon.

There were two reasons for this. First, they were furious at the fact that Napoleon, through the Treaty of Tilsit, had created the duchy of Warsaw and instituted his liberal civil code there. They viewed Napoleon's reforms as a threat, especially his egalitarian principles. With these reforms the Jews and serfs, who were peasant laborers bound to duty, would gain freedoms unheard of in Russia, and Warsaw was simply too close for comfort. Second, the nobles were opposed to the Continental System and had already forced Alexander into not only accepting British trade, but levying huge taxes on French trade as well. After all, the embargo on Britain was hurting them economically.

Ultimately, Alexander gave in to the pressure and on April 8, 1812, issued an impossible ultimatum to Napoleon: either give up the duchy of Warsaw or Russia would break peace with France. Napoleon knew that Russia was already negotiating alliances with Sweden and England, and soon they would do so with Prussia. He also knew that they were preparing to invade Warsaw. In addition, he knew that Alexander had expansionist ideas of his own. Last but not least, Napoleon had made a promise to the Poles to establish a Polish state, and giving up Warsaw to Russia would break that promise.

Napoleon offered countless peace proposals to Russia, always within the constraints of the Tilsit agreement, but stopping short of supporting Poland's pleas for an independent kingdom. He received no response. Thus, he made the difficult decision that he needed to invade Russia if he were to preserve all that he had done so far and protect his empire and the democratic way of life.

THE BEST-LAID PLANS

But Napoleon would not let it be a reckless folly. First, he knew that he had never lost to the Russians and that he understood their fighting techniques. Second, he conducted extensive research on Russian roads, past battles, and weather patterns over the previous twenty years, and arranged his logistics accordingly. Third, he used persuasive diplomacy to assemble the largest army known to man, increasing his *Grande Armée* to nearly six hundred thousand strong, made up from more than twenty countries—even including Prussia and Austria. The fact that some of his troops were still mired in the Peninsular War didn't thrill him, but he saw no choice. Napoleon said:

> *Let it be said once more: it was against my will that I undertook war with Russia. I knew better than anyone that Spain was a gnawing cancer that must be healed before one could enter upon such a terrible war in which the first battle would be fought at a distance of 500 leagues from my frontier . . . I should have been a fool if I had begun the war of 1812 to obtain something that I could easily have got by friendly negotiations.*

Thus began the invasion that would be immortalized in Tchaikovsky's *1812 Overture.* Having done his research, Napoleon developed a prudent plan. He knew that Charles XII, the king of

Sweden, attempted to invade Russia in 1709, but lost his horses during the brutal Russian winter. As a result, Charles XII had to abandon his ammunition. Without horses and ammunition, and in the crippling cold, thousands of troops perished. Determined not to suffer the same fate, Napoleon planned to take his troops no farther than Smolensk, which was still a few hundred miles from Moscow. There, he thought, he could wait for the Russians to come, defeat them, renew peace discussions, and return before winter.

He planned extensively. He would bring food and supplies in trains that would lag behind the army, and as a contingency the troops and horses would live off the land, just as they had in previous campaigns. Furthermore, each soldier would carry a four-day ration of food, just in case. He would also leave troops in Warsaw and at each village to maintain his line of communication, which is why he needed such a large army. He planned to send a total of four hundred thousand men across the Polish border into Russia. Little did he know, only ten thousand of those men would return.

LESSON: THE IMPORTANCE OF RISK ANALYSIS

Napoleon's decision to invade Russia wasn't necessarily a bad one. He had come to the realization that he really didn't have much choice, despite the dangers of fighting a war on two fronts. Also, his plan seemed sound and he prepared extensively, as was his nature. But the few questions that he didn't think to ask ended up causing disaster. It is true that some risks are indeed unknowable, and Napoleon could hardly be faulted for not expecting the Russians to destroy their own villages. And he was probably aware of the dangers of an undisciplined, multinational army, but he might have felt it was a risk worth taking. But he could have asked more "what if" questions, such as: What if we get to Smolensk, and there's no sign of the Russians? Do we turn around and go home, or do we remain in rains fell, making the roads muddy and impassable. Then summer came early, bringing stifling heat and burning out crops. Men and horses perished in the mud and heat, with many troops suffering from outbreaks of dysentery and influenza. To make matters worse, the Russians had adopted a scorched-earth policy, destroying their own villages and burning crops as they retreated toward Moscow. Since Napoleon's supply trains were unable to progress in the mud, and eating off the land wasn't an option, more men and horses perished.

This was also when the disadvantages of such a large army became evident. Again, there was a shortage of effective leaders, but this time it was made worse by the fact that two-thirds of the *Grande Armée* consisted of foreign troops, most of whom didn't even speak French. Undisciplined and untrained, they ate their four-day food rations the first day. And discouraged by the heat, sickness, and confusion, many of them began deserting. After all, they didn't have the same stake in the matter as the French troops, especially the Prussians and Austrians. When the army did get into skirmishes with the Russians, nothing came of it, and through disorganization, the Russians were allowed to flee.

LESSON: MANAGING LARGE TEAMS

As Napoleon discovered, there are inherent dangers in having a large team. First, a good leadership staff is required to inform and motivate the respective sub-teams, as the leader cannot be everywhere. Second, mission commitment and self-discipline are required of all team members, as their duties are typically more widely distributed than on a small team. Third, planning is required to keep everyone engaged over the long haul, as people quickly become demoralized if not actively accomplishing something. If they can't be engaged in something, then frequent communication becomes critical.

Smolensk? In either case, what would happen then? Do we need t
pack for winter? What are the dangers of staying so far from home?

This is the level of detail we need to contemplate when undertaking a major project—and to Napoleon's credit, the level of detail
he usually considered. We can't think of everything, but the more
we meditate on the possible risks, the more likely we'll increase our
chances of being successful. We need to think through the entire
scenario, asking ourselves "what if" questions and any subsequent
questions that are generated, such as: What if we create this won-
derful software product, and people in our company don't use it?
How will we ensure that it's used so we can gain the promised benefits? What if we put together a project team of superstars and none
of them get along? How can that risk be avoided or reduced?

Notice that many of these questions revolve around people. That's
because people are typically the most unpredictable variable in any
endeavor. Of course, in some industries, it may be the weather or
some other uncontrollable factor. When contemplating these scenarios, we need to constantly remind ourselves to consider the different
ways people may act—or the way in which weather can impact us,
and so forth—and plan accordingly. This is not to say that we should
become so afraid that we never get started, merely that we need to
take the time to think about the possible scenarios. And, with large
projects, the time spent doing so should be accordingly greater.

What actually happened when Napoleon took his army into Russia?

DISASTER IN RUSSIA

With the decision made and preparations completed, Napoleon's
army began their march to Smolensk. They would have stopping
points at the villages of Kovno, Vilna, and Vitebsk. Everything had
gone quite smoothly by the time the massive army made it to Kovno.
Then, when they left Kovno for Vilna, things became worse. Heavy

Napoleon had everything going against him. Although he had plenty of heroes, he lacked effective leaders, especially among the foreign units. In addition, two-thirds of his army now consisted of foreigners who had a minor commitment at best, as was evident by the level of desertion—and this included their leaders. They also lacked self-discipline, as was evident by their rapid consumption of food rations. To make matters worse, since they didn't speak French, many important factors were lost in the communication. As the march continued amid heat, hunger, and exhaustion, and with poor communication and no clear indications of success, people lost hope. That is a dangerous state of affairs for a team about to embark on a major endeavor.

This situation is not unique to the battlefield. Whether in business or government, we will often have a large team distributed among various locations and/or organizations, and wonder to ourselves how we'll coordinate such an effort and keep everyone focused on the mission. The answers are the same as they were for Napoleon. We need an effective leadership team. We need to confirm the commitment of vendors, part-time resources, and remote team members, making sure they understand the protocols and policies we establish. We need to keep everyone engaged through the long haul with frequent milestone checkpoints, and, most importantly, we need to communicate frequently. No doubt, there are challenges with large and widely distributed teams, but with these precautions, we should be able to reduce the risks.

NAPOLEON PRESSES ON

When Napoleon and his army arrived in Vilna, they found an abandoned town, with stores and houses destroyed by the Russians. Napoleon decided to wait a bit to see if Alexander would respond to his peace offerings. After staying in Vilna for eighteen days, Napoleon decided to continue on to Vitebsk. Again his armies got into skir-mishes with the Russians, and again the Russians were allowed to flee. Even worse, another eight thousand horses were lost. Through it all, Napoleon remained optimistic and promised the troops rest when they got to Vitebsk. This optimism didn't spread to his troops, though, as they were discouraged and hungry. Even more critical, they weren't combat ready.

Just as at Vilna, Vitebsk was demolished and devoid of any food or supplies aside from flour, which the men cooked with water into a soup. Napoleon decided to wait in Vitebsk until the few remain-ing supply trains caught up, which wasn't until a week later. At this point, Napoleon's staff argued that it would be best to call the mis-sion to a halt, declare mild success, and wait for reinforcements.

LESSON: KNOWING WHEN TO CUT YOUR LOSSES

It's clear that at this point in the journey Napoleon's troops were exhausted. The decision to continue to Vitebsk wasn't necessarily a bad one. Once they got to Vitebsk, however, and waited for the food to arrive, it was time to consider halting the mission and developing a new plan. Napoleon's staff recognized it, and later even Napoleon realized it; he said in his memoirs, "I should have remained in Vitebsk."

> "Nothing is more difficult, and therefore more precious, than to be able to decide."
> —NAPOLEON

It is one thing to set outrageous goals, and even desirable if one wants to achieve greatness, but it is another to recognize when to scale back and set a more realistic tar-get. Sometimes, it may make sense to stop the project, rethink it, and take a new approach. Other times, it is best just to bring the project to a halt and cut your losses. All too often, a project continues even after it is obvious that the targets are not going to be achieved. In the end, there's nothing but wasted time and money and a bunch of demoralized people. Just as Napoleon should have stopped at Vitebsk, we need to know when to stop and regroup. As Napoleon said, "Nothing is more difficult, and therefore more precious, than to be able to decide."

SMOLENSK AT LAST

After a two-week rest in Vitebsk, Napoleon led his army toward Smolensk, an ancient walled city, where the Russians were now entrenched. After some heavy fighting in the suburbs, the French finally arrived at Smolensk, only to find that the Russians had retreated once more. Once again, they had destroyed their own city, this time setting fire to it. And once again, this was an opportunity to call the mission to a halt. First, this was as far as Napoleon said he would go to avoid the fate of Charles XII. Second, his army was not prepared for winter travel, since he had expected to return before winter. Worse, they were burned out and felt that enough was enough.

Napoleon thought about halting the mission, but he felt to remain there for an extended stay would have increased the chances of further intrigue in Paris. Besides, he didn't want his army stranded hundreds of miles from home, taking a chance that the Russians would gain reinforcements. With the Russians heading toward Moscow, 280 miles away, Napoleon decided to pursue them.

LESSON: THE DANGERS OF DRIVING TOO HARD

If it is true that Napoleon should have remained at Vitebsk, then he certainly should have gone no farther than Smolensk, which was where he had originally intended to stop. All of the concerns that he now raised about the risks of staying in Smolensk should have been addressed before the campaign began. Now Napoleon was so obsessed with pressing on that he was blind to the sentiments of his staff and the condition of his troops.

In the business world, we can equate this to the practice of forced overtime. How many times have we seen a project where people were forced to work long stretches of overtime in order to meet an objective? Could there have been other solutions, such as scaling back the objectives, making the targets more realistic, or bringing in additional resources? Sometimes the target date is less flexible, such as a need to meet a government regulation or a need to get a product on the market quickly. But these targets should not be at the expense of our most valuable resource—our people.

If people need to put in extra effort over a short duration, are given incentives to meet certain targets, or are grouped in a collaborative setting so as to gain productivity, that is one thing, and quite appropriate. It is also appropriate to raise a sense of urgency, which can serve to motivate some people to voluntarily work extra hours. But to drive people to the point of exhaustion is not only unnecessary; it is counterproductive. According to the American Federation of Teachers (AFT) Web site, "Mandatory overtime has been linked to poorer general health, increased injury rates, greater levels of illness, and even increased levels of mortality."[1] The site goes on to link mandatory overtime with job performance problems. The U.S. Healthcare Workers Council stated similar findings.

This is not surprising. Parkinson's Law dictates that work expands to fill the time allotted. If people are expected to work twelve hours a day, they'll find ways to fill that time, but be less motivated, make more mistakes, and still accomplish only about six to eight hours of real work. Earlier, we spoke of moral force being achieved through order, purpose, recognition, and rewards, but even those elements aren't enough to compensate for an exhausted team. Although we need to drive toward our goals, we cannot drive so hard that we lose sight of our people's morale and well-being. Napoleon made this mistake, and it cost him dearly.

THE AVOIDABLE CONSEQUENCES

Now that we've explored the lessons from the Russian invasion, namely the importance of risk analysis, the dangers of large teams, knowing when to cut your losses, and the potential impact of driving too hard, let's briefly look at the results of these omissions on Napoleon's part—results that were entirely avoidable. We'll return to Napoleon and his exhausted army as they chased the Russians in the ninety-degree heat, encountering one burned-out village after another.

THE FRUITLESS BATTLE OF BORODINO

Under pressure from his nobles to defend Moscow and stop retreating, Alexander finally decided to take a stand. He sent his armies out to meet Napoleon at Borodino, seventy miles from Moscow. Finally, Napoleon would have his battle. The battle was brutal, lasting nearly twenty-four hours. By the battle's end, the Russians had lost forty-four thousand men and the French thirty-three thousand, including forty-three generals. What remained of the Russian army retreated to Moscow. Napoleon's troops, in no shape to bring about a decisive victory, were now so deep into Russia that there was not much hope of returning to Paris before winter. This was truly a no-win situation that never should have happened. Unfortunately, things would get worse.

THE BURNING OF MOSCOW

If everything up to now had dampened the troops' spirits, the sight of Moscow, with its glistening domes and glorious architecture, renewed them. On September 14, 1812, approximately one hundred thousand men entered Moscow—a far cry from the four hundred thousand that had begun the journey. Not surprisingly, Moscow was abandoned. Soon, fires began to erupt, and after a while, it became obvious that the Russians were burning their glorious city. Even Napoleon could not have predicted this. The fires spread for three days, destroying four-fifths of Moscow.

Napoleon and his troops eventually found shelter in the few houses that remained, where they found an abundance of food in underground cellars. Napoleon wrote to Alexander and waited for a response, but received none. Finally, after more than a month in Moscow waiting for a response, he made the decision to head back to Smolensk, which would at least shorten the line of communication back to Paris. It was now October, and Napoleon's research had shown that winter typically came in late November, so this would have seemed to be a safe assumption. Unfortunately, winter came a month early, bringing snow and freezing temperatures.

THE ATTACK OF "GENERAL WINTER"

Napoleon's troops marched through decimated villages with no food or water. Men and horses froze to death in their tracks. And, just as had happened to Charles XII, the lack of horses forced Napoleon's troops to abandon their ammunition. By the time the troops finally arrived at Smolensk, the temperature had reached -26 degrees Centigrade (-15 degrees Fahrenheit). Smolensk was uninhabitable, and the little food remaining had been eaten by the advance troops. Worse yet, the Russians had three approaching columns that outnumbered Napoleon's army, now reduced to about fifty thousand men, three to one.

At this point, without ammunition and horses, Napoleon's army wasn't really an army at all. Victory was no longer even a consideration. Now the goal was simply to survive.

THE LONG ROAD HOME

Napoleon's army fled west toward Vilna, where an abundance of food awaited. But first, they would need to cross the Berezina River, which Napoleon had naturally assumed would be frozen. Unfortunately, the weather had warmed just enough to turn the river into icy slush. When one of Napoleon's staff heard from a local peasant about a shallow point nine miles to the north, Napoleon had his men construct a makeshift bridge there. At the same time, he had a separate unit create some fires farther south to set up a diversion for the Russians.

Sure enough, the Russians saw the flames and headed south. Meanwhile, the bridge was constructed, and by the time the Russians realized they had been duped, many of Napoleon's men had crossed the bridge, with Marshal Ney heroically fending off the Russians from the rear. The Russians chose not to follow. After their amazing feat, the thirty thousand men who made it across the bridge now headed for Vilna, where they would finally get some food and shelter. Unfortunately, the temperatures dropped again, so many more perished on the way. Ultimately, only ten thousand men returned to Kovno.

FINAL OBSERVATIONS ON THE RUSSIAN INVASION

Nobody could have predicted the Russians' burning of Moscow, the early winter, or the unusual thaw that melted the Berezina. All of this could have been avoided, however, if the right questions had been asked up front, or if Napoleon had chosen to remain in Vitebsk when it was obvious the mission should have been halted. Napoleon later realized this, and hopefully, we can benefit from it as well. We cannot underestimate the need to ask pressing questions when planning a project, or to recognize when the project looks as though it will not meet its targets. Napoleon did this to a degree, but a combination of overconfidence and wishful thinking clouded his judgment.

THE WATERLOO DEBACLE

We've seen the disastrous Russian Campaign of 1812, but surprisingly, that wasn't the end of Napoleon's career. To his credit, he was able to rebuild a sizable army of about three hundred thousand men, and in the following year, defeat the Russians and Prussians in Germany. Russia, Prussia, Austria, and England, however, then formed an alliance that would become the Sixth Coalition. Worse, Wellington, who had emerged victorious in Spain, was now threatening to invade France. Napoleon's marshals, sensing the futility, called a meeting and declared to Napoleon that they were no longer willing to fight. They asked Napoleon to voluntarily abdicate in order to save France. Not wanting to penalize France by his presence, Napoleon agreed to a voluntary exile on the island of Elba, with the title of Emperor of Elba. This exile would be short-lived.

THE NEW, IMPROVED NAPOLEON

After several months on Elba, Napoleon grew concerned. First, he heard that Tallyrand, who now had a position of influence, was plotting to have him moved to a more remote island and possibly even assassinated. Second, Louis XVIII, the new king, had not paid Napoleon or his family any of the agreed-upon allowances as stated in the treaty. Then a moment of opportunity came. Napoleon heard that the people of France were so upset by the restored aristocracy that they had begun a strong movement calling for his return, and he decided to act.

He made a daring return with the eleven hundred troops accorded him on Elba. They landed in the south of France and made their way north. In a dramatic moment when French troops—now under Louis XVIII—were sent to arrest him, they embraced him instead, shouting, *"Vive l'Empereur!"* (Long live the Emperor!). From that moment on, all of France rallied around Napoleon, and Louis XVIII fled. It was nothing short of a miracle. Napoleon declared, "A great many foolish things have been done, but I have come to put everything right." And he did.

For the next period of time, known as the Hundred Days, despite being sick and worn out, Napoleon spent all of his efforts making peace offerings throughout Europe, even agreeing to the original borders that existed before the Revolution. In addition, he made good on his word in France, abolishing censorship, expanding the electorate, and establishing trials by jury. For a while, the rest of Europe considered his offers. Tallyrand convinced them otherwise. Then, when Murat stupidly took it upon himself to attack Austria, Napoleon's fate was sealed. In March 1815, the coalition declared Napoleon an international outlaw and prepared to invade France. Once again, Napoleon had to reluctantly prepare for war. And once again, we are offered a valuable lesson.

WATERLOO: THE FINAL BATTLE

Napoleon knew that the Russians and Austrians were amassing an army of four hundred thousand troops. Also, the British, led by Wellington, were much closer in Waterloo, Belgium; and the Prussians were coming to join them. This was the seventh and final coalition against France. Napoleon needed to act quickly. As usual, his plan would be to attack the British with most of his forces, send a small army to delay the Prussians, and then use his combined forces to attack the Prussians. There were several problems.

First, he didn't have the services of Berthier, who had leaped from a window to his death—some say he was pushed. Second, because

Napoleon was exhausted during the Hundred Days, he had made some less-than-astute decisions regarding placing the right people in the right positions. As a consequence, there was one miscommunication after another, at times even resulting in conflicting orders. Finally, because he was tired, Napoleon made the uncustomary decision to delay when rain had washed out the roads.

Because of the delays, Marshal Grouchy, who was sent to head off the Prussians, ended up overshooting them by miles, allowing the Prussians to join forces with the British. It was not helpful that Grouchy, clearly the wrong man for the job, did not display any sense of urgency. Until then, despite the setbacks, Napoleon's army had been making progress against the British—even Wellington called the battle a "near run thing." But it was all over once the Prussians arrived. Napoleon's army fled, and there ended the battle of Waterloo.

LESSON: THE IMPACT OF BURNOUT

Although the Waterloo campaign was doomed by several factors, including the wrong people in the wrong positions, excessive delays, and miscommunication, the root cause for all of this was burnout on Napoleon's part. According to eyewitnesses, Napoleon was lethargic and unsure of himself toward the end of the Hundred Days. This was obvious in his random assignment of personnel and his uncustomary delays. And not only was Napoleon burned out, but his marshals and his troops were as well. Year after year of fighting battles will do that to anyone, especially when there seems to be no end in sight. If Napoleon had not lost at Waterloo, it would have happened soon thereafter.

Those of us in leadership and management positions tend to be more driven than others. We find ourselves working at night to catch up, since we're in meetings all day. Like Napoleon, we often live our work. But it's a dangerous habit that can get out of hand if we're not careful. Putting in some extra hours may be fine, especially if we're inspired to accomplish great things. But we also need to make time for our families and leisure activities. We won't be able to maintain our level of effectiveness in the long term without this sense of balance.

EXECUTIVE SUMMARY

As we learned from the events in this chapter, the decision to invade Russia wasn't necessarily a bad one. Napoleon fell short, however, in four key areas.

First, he omitted some important "what if" questions during his campaign preparation, especially involving the potential response by the Russians. Second, he proceeded despite the dangers of having a large, multinational force. Third, he didn't know when to halt the mission and cut his losses. Fourth, and finally, he drove his team too hard when it was obvious they were no longer in fighting shape. As a result, his once-invincible *Grande Armée* was no longer an army at all by the time they reached Moscow, and those who survived had to endure ice, numbness, and death on the long march home.

These four mistakes have taught us some valuable lessons, since we also must ask "what if" questions; manage large, distributed teams; know when to cut our losses; and recognize when we're driving our teams too hard. Without these things, we can follow all of the Six Winning Principles and still come up short. Although Napoleon was able to rebuild his army, his marshals—tired of fighting the world—refused to fight any longer. And by the time Waterloo came along, Napoleon was burned out as well. This brings us another lesson, as all too often we get so caught up in our work that we forget the need for a sense of balance in our lives. We can't maintain our effectiveness in the long run without it.

In the next chapter, we'll explore the Four Critical Warning Signs that can help us avoid falling into the same traps that Napoleon did. Then, in the final chapter, we'll see the aftermath of Waterloo and the legacy that Napoleon left for the world and for us.

MARCHING ORDERS

UNDERSTAND THE IMPORTANCE OF RISK ANALYSIS

Don't forget to analyze possible alternative scenarios when planning a project.

- Pay special attention to those factors that are unpredictable, such as people and weather.
- Ask plenty of "what if" questions.
- Spend the time appropriate to the size of your project.

RECOGNIZE THE DIFFICULTIES OF LARGE TEAMS

If managing a large and/or distributed team, take the necessary precautions.

- Assure that you have an effective leadership staff, capable of leading and managing their respective sub-teams.
- Confirm the commitment of vendors, part-time resources, and remote team members, and make sure they understand the correct protocols and policies.
- Keep everyone engaged through the long haul with frequent milestone checkpoints.
- Communicate frequently.

KNOW WHEN TO CUT YOUR LOSSES

Don't continue a project past the point of realization that your targets will not be achieved.

- Setting outrageous goals may be good, but know when it is time to scale back to a more realistic plan.
- Once it is realized that your targets will not be achieved

under the current course of action, either develop a new plan or end the project.

BEWARE THE DANGERS OF DRIVING TOO HARD

Don't force excessive mandatory overtime or you'll burn out your team.

- Mandatory overtime has been linked to health problems and has been proved to decrease productivity.
- Instead, raise a sense of urgency, which will inspire some to voluntarily work extra hours.
- Consider scaling back the objectives, setting a more realistic target date, or bringing in additional resources.

DON'T UNDERESTIMATE THE IMPACT OF BURNOUT

To ensure long-term effectiveness, keep a sense of balance in your life.

- Putting in extra hours may be fine, but make time for family and leisure activities.
- Burnout leads to rash decisions and impatience with others.
- Burnout can lead to health problems, for you as well as your team members.

CHAPTER 14

The Four Critical Warning Signs

Great ambition is the passion of a great character. Those endowed with it may perform very good or very bad acts. It all depends on the principles that direct them. —NAPOLEON

Nobody could accuse Napoleon of not being ambitious. Yet, throughout his rise, the Six Winning Principles kept him on the right path. Unfortunately, at the height of his power, he fell into the traps that often accompany such heights. It happened so quickly that even he didn't realize his principles had been compromised. It was too late by the time he did realize it. Perhaps his fall was inevitable, just a reminder of the futility of trying to bring about a major culture change without buy-in from key stakeholders—in Napoleon's case, the other monarchs of Europe. But it is quite possible that he could have succeeded in his goals if he hadn't fallen into some of these traps.

Fortunately for us, these failings carry lessons that are just as valuable as those from his triumphs. Just as we've learned how to boost our chances of success through Napoleon's Six Winning Principles, we can learn how to avoid failure by observing certain warning signs. These warning signs can serve as triggers to remind us that we may need to take some action to stay on course.

Specifically, there are Four Critical Warning Signs we need to watch for:

1. Power—leading to separation, self-righteousness, and impatience
2. Overzealousness—leading to grandiose ideas, obsession, and impulsiveness
3. Scarcity of effective leaders—leading to disorder, mistrust, and micromanagement
4. Unbalanced lifestyle—leading to burnout, loss of composure, and loss of health

Any one of these conditions can undermine our abilities to stay on target with the Six Winning Principles. Let's consider each in more detail.

POWER

As Napoleon found out, power can bring with it many unwanted side effects. This doesn't have to defeat us, however, as long as we curb that power by taking certain precautions, which is why we must consider power a warning sign. If we are in a position of power or even imagine ourselves to be in a position of power, we need to be aware that subtle changes can occur that produce negative impacts.

With increased responsibility, we can find ourselves becoming so busy or thinking at such a high level that we unwittingly isolate ourselves from our teams. This tends to lead to impatience, as we become more focused on our own goals and needs and don't have time for the details "the little people" are struggling with. Ultimately, if we allow this to happen, we are more susceptible to becoming caught up in our own self-righteousness, thinking that our view is always

the right view and making rash decisions as a result. It is this deadly trio of separation, impatience, and self-righteousness that has caused many leaders to falter at the height of their power. It is certainly worth a brief exploration of each of these three elements.

SEPARATION

As we saw with Napoleon following Austerlitz, power often requires us to move to another plateau, which can isolate us from our close associates. As a result, we tend to lose our sense of empathy and ignore the plight of those who are laboring in the details. As people grow frustrated, morale and productivity suffer.

To avoid this fate, we need to recognize when we're beginning to isolate ourselves from the people around us. But this is not always so easy. It can happen without our even realizing it. This is why the best cure for separation is to prevent it before it happens. We can do this by scheduling specific times to be available to others and listen to their concerns. Some busy leaders have scheduled regular "doctor's in" sessions, when staff can come to them with issues, or set up public forums for people to share concerns. Napoleon did this in his earlier days, but he had to curtail the practice as his power grew and his attentions were focused on Spain and Russia. Unfortunately, his relationships with his staff suffered for it.

To summarize, if we want to avoid the downward spiral that separation can lead to, it is critical that we make time for the people who rely on us—and this is usually best accomplished by scheduling specific times to do so.

IMPATIENCE

Another by-product of power is that it often leads to impatience, as we find we no longer have time to get caught up in people's

concerns or debates. It is too easy to simply decree what we want done. When separation and impatience are combined, it is a lethal combination, as we find ourselves inflicting our will on people who no longer feel comfortable voicing their concerns. As they begin to realize that we're out of touch with their needs, they become frustrated and disillusioned, which leads to further separation. It's truly a vicious circle.

To a degree, we saw this in the way Napoleon treated Prussia and Austria after his successes at Austerlitz. This could perhaps be excused because Prussia and Austria had been perceived as a national threat, but his win-lose approach with them caused problems later. Of more concern was the fact that he was beginning to do the same with some of his generals. As Napoleon's power grew and his distractions increased, he didn't have the time to build their leadership skills and began barking out unrealistic orders, especially during the Peninsular War.

Napoleon's growing impatience also extended to his treatment of those countries that didn't adhere to his Continental System, such as Portugal and Spain. Until then, the Continental System was beginning to take its toll on England, and waiting a little longer might have brought Napoleon the results he desired. Instead, he decided to push the issue and invade Portugal and Spain because he had the power to do so.

Making snap decisions is one thing, but doing so in a way that makes others feel uncomfortable and raises general concerns is an abuse of power. And sometimes we do this without even realizing it. If we do find ourselves getting impatient, we need to stop and think about what is making us that way and slow down if possible. Most importantly, we need to be rational and think before we act— or speak. And if we avoid the separation that so often goes with power and make time to listen to others, we'll be less likely to grow impatient in the first place.

SELF-RIGHTEOUSNESS

Perhaps the greatest danger of power is that it tends to lead to self-righteousness. Especially with successes under our belts, we think we can do no wrong. We tend to feel that our way is best and thus disregard the cautions and perspectives of others. For example, Napoleon was so caught up in his Continental System and with spreading the values of democracy throughout Europe that he no longer felt the need to negotiate. Nowhere was this more evident than in his invasion of Portugal and the ill-fated takeover of Spain. He began to see himself as God, bringing liberty and equality to the world merely by his declaration.

It is good to believe in ourselves, but we need to be aware of the dangers of self-importance. In his *Harvard Business Review* article "Narcissistic Leaders: The Incredible Pros, the Inevitable Cons," Michael Maccoby, author of *The Productive Narcissist*, pointed out that narcissistic leaders—those visionaries who dream of changing the world and leaving behind a legacy—can be extremely valuable, provided they take necessary precautions. He suggested finding a trusted sidekick who might be more grounded in reality; sharing philosophies with the team ("indoctrinating the organization"); and seeking counsel to build listening skills and overcome character flaws, such as a need for perfection or a feeling that only we can do the job correctly.[1]

These are good suggestions. We can decrease the chances of succumbing to self-righteousness by surrounding ourselves with one or more trusted associates with temperaments different from ours and listening to their input, by sharing our philosophies so that others will understand us, and by seeking to understand our own character flaws.

Overall, we can greatly reduce the chances that power will defeat us with decreased separation, more patience for those around us, and better control of our own weaknesses. The key point is that with power comes great responsibility, and that means the responsibility to limit separation, impatience, and self-righteousness. With that in mind, we should consider power as the first warning sign that we need to watch out for these three harmful side effects. The next critical warning sign is overzealousness.

OVERZEALOUSNESS

There is a fine line between passion and overzealousness, and it is not often easy to tell when we've crossed that line. Suffice it to say that if we're extremely excited about a project or an idea, we need to be aware that it can lead to some negative side effects. Just as power can lead to separation, impatience, and self-righteousness, being passionate about a project or an idea can lead to other traps. What makes this difficult is that, as leaders, it is important for us to be passionate. In fact, it is vital, since passion on the part of the leader can inspire a whole team to greatness. But trouble can ensue if that passion evolves to the point where we develop grandiose ideas, become obsessed with achieving our goals at all costs, and begin making impulsive decisions. This is when passion becomes overzealousness.

So, if we notice that we're extremely excited about a project or an idea, we need to assume that we are in danger of developing those unwanted by-products. But how do we tell if we've gone too far? How can we tell if our ideas seem grandiose, if we're becoming obsessed with our goals, or if we're becoming impulsive? Let's explore each of these in more detail and find out.

GRANDIOSE IDEAS

Consider Napoleon's vision of creating a democratic Europe. There's nothing wrong with that vision, but he might have had better chances of achieving that vision if he had scaled back his plans to focus on securing his empire's borders, making improvements within the empire, and improving relationships with his enemies, much as he did in his earlier days. Instead, he tried to force the issue once he had the power to do so. Although it is important to have big goals, we need to know when it is time to scale those goals into something more realistic—this is where a sidekick can come in handy. Perhaps we need to break a project into separate, sequential projects in order to gain interim successes and slowly build toward our overall vision. Or maybe we need to limit the scope of our project. The challenge is that as leaders we are taught to think big and to aim for the skies, but those grandiose ideas need to be tempered with a dose of reality.

This is more an art than a science. Fortunately, we can control this to a degree by having a project scope statement that is validated by key stakeholders and signed off on by the sponsor. And a rigorous change management process should be followed that requires sign-off and approval for all changes, in order to keep the scope of the project from escalating as new ideas develop—the dreaded "scope creep."

OBSESSION

Another sign of overzealousness is that we become so obsessed with our goals that we don't know when it's time to cut our losses or when we're driving our people too hard. Nowhere is this more evident than in Napoleon's Russian campaign. Several times he had the opportunity to halt the mission and regroup, but he could not accept failure and kept driving his army farther into Russia (see Chapter 13). Like the mythical Icarus, who flew too close to the sun, or a gambler who wants just one more chance to win his money back, Napoleon was lured deep into Russia. By the time the troops reached Moscow and winter arrived, a strategic military campaign had turned into a deadly fight against the elements.

As leaders, we need to know when to cut our losses and recognize when our teams are suffering. Most important, we need to recognize when we're becoming obsessed, so we can avoid these situations before they happen. That's easier said than done. Perhaps the first warning should be if we're passionate about something and others are voicing concerns. If this happens, it's time to stop, look, and listen. If we notice that our people are always absent or sick, or are growing doubtful that our mission can be achieved, it's a sign that we may be driving them too hard. We discussed the impact of mandatory overtime in Chapter 13, but we also need to consider whether our people are burning themselves out trying to reach an unrealistic goal.

We also discussed knowing when to cut our losses and ending a project as soon as we realize that its value will not be achieved. We can assure that this happens by establishing a stage gate process—at predefined points throughout the project, a steering committee evaluates whether the project should be ended or deferred to a future date.

IMPULSIVENESS

The final indicator of overzealousness is impulsiveness. Nowhere is this more evident than in Napoleon's decision to take over Spain, his ignorance of the sentiment of the people, and his ignorance of the risks when preparing for the Russian invasion. In all these cases, he was so caught up in his own goals that he overlooked important risks and the human aspect of his decisions. We need to watch out for this as well. If we're managing a project and become so caught up in its goals that we bypass getting the appropriate buy-in, issue insensitive communications, or ignore key risks, we are setting ourselves up with a severe handicap.

There's something to be said for speed and spontaneity, but this should not be confused with impulsiveness. For example, all too often an overzealous project manager will jump right into the design phase without consulting others or thinking of potential risks, or will send an organization-wide memo that doesn't consider how people might react. Such impulsive actions can undermine an otherwise brilliantly executed project. We must think before we act, and we must deliberate with others appropriately. Most importantly, we need to consider the potential long-term impact of our actions.

It is plain to see that all of these elements—having grandiose ideas, being so obsessed with our goals that we have a "win at all costs" attitude, and making impulsive decisions—are driven by an excessive amount of passion, which we can call overzealousness. We should consider overzealousness a critical warning sign that can lead to trouble if left unchecked. Fortunately, as we have learned, there are ways to avoid such trouble. Now let's explore another critical warning sign—one that caused Napoleon much grief: scarcity of effective leaders.

SCARCITY OF EFFECTIVE LEADERS

As Napoleon's army grew, the lack of effective leaders caused him myriad problems (see Chapter 12). First, because his leaders weren't strategic thinkers, they made foolish decisions and began creating their own interpretations of what they thought Napoleon wanted. And because they lacked people skills, they weren't effective at carrying Napoleon's message across. Disorder ensued, which was evident at Spain and Waterloo. As Napoleon began to lose trust that these leaders could execute his plans appropriately, he started to micromanage, which was a futile exercise since he couldn't be everywhere at once. Finally, his micromanagement began to frustrate his leadership staff, and they grew skeptical and disheartened.

This vicious chain of disorder, mistrust, and micromanagement can be avoided if we simply take the time to either build or obtain effective leadership teams. As we learned in Chapter 12, we can't put people without soft skills or strategic thinking ability in leadership positions. At the very least, we need to invest the time and money in building these skills. We can also invest more time in sharing our philosophies, so that these leaders will be better equipped.

This may not be an issue if we are managing a small project, but for a large project or a major program, we need to rely on other leaders to accomplish our mission. Besides, we need to build leaders now if we want to take on larger projects in the future. Otherwise, our teams are not scalable to larger efforts, and neither are we.

There were several reasons Napoleon lacked effective leaders. First, good leaders were scarce, just as they are today. Second, he was so busy that he hadn't taken the time to select those with leadership potential and hone their skills. And third, he felt that a great soldier could inspire others to greatness. He later realized that this was not the case. Ultimately, he kept those soldiers in leadership positions because he had no other choice. He suffered for it in Spain.

We need to consider it a critical warning sign if we look around and discover a lack of effective leaders we can rely on. This means that our team is not scalable to larger projects, and that we'll most likely end up with disorder, mistrust, and micromanagement. To avoid this fate, we need to make sure we take those who have a combination of people skills and analytical ability and invest some time and money in building their skills. If no candidates exist, we may need to recruit leaders from elsewhere in the organization. We should avoid micromanagement, however, at all costs. It is better to set up regular mentoring sessions with those we choose as leaders and make sure they understand our philosophies.

Now that we've seen the importance of effective leaders, let's look at the final critical warning sign, one that tends to affect us all: an unbalanced lifestyle.

UNBALANCED LIFESTYLE

In the preceding chapter, we saw how Napoleon's burnout led to his mistakes at Waterloo, especially in his delays and his assignment of personnel. But fortunately, we can do something about burnout before it happens. We just need to recognize when we're leading an unbalanced lifestyle. Napoleon said, "Work is my element. I was born and made for work. I have recognized the limits of my eyesight and of my legs, but never the limits of my working power." Perhaps this was part of the problem.

Despite a million books on the subject, leading a balanced lifestyle is not complicated. It boils down to four things: a healthy diet, moderate exercise, adequate sleep, and a balance of work and play. Unfortunately, these four simple things elude us more often than not. If these things don't come naturally—and usually they don't—then we need to tilt the scales in our favor with good time management, especially with regard to making time for moderate exercise, play, and sleep. If we do that, the diet and everything else will probably fall into place.

Napoleon was known to sleep very little—many nights only getting two to three hours of sleep. He cautioned his family members to take time for leisure activities but didn't do so himself. Because of the burnout caused by years of such abuse, Napoleon began to lose his composure more frequently. For example, when he met with Metternich, the Austrian foreign minister in charge of settling affairs, following his defeat at Waterloo, he shouted, "How much are the English giving you?" Even Napoleon later admitted, "My righteous anger was no excuse . . . One should never humiliate anyone whom one wishes to win over." This outburst was clearly an example of burnout.

The loss of composure caused by an unbalanced lifestyle can be deadly. If we find ourselves getting overloaded to the point where we're short with people, or say things we regret—whether it's with colleagues or with our families—it's time to examine our lifestyles and see if they're out of balance.

Perhaps the worst risk of leading an unbalanced lifestyle is to our health. It is one thing to go through a stressful period during a major project, but to go years without making time for family and vacations can ultimately affect our health, whether it is in the form of repetitive injuries, heart disease, or mental health. It simply is not worth it.

We need to make time for leisure and we need to take care of ourselves, or we won't be any good at work or at home. And as busy leaders, we're in danger of this more than anyone.

EXECUTIVE SUMMARY

As we've seen in the last several chapters, there were some clear warning signs that, if observed, could have enabled Napoleon to achieve his goals. In this chapter, we've narrowed those warning signs down to four root causes: power, overzealousness, scarcity of effective leaders, and an unbalanced lifestyle. Just as Napoleon's Six Winning Principles are interconnected, so are these warning signs. For example, power can easily evolve into overzealousness. And both power and overzealousness can cause us to skip important details, such as grooming effective leaders. Ultimately, with busier schedules and no effective leaders to support us, we put all of our energy into our work just to make ends meet. And thus we end up with an unbalanced lifestyle.

We can augment our chances of success using the Six Winning Principles effectively if we are aware of these Four Critical Warning Signs and take precautions accordingly. It certainly would have helped Napoleon.

In our next and final chapter, we will learn what became of Napoleon after Waterloo and explore the legacy he has left for the world—and for us. The chapter includes two useful maps: a map of the Six Winning Principles and a map of the Four Critical Warning Signs. These maps can help guide us to success in any project we undertake.

MARCHING ORDERS

BEWARE OF POWER

Power can lead to separation, impatience, and self-righteousness.

- Reduce separation by scheduling time to be available to others.
- Curb impatience by slowing down and thinking about what is making you that way; think before you act or speak.
- Avoid self-righteousness by surrounding yourself with levelheaded associates, sharing your philosophies, learning to listen, and getting counseling for dealing with perfectionism—or the "Only I know how to do it" syndrome.

WATCH OUT FOR OVERZEALOUSNESS

Overzealousness leads to grandiose ideas, obsession, and impulsiveness.

- Scale back grandiose ideas by restricting the scope of your effort or breaking the effort into multiple projects. Have an agreed-upon scope statement that defines the boundaries of the project's scope, and a rigorous change management process to avoid scope creep.
- If you're passionate about something, pay special attention to knowing when to cut your losses or ease up on your team; don't adopt a "win at all costs" attitude. Have an objective stage gate process for deciding at predetermined points whether your project should continue, end, or be deferred.

- Watch out for impulsiveness, such as bypassing attaining the appropriate buy-in, issuing insensitive communications, or ignoring key risks; impulsiveness is a sure sign of overzealousness.

TAKE NOTICE IF EFFECTIVE LEADERS ARE SCARCE
A lack of effective leaders brings about disorder, mistrust, and micromanagement.

- Select leaders with people skills and an ability to think strategically.
- If no such leaders exist, find those people who most qualify and invest the time and money in building their leadership skills.
- As a last resort, obtain leaders from elsewhere in the organization.
- Rather than micromanage, set up mentoring sessions and share your philosophies.

AVOID AN UNBALANCED LIFESTYLE
An unbalanced lifestyle can lead to burnout, loss of composure, and health problems.

- Strive for a fairly healthy diet, moderate exercise, adequate sleep, and a balance of work and play.
- Be sure to schedule time for exercise and leisure activities.
- If you find yourself getting short with people or getting frustrated easily, it's time to examine your lifestyle.

CHAPTER 15

Napoleon's Legacy

What will history say? What will
posterity think? —Napoleon

After Waterloo, Napoleon returned to Paris. He knew his days as a political leader were over. His supporters, in the meantime, were hopeful. They created an interim French government and asked the allies to let France keep its independence and choose its next leader. The request was denied. Instead, the allies chose to put Louis XVIII back on the throne. Once again, Napoleon agreed to a voluntary exile in order to spare France from any further disaster. After a week of negotiations, he agreed to be exiled to the English countryside. Little did he know that plans had been made to send him to the remote, dreary isle of St. Helena, fifteen hundred miles off the coast of Africa.

On St. Helena, deprived of the respect and niceties of life that he was accustomed to, and under close guard by the British, he grew increasingly depressed. To lift his spirits and pass the hours, he began writing his memoirs. St. Helena was a desolate place, and Napoleon was getting sicker by the day—doctors attributed it to stomach cancer, and although later DNA tests uncovered traces of arsenic in his hair, more recent research seems to confirm the doctors' original findings. During this time, he reflected on his career and his life, often proudly, but other times going over countless "what if" scenarios in his head—how he could have won at Waterloo, and what he would have done differently throughout his career. Most of all, he used this opportunity to clear his name for posterity, and to explain the reasons for some of his decisions. It is through these memoirs that he finally achieved the immortality he hoped for, and it is to our benefit that he did.

Napoleon died at St. Helena on May 5, 1821, at the age of fifty-two. His final words were, "France . . . army . . . head of the army . . . Josephine." As mandated by the British, he was buried in an unmarked grave on St. Helena. Years later, in 1840, his body was taken to Paris amid great ceremony. A glorious state funeral was held, cannons were fired, and bells rang throughout Paris. The procession wound its way through the city, under the Arc de Triomphe, and ultimately to St. Jerome's chapel, where he was laid to rest until his tomb was ready. The elaborate tomb was completed in 1861 and Napoleon was moved there permanently. Napoleon's coffin remains on display to this day under the dome of Les Invalides in Paris.

Napoleon knew his legacy would be debated for years to come. He was well aware of the negative propaganda spread by Tallyrand and the aristocracy of Europe. But he was hopeful that his accomplishments would ring loud and true. As he put it, "In whatever way I may be distorted, suppressed, or mutilated, my enemies will find it a difficult matter to make me disappear completely; for actions speak, they shine like the sun."

And what were Napoleon's accomplishments? In addition to more than fifty battles, most of which he won, he crafted a civil code that is still used in France and that is the basis for most civil codes today. He brought order out of chaos after the French Revolution. He was the forefather of modern military and business strategy, and he used concepts such as Economy of Force, Earned Value, and Critical Chain before they were established in modern times. He led the creation of countless bridges, roads, marinas, ports, museums, and monuments, and changed the face of modern Europe. His troops discovered the Rosetta stone, which led to the deciphering of hiero-glyphics and an understanding of Egyptian history. About the only thing he didn't achieve was his ultimate dream of creating a united and democratic Europe. But even that would ultimately come to be.

In 1950, more than a century after Napoleon's death, French for-eign minister Robert Schuman proposed creating an integrated Europe, in hopes of assuring lasting peace after seeing the destruc-tion of World War II. That evolved into what is known today as the European Union (EU), which serves to unite Europe under a com-mon set of trade policies, a common currency, and common laws on civil liberties and justice. Napoleon would have approved.

Napoleon had extraordinary abilities, and his sheer breadth of accomplishments will probably never be repeated. Even his greatest adversary, the Duke of Wellington, when asked who the greatest general of his day was, responded: "In this age, in past ages, in any age, Napoleon." Perhaps that is why countless military leaders throughout history have studied and benefited from Napoleon's principles and techniques, and why many modern leadership and marketing books quote Napoleon to this day.

And what of *our* legacy? As leaders and project managers, we can-not underestimate the importance we have to our teams and our organizations. We are in a unique position to change people's lives, either positively or negatively, depending on our actions. Everything we do has a potential domino effect. And if we follow Napoleon's Six Winning Principles and observe the Four Critical Warning Signs, it is more than likely that the effect will be positive. To assist with this, I've provided handy diagrams (maps) for both at the end of this chapter.

Napoleon said, "Peruse again and again the campaigns of Alexander, Hannibal, Caesar, Gustavus Adolphus, Turenne, Eugene, and Frederick. Model yourself upon them. . . . Your own genius will

be enlightened and improved by this study, and you will learn to reject all maxims foreign to the principles of the great commanders." He should have added his own name to this list. And now, through our study of Napoleon's triumphs and his failures, we have done as he suggested. The rest is up to us.

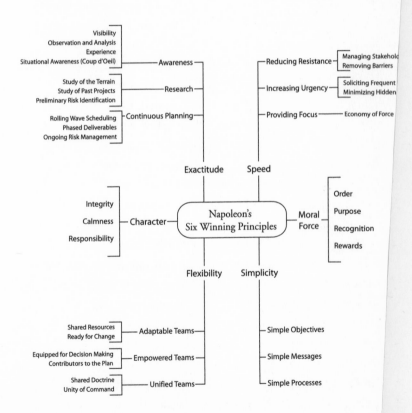

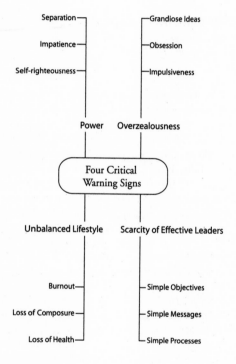

NOTES

Introduction

1. Stephen R. Covey, from his book review on Amazon.com for the book *The Project Management Scorecard*, by Jack J. Phillips, Timothy W. Bothell, and G. Lynne Snead.

Chapter 1

1. Quentin W. Fleming and Joel M. Koppelman, *Earned Value Project Management* (Newtown Square, PA: Project Management Institute, 2000).
2. Tom Peters and Robert H. Waterman Jr., *In Search of Excellence: Lessons from America's Best Run Companies* (New York: Warner, 1988).
3. Geoffrey Moore, *Crossing the Chasm* (New York: Harper Business, 2002).
4. Edward R. Tufte, *Visual Explanations: Images and Quantities, Evidence and Narrative* (Cheshire, CT: Graphics Press, 1997).
5. Dean Anderson and Linda Ackerman-Anderson, *Beyond Change Management* and *The Change Leader's Roadmap* (San Francisco: Pfeiffer, 2001).

Chapter 2

1. Ken Blanchard and Jesse Stoner, *Full Steam Ahead: Unleash the Power of Vision in Your Company and Your Life* (San Francisco: Berrett-Koehler, 2004).
2. Peter M. Senge, *The Fifth Discipline* (New York: Currency, 1994).
3. Ram Charan, *What the CEO Wants You to Know: How Your Company Really Works* (New York: Crown Business, 2001).
4. Project Management Institute, *A Guide to the Project Management Body of Knowledge (PMBOK, Guide)*, 2000 Edition (Newtown Square, PA: Project Management Institute, 2000).
5. Baron Agathon-Jean-François Fain, *Napoleon: How He Did It: The Memoirs of Baron Fain* (San Francisco: Proctor Jones, 1998).
6. Dean Anderson and Linda Ackerman-Anderson, *Beyond Change Management*: Advanced Strategies for Today's Transformational Leaders; and Senge, *The Fifth Discipline*.
7. Robert S. Kaplan and David P. Norton, *The Balanced Scorecard: Translating Strategy Into Action* (Watertown, MA: Harvard Business School Press, 1996).

8. J. M. Thompson, ed., *Napoleon's Letters* (London: Prion, 1998).
9. Ibid.
10. John P. Kotter and Dan S. Cohen, *The Heart of Change: Real-Life Stories of How People Change Their Organizations* (Watertown, MA: Harvard Business School Press, 2002).
11. Harry Beckwith, *What Clients Love* (New York: Warner Business, 2003).
12. Jonathan Tate, "Strange Days: Are Businesses Equipped to Catch Opportunity in an Unpredictable World?" PricewaterhouseCoopers: http://www.pwc.com, 2002.

Chapter 3
1. Geoffrey Moore, *Crossing the Chasm* (New York: Harper Business, 2002).

Chapter 4
1. Karl von Clausewitz, *On War* (London: Penguin, 1982).
2. Baron Antoine Henri de Jomini, *The Art of War* (London: Greenhill, 1996).
3. Eliyahu Goldratt, *Critical Chain* (Great Barrington, MA: North River Press, 1997).
4. Clausewitz, *On War*.

Chapter 5
1. Jomini, *The Art of War*.
2. Ibid.

Chapter 6
1. Tom Peters, *In Search of Excellence* (New York: Warner, 1993).
2. Arthur Conan Doyle, *A Scandal in Bohemia* (New York: Oxford University Press, 1998).
3. Brian W. Hallmark and James C. Crowley, *Company Performance at the National Training Center: Battle Planning and Execution* (Washington, DC: RAND Corporation, 1997).
4. Karl von Clausewitz, *On War* (London: Penguin, 1982).
5. Ibid.
6. Rita Mulcahy, *Risk Management: Tricks of the Trade, for Project Managers* (Minneapolis: RMC Publications, 2003).
7. Fain, *Napoleon: How He Did It*.
8. Ibid.
9. Fleming and Koppelman, *Earned Value Project Management*.

Chapter 7
1. Alan Axelrod, *Patton on Leadership: Strategic Lessons for Corporate Warfare* (New York: Prentice Hall, 2001).

2. Anderson and Ackerman-Anderson, *Beyond Change Management* and *The Change Leader's Roadmap.*
3. Goldratt, *Critical Chain.*
4. Jomini, *The Art of War.*
5. Moore, *Crossing the Chasm.*
6. Jomini, *The Art of War.*
7. Frederick Brooks, *The Mythical Man Month: Essays on Software Engineering* (Boston: Addison-Wesley Professional, 1995).

Chapter 8

1. John Lennon, from his song "Beautiful Boy" on the *Double Fantasy* album
2. Carl H. Builder, Steven C. Bankes, and Richard Nordin, *Command Concepts: A Theory Derived from the Practice of Command and Control* (Washington, DC: RAND Corporation, 1999).
3. David Chandler, *The Military Maxims of Napoleon* (London: Greenhill, 1987).

Chapter 9

1. Jaclyn Kostner, *Virtual Leadership: Secrets from the Round Table for the Multi-Site Manager* (Bridgewater, NJ: Replica, 1998).
2. Harry Beckwith, *Selling the Invisible: A Field Guide to Modern Marketing* (New York: Warner Business, 1997).
3. Fain, *Napoleon: How He Did It.*

Chapter 10

1. Conan Doyle, *The Adventures of Sherlock Holmes.*
2. Covey, *The 7 Habits of Highly Effective People.*

Chapter 11

1. Clausewitz, *On War.*
2. Axelrod, *Patton on Leadership.*
3. Jomini, *The Art of War.*
4. Moore, *Crossing the Chasm.*

Chapter 13

1. www.aft.org (American Federation of Teachers).

Chapter 14

1. Michael Maccoby, "Narcissistic Leaders, The Incredible Pros, the Inevitible Cons," *Harvard Business Review.*

BIBLIOGRAPHY

Leadership and Project Management Books

Ackerman-Anderson, Linda, and Dean Anderson. *The Change Leader's Roadmap.* San Francisco: Pfeiffer, 2001.

Anderson, Dean, and Linda Ackerman-Anderson. *Beyond Change Management.* San Francisco: Pfeiffer, 2001.

Beckwith, Harry. *Selling the Invisible: A Field Guide to Modern Marketing.* New York: Warner Business, 1997.

————. *What Clients Love.* New York: Warner Business, 2003.

Blanchard, Ken, and Jesse Stoner. *Full Steam Ahead: Unleash the Power of Vision in Your Company and Your Life.* San Francisco: Berrett-Koehler, 2004.

Brooks, Frederick. *The Mythical Man Month: Essays on Software Engineering.* Boston: Addison-Wesley Professional, 1995.

Carnegie, Dale. *How to Win Friends and Influence People.* New York: Pocket Books, 1981.

Charan, Ram. *What the CEO Wants You to Know: How Your Company Really Works.* New York: Crown Business, 2001.

Collins, Jim. *Good to Great: Why Some Companies Make the Leap and Others Don't.* New York: Harper Business, 2001.

Covey, Stephen R. *The 7 Habits of Highly Effective People.* New York: Free Press, 1990.

DeLuca, Joel R. *Political Savvy: Systematic Approaches to Leadership Behind-the-Scenes.* Berwyn, PA: EBG, 1999.

Fleming, Quentin W., and Joel M. Koppelman. *Earned Value Project Management.* Newtown Square, PA: Project Management Institute, 2000.

Goldratt, Eliyahu. *Critical Chain.* Great Barrington, MA: The North River Press, 1997.

Jennings, Jason. *Less Is More: How Great Companies Use Productivity as a Competitive Tool in Business.* New York: Portfolio, 2002.

Kaplan, Robert S., and David P. Norton. *The Balanced Scorecard: Translating Strategy into Action.* Watertown, MA: Harvard Business School Press, 1996.

Kostner, Jaclyn. *Virtual Leadership: Secrets from the Round Table for the Multi-Site Manager.* Bridgewater, NJ: Replica, 1998.

Kotter, John P., and Dan S. Cohen. *The Heart of Change: Real-Life Stories of How People Change Their Organizations.* Watertown, MA: Harvard Business School Press, 2002.

Maccoby, Michael. *The Productive Narcissist: The Promise and Perils of Visionary Leadership.* New York: Broadway, 2003.

Moore, Geoffrey. *Crossing the Chasm.* New York: Harper Business, 2002.

Mulcahy, Rita. *Risk Management: Tricks of the Trade, for Project Managers.* Minneapolis: RMC Publications, 2003.

———. *PMP Exam Prep* (4th ed.). RMC Publications, 2003.

Newell, Michael W. *Preparing for the Project Management Professional (PMP) Certification Exam,* (2nd ed.). Amacom, 2005.

Peters, Tom. *The Project 50 (Reinventing Work): Fifty Ways to Transform Every "Task" into a Project That Matters!* New York: Knopf, 1999.

Peters, Tom, and Nancy Austin. *A Passion for Excellence: The Leadership Difference.* New York: Random House, 1985.

Peters, Tom, and Robert H. Waterman Jr. *In Search of Excellence: Lessons from America's Best Run Companies.* New York: Warner, 1988.

Project Management Institute. *A Guide to the Project Management Body of Knowledge (PMBOK, Guide)* – 2000 ed. Newtown Square, PA: Project Management Institute, 2000.

Senge, Peter M. *The Fifth Discipline.* New York: Currency, 1994.

Tufte, Edward R. *Envisioning Information.* Cheshire, CT: Graphics Press, 1990.

———. *Visual Explanations: Images and Quantities, Evidence and Narrative.* Cheshire, CT: Graphics Press, 1997.

———. *The Visual Display of Quantitative Information.* Cheshire, CT: Graphics Press, 2001.

Napoleonic, Military, and Other Sources of Reference

Asprey, Robert. *The Reign of Napoleon Bonaparte.* New York: Basic Books, 2000.

———. *The Rise of Napoleon Bonaparte.* New York: Basic Books, 2000.

Axelrod, Alan. *Patton on Leadership: Strategic Lessons for Corporate Warfare.* New York: Prentice Hall, 2001.

Bourrienne, Louis Antoine Fauvelet de. *Memoirs of Napoleon Bonaparte.* New York: Charles Scribner's Sons, 1890.

Brandt, Heinrich von. *In the Legions of Napoleon: The Memoirs of a Polish Officer in Spain and Russia, 1808–1813.* London: Greenhill, 1999.

Builder, Carl H. *The Masks of War: American Military Styles in Strategy and Analysis.* Baltimore, MD: Johns Hopkins University Press, 1989.

Builder, Carl H., William M. Hix, Morlie H. Levin, and James A. Dewar (ed.). *Assumption-Based Planning: A Planning Tool for Very Uncertain Times/MR-114-A.* Washington, DC: RAND Corporation, 1993.

Builder, Carl H., Steven C. Bankes, and Richard Nordin. *Command Concepts: A Theory Derived from the Practice of Command and Control.* Washington, DC: RAND Corporation, 1999.

Castle, Ian, and Christa Hook (illust.). *Austerlitz 1805: The Fate of Empires.* Oxford, UK: Osprey Publishing, 2002.

Chair, Somerset de, ed. *Napoleon on Napoleon.* London: Brockhampton, 1992.

Chandler, David. *The Military Maxims of Napoleon.* London: Greenhill, 1987.

Clausewitz, Karl von. *On War.* London: Penguin, 1982.

Coignet, Capt. Jean-Roch. *The Note-Books of Captain Coignet: Soldier of the Empire, 1799–1816.* London: Greenhill, 1998.

Conan-Doyle, Arthur. *The Adventures of Sherlock Holmes.* New York: Oxford University Press, 1998.

Cronin, Vincent. *Napoleon.* London: HarperCollins, 1994.

Elting, John R. *Swords Around a Throne: Napoleon's Grande Armée.* New York: Da Capo Press, 1997.

Englund, Steven. *Napoleon: A Political Life.* New York: Scribner, 2004.

Epstein, Robert M. *Napoleon's Last Victory and the Emergence of Modern War.* Lawrence, KS: University Press of Kansas, 1994.

Esdaile, Charles. *The Peninsular War: A New History.* New York: Pallgrave Macmillan, 2003.

Esposito, Vincent J., and John R. Elting. *A Military History and Atlas of the Napoleonic Wars.* London: Greenhill, 1999.

Fain, Baron Agathon-Jean-François. *Napoleon: How He Did It: The Memoirs of Baron Fain.* San Francisco, CA: Proctor Jones, 1998.

Geyl, Pieter. *Napoleon: For and Against.* New Haven and London: Yale University Press, 1949.

Hallmark, Brian W., and James C. Crowley. *Company Performance at the National Training Center: Battle Planning and Execution.* Washington, DC: RAND Corporation, 1997.

Howard, Michael. *Clausewitz: A Very Short Introduction.* New York: Oxford University Press, 2002.

Howarth, David. *A Near Run Thing.* London: Collins, 1968.

Johnston, R. M., ed., and Philip J. Haythornthwaite (intro). *In the Words of Napoleon: The Emperor Day by Day.* London: Greenhill, 2002.

Jomini, Baron Antoine Henri de. *The Art of War.* London: Greenhill, 1996.

Jones, Proctor Patterson. *Napoleon: An Intimate Account of the Years of Supremacy, 1800–1814.* San Francisco: Proctor Jones Publishing Company, 1992.

Jonge, Alex de, transl. *Napoleon's Last Will and Testament.* London: Paddington, 1977.

Kircheisen, F. M., and Napoleon. *Memoirs of Napoleon I: Compiled from His Own Writings.* London: Hutchinson & Co., 1931.

Laufer, Alexander. *Simultaneous Management: Managing Projects in a Dynamic Environment.* New York: American Management Association, 1996.

Laufer, Alexander, and Edward J. Hoffman. *Project Management Success Stories: Lessons of Project Leaders.* New York: John Wiley & Sons, 2000.

Leonhard, Robert R. *The Principles of War for the Information Age.* New York: Ballantine, 1998.

Ludwig, Emil, Eden and Cedar Paul (transl.). *Napoleon.* New York: Boni & Liveright, 1926.

Luvaas, Jay, ed. *Napoleon on the Art of War.* New York: Free Press, 1999.

Machiavelli, Niccolò. *The Prince.* London: Penguin Classics, 1999.

Markham, Felix. *Napoleon.* New York: Mentor, 1966.

Markham, J. David. *Imperial Glory: The Bulletins of Napoleon's Grande Armée 1805–1814.* London: Greenhill, 2003.

———. *Napoleon's Road to Glory: Triumphs, Defeats & Immortality.* London: Brassey's, 2003.

Marshall-Cornwall, James. *Napoleon as Military Commander.* New York: Barnes & Noble, 1998.

Menéval, Baron C-F de. *Memoirs of Napoleon Bonaparte.* New York: P. F. Collier & Son, 1910.

Neillands, Robin. *Wellington and Napoleon: Clash of Arms 1807–1815.* New York: Barnes & Noble, 2002.

Pendry, J. D. *The Three Meter Zone: Common Sense Leadership for NCOs.* California: Presidio Press, 2000.

Sanborn, Keith, transl. *How to Make War.* New York: Ediciones La Calavera, 1998.

Santamaria, Jason A., Vincent Martino, and Eric K. Clemons. *The Marine Corps Way: Using Maneuver Warfare to Lead a Winning Organization.* New York: McGraw-Hill, 2004.

Thompson, J. M. *Napoleon Bonaparte.* Gloucestershire, UK: Sutton, 2001.

Thompson, J. M., ed. *Napoleon's Letters.* London: Prion, 1998.

Tsouras, Peter G. (ed.). *The Greenhill Dictionary of Military Quotations.* London: Greenhill, 2000.

Woloch, Isser. *Napoleon and His Collaborators: The Making of a Dictatorship.* New York: W. W. Norton, 2001.

Articles and Web Sites

The Fondation Napoléon (Napoleon Foundation): http://www.napoleon.org

International Napoleonic Society: http://www.napoleonicsociety.com/

Napoleon Bonaparte Internet Guide: http://come.to/napoleon/

The Napoleon Series: http://www.napoleonseries.org/

Napoleonic Guide: http://www.napoleonguide.com/

PBS Empires: Napoleon: http://www.pbs.org/empires/napoleon/

Tate, Jonathan, "Strange Days: Are Businesses Equipped to Catch Opportunity
    in an Unpredictable World?" PricewaterhouseCoopers:
    http://www.pwc.com/extweb/newcolth.nsf/docid/F7985B3F3F01799C85256
    C3F006E27F3, 2002

ABOUT THE AUTHOR

L eadership doesn't come easy. Of course—and ask anyone in the field—neither does project management. Drawing on his vast experience and self-led education, Jerry Manas has found a way to help others strive toward excellence in both areas. It is an endeavor he has pursued himself for more than twenty-five years—successfully; an endeavor that has earned him a significant number of commendations and achievements throughout his career; an endeavor that has brought many observations and lessons that he'll gladly share with those who would welcome the input and guidance.

A certified Project Management Professional (PMP) through the Project Management Institute, he has provided project management, leadership, training, and product development services to the Information Technology sector for a wide range of organizations, from small domestic businesses to international Fortune 500 companies. He has managed projects of all types, from small software development projects to large-scale, global projects spanning Europe, Asia/Pacific, Latin America, and North America. Jerry is cofounder of PMThink! (www.pmthink.com), a thought leadership Web site, where topics such as Project Management, Portfolio Management, and Governance are discussed.

To stay abreast of the ever-changing industry, he remains actively involved with the Project Management Institute, and currently serves on the Board of Directors for PMI's Aerospace and Defense SIG. He has also contributed to several of PMI's international standards, including their Organizational Project Management Maturity Model (OPM3), where he assisted with the integration of the model and helped define the glossary; and the new Program and Portfolio Management Standards, where he was recruited to help lead the program (consisting of more than three hundred volunteers around the world) as part of a small leadership team.

Like other pioneers in the business community, Jerry's ultimate goal is to make a lasting contribution—specifically by opening other professionals' eyes to new perspectives about project management and leadership: that, to do either well, both are required. Realizing that this effort takes a solid leadership approach in itself, he has examined the craft—its issues and philosophies—and combined a few other passions to create an entertaining and uplifting experience for the educated reader.

His affinity for history, his pursuit of fresh perspectives on leadership, and his understanding about the effectiveness of simplicity create a powerful and wise approach to understanding the complexities of today's leadership issues, especially in the project management industry. Underlying all of this is his strong belief that some of the most relevant lessons for today's project managers and leaders can be learned from an exploration of historical figures—their triumphs and their failures.

When he's not managing projects, writing articles, giving presentations, or contributing his expertise to various professional organizations, he might be found enjoying his enthusiasm for art, movies, or music. But yes, even those passions are well explored. As an art major in college, a wine connoisseur, a serious home theater buff, an accomplished songwriter, and a member of the National Academy of Recording Arts and Sciences, there doesn't seem to be any pursuit that Jerry takes on with anything less than excellence and enthusiasm.

**For a bonus essay on Napoleon, please see
www.manasbooks.com.**

ACKNOWLEDGMENTS

$\mathbf{M}$any authors have stated in their acknowledgments that a book is never written in isolation, and that they've stood on the proverbial "shoulders of giants"—to borrow a phrase from Sir Isaac Newton. And now I know exactly what they mean.

First and foremost, I must thank my wife, Sharon, for her encouragement and endless support while I wrote this book. She truly deserves a Legion of Honor medal. Thanks to my parents, Sid and Barbara, for their love and encouragement; and to my in-laws, Norman and Sallie Olson, for always being there—especially for watching our daughter on my writing days when Sharon had to work.

I'd like to thank Lori Lisi, without whose expert consulting and guidance this would have been a very different book.

I'd like to thank my agent, Daniel Bial; and my publisher at Nelson Business, Victor Oliver, who believed in this book and gave me the opportunity to share it with the world. Special thanks to Kristen Parrish, my editor at Nelson, who guided me through the editing process, made excellent suggestions, and addressed any question I threw at her. Also, I'd like to thank Brandi Lewis, marketing director for Nelson Books; Belinda Bass, for the inspired book cover design; Michael Aulisio, marketing specialist; and Melanie Bryant, publicist.

Special thanks to those who acted as my sounding board, kindly correcting me if I had my facts wrong: Dr. Norman Olson, my father-in-law and an armchair historian; Graham McHardy, who always reminded me about the British perspective; Pierre Duchesne, who always reminded me about the French perspective; and my brother,

Eric, a research scientist, for dropping to my level of understanding to make sure my physics examples weren't too far off base.

Thanks to Ed Youngberg, my editor at Gantthead.com, for getting my writing career started; and to Donna Boyette, a fellow Gantthead writer, for encouraging me to write. Thanks also to Brian Dimeo, who designed my Web site and anything else I asked him to design at a moment's notice; and to Blythe Camenson, for helping me through the query-letter process. Thanks to Ruth Rogers for all the moral support and for being a true friend.

I owe a special debt of gratitude to two extremely talented teams I've had the pleasure of working with during the last year—and who have inspired many of the ideas in this book: PMI's Program and Portfolio Management Standard (PPMS) Leadership Team (Paul Shaltry, Tom Vanderheiden, Dave Whelbourne, Clarese Walker, Mike Yinger, Beth Oulette, Claude Emond, Nancy Hildebrand, Patricia Mulcair, Larry Goldsmith, Kristin Vitello, and program manager extraordinaire, Dave Ross) and the PMO Implementation Team at Rohm and Haas (Tom Reedy, Dawn Bordogna, Sharon Gaudino, Tom Ciamaricone, Bill Gundrum, Sam Spurlock, Dawn Freeman, Wendy Smith Lawson, Paul Haywood, Lois Donnelly, Rick Pivek, Frank Miller, Ting Hooi Looi, Margie Gale, Phiny Abraham, and PMO director, Ralph Ruocco). I'd also like to thank Rita Mulcahy, for allowing me to contribute to her recent book on risk management.

I'm indebted to those authors who have so expertly documented Napoleon's life and career, making my job much easier. Although I referred to many books while writing this one, I especially relied on those by J. David Markham, Vincent Cronin, F. M. Kircheisen, R. M. Johnston, Baron Fain, Proctor Jones, James Marshall-Cornwall, David Chandler, and J. M. Thompson. I could not have written this book without them. Likewise, the *Greenhill*

Dictionary of Military Quotations, edited by Peter Tsouras, was an invaluable source of information.

Finally, I would be remiss if I didn't thank a certain someone, who, though short in stature, inspires me to do my best and make this world a better place. No, I'm not referring to Napoleon—I'm referring to my daughter, Elizabeth, who brightens each and every day for me.

Oh, and I suppose I should thank Napoleon.